MW00635996

GAMESMASTER
THE ORAL HISTORY

Written by Dominik Diamond
Edited by Jack Templeton

Foreword by Robbie Williams

100 illustrations

**T**here is nothing more nineties than *GamesMaster*. Well, that and perhaps the clientele at Soho House Farm on any given weekend in August. But long before that clientele became mums and dads – and maybe even grandparents – there were some profoundly serious matters to contend with. Like ...

'Did I just piss on my Patrick Cox loafers?', 'Why am I "Wanker of the Week" on *The Girly Show*?' and 'I'm in a toilet cubicle with Shaun Ryder ... surely I'm cool now, right? (OK, perhaps that was just me.)

Of all the things I pondered through the very naughty nineties, one thing I didn't have to scratch my head about was: 'Which member of Take That owns a *GamesMaster* Golden Joystick?' Because it's fucking me. That's right, Jason Orange ... Me!

I am 46 years old, lying on my bed, a father of four, and reliving that moment in my head. I've just leaned back and exhaled in an almost post-coital glow.

I own 19 Brit awards, countless MTV moonmen and have been given the freedom of the city of Stoke-on-Trent. But nothing, and I'm not kidding, nothing has brought out more excitement and joy from acquaintances and friends visiting my house than gazing at that perspex box and what lays inside. To be honest it's the 'award' that's given me the most joy. Mainly because I genuinely felt like I deserved it. Music awards are just an opinion, but proving I was the best games player was all down to me. Because I actually *did* win. And I beat Jason Orange ... Did I mention that?

So, here's to you, *GamesMaster*, for keeping me entertained and giving me probably my favourite moment of my Take That life. You lads took one hell of a beating. And here's to you too, Sunbury Pumping Station, for being the venue of that titanic battle, fought twice because of technical difficulties. Yeah. I had to win it fucking twice.

And here's to you too, Jason Orange. You have my address. Come visit the joystick any time. It's next to my *Smash Hits* Best Haircut 1993 award.

Robbie Williams
Age 46 and three-quarters

HEWLAND
INTERNATIONAL

GAMESMASTER   Tuesday 7 January, 6.30 - 7.00pm

Gamesmaster is a new 10 week series which shows the very best computer and
video games played by some of the country's very best players.

A recent survey revealed that 22% of British households harbour some form
of computer games playing system while, in the build-up to Christmas, sales
of computer games systems such as Game Boy (Nintendo) and Game Gear (Sega)
are slugging it out for an anticipated £150m total market. What better
time then for the first ever computer and video games magazine programme on
television, the one medium which can recreate the astonishingly realistic
graphics of today's games?

Hosted by newcomer to television DOMINIK DIAMOND, each programme features
three game-playing sequences, either individual or head-to-head, covering a
variety of games both computer and video. As well as skilled players,
celebrities are asked to try their hand at games they either play in real
life or endorse. So can ANNABEL CROFT win at tennis? Who is the best
baseball player, ex-Wimbledon champion PAT CASH or his wife EMILY? Can
Wimbledon's JOHN FASHANU steer a football side to glory? And can ASHLEY
PASKE (Matt from Neighbours) successfully negotiate Ramsay Street?

Gamesmaster isn't, however, just about playing games. Every week, there'll
be a look at new releases, a rundown of the Top Ten sellers, news on trends
and developments and, for those who need advice, a chance for a
'Consoletation' with THE GAMESMASTER. Created from virtual reality and
therefore more lifelike than any previously seen computer-generated being,
THE GAMESMASTER is an omnipotent being who knows every answer to every
problem. Regular television viewers may notice a close resemblance to
Britain's best known astronomer PATRICK MOORE. The similarity is definitely
not a coincidence.

Filmed in a disused church, Gamesmaster has a Gothic, eerie feel to it. But
it offers viewers of all ages a glimpse into a world where computer and
video games are as interactive and exciting as life itself. The future of
entertainment is here: Gamesmaster fully explores it.

Prod Co: Hewland International
Press Contact: Steve Pinder, C4, 071-927 8888
C4 commissioning editor: Mike Miller

SERIES
ONE

JANUARY 1992

I wanted to be a star. I hate that my ambitions were so shallow. But apparently, when people asked me what I wanted to be when I grew up, I was that kid who said 'famous'. I don't think I was alone in that in terms of my peers. I grew up on a council estate in Arbroath, a wee fishing town on the east coast of Scotland. Like many kids born into those towns in the seventies, I was born into a family that had been born there, went to school there, worked there and died there. My generation were different. My generation of kids were – thanks in no small part to the hard work and support of our mums – the first generation in that part of Scotland who wanted to do something different. To learn something new. To live somewhere new. To leave an arseprint in the sands of time. I didn't really know how I was going to do that, I just knew it would involve being famous, so from an early age I acted, I sang, I played classical guitar, I entered impromptu speech contests as a 10-year-old, and from as soon as I could talk, according to family tales, I would set out to entertain every room I entered.

By the time I arrived at Bristol University in 1988, my ambitions had narrowed into becoming the next great British stage actor – the next Olivier. I had acted in all manner of school and local plays and I just loved how it felt to be on stage and be able to hold the attention and emotions of an audience. Then, at the first Bristol University Department of

Drama Students' Cabaret I got drunk and broke the golden rule that First Years Do Not Perform. I leapt on stage and started telling jokes. Half of them nicked from Billy Connolly, the other half being my observations on buying condoms in a small town like Arbroath. Everyone laughed. And that was it. I just wanted to do standup. It was all the rush of steering an audience by acting in a play ... but more intense. More personal. More selfishly, egotistically rewarding. I actually ended up studying comedy as a module at Bristol. We looked into what constitutes a joke, how they work and why people laugh. It was all quite deconstructed and intellectualized. I just felt that if you can make people laugh you are making them happy, and if you make people happy then they like you. And we all just want to be liked, don't we? It doesn't matter where you are, in what situation. I mean, I have been in Canada for over 10 years. Came here as a complete unknown immigrant. And we've had a great life. Because I have made people laugh. Personally. Professionally. It's all about the funny.

But at the start of the nineties? I was also working class. And Scottish. From a council estate. I had that angry chip on my shoulder about the wrongs of the world, so I wanted to do dangerous anti-establishment comedy in the mode of Bill Hicks or Ben Elton, basically. Something that shook things up. Something that was a bit different.

SMELLS LIKE TEEN SPIRIT

> It has been frustrating at times. I could see quite clearly the enormous growth in popularity of videogames, and therefore the potential for a TV series. At the time we were developing our series, I was terrified someone else would spot what we had spotted and move in ahead of us. But we were lucky and Channel 4 have been fantastically supportive. They always said they would commission the series as soon as they could find the funds and they have kept their word.
>
> Jane Hewland, *New Computer Express*, 1991

H.H. **Harry Hewland** I was a child videogame addict. All my friends were the same. It was a time when games consoles were like alchemy. Finally you could create the arcade experience at home.

J.H. **Jane Hewland, Executive Producer** It was 1990 and Harry was 10 at the time. He was pestering me to get him a NES for Christmas, which came with two games: *Duck Hunt* and *Gyromite*. As I was watching him shoot these ducks I was thinking, *Oh, I'm getting excited about this*. There was something in watching him try and beat this challenge, and it hit me that this could be a television programme.

Jane Hewland changed my life. I was one of a generation of people who got their first break in telly from her because she spots quirky talent like no one else. She is the smartest, bravest, toughest, not-give-a-fuck person I have ever worked for. Jane worked on so many things that were perceived as cool, which she never set out to make cool because she herself is proudly uncool.

H.H. My mum created a lot of television over the years. Shows way ahead of their time like *Network 7* – a live youth magazine show on Channel 4 – that she developed with Janet Street-Porter. As a single mum she took me into cutting rooms from when I was a baby, so I grew up in and around TV.

C.M. **Cameron McAllister, Series Director (Series 1–2)** Jane was fixated on how exciting youth television could be. She could see videogames was a massive growth area and would ask, 'Why is no one doing this?'

J.H. Harry obviously wanted more games to play, so I took him to videogame shops where these places were packed with kids pulling out £50 notes. This was during a major recession so I knew there was money in it and a commercial opportunity, because in a recession people don't stint on their kids, they stint on themselves.

M.M. **Mike Miller, Head of Sport** Channel 4 was set up to provide programming that people wouldn't see elsewhere. There weren't hundreds of channels. There was BBC One, BBC Two, ITV and then Channel 4. The BBC and ITV aimed at a mass market. BBC Two was a little more adventurous – some would say highbrow – but Channel 4 launched on the idea of giving a voice to cultures and people that otherwise weren't heard.

J.H. I made a pilot tape of Harry's 11th birthday party. I took him and his friends out to Laser Quest and filmed it all, intercut with interviews of all these kids talking passionately of their love for videogames. It really brought the whole thing to life. I tried to get the BBC and ITV interested but they had no clue who Nintendo were or what I was talking about.

M.M. I was the second commissioning editor for sport at Channel 4. My remit was to show content audiences had already seen in a new and different light. So we showed things like Gaelic football, sumo wrestling and kabaddi. But we couldn't just show the footage itself because people didn't know the rules, the culture or the individuals. To connect with sport you need to either love or hate the people that you're watching. You need some sort of an emotional connection. So we packaged up all those different elements to introduce it to the audience.

J.H. Mike was Canadian so he understood the videogames craze, given North America and Canada were culturally six months ahead of us.

M.M. I don't know why other people didn't see it. It was obvious to me that videogames were an interesting, booming area.

C.M. Jane sold to him a genius idea that this would come under Channel 4's sports remit, because watching people play videogames was a spectator activity.

J.H. It was an odd way to go but it worked. It would never have made it to air without him.

M.M. I was convinced straight away that this was something we should be doing. Then it was a question of convincing the people above me. Michael Grade, the chief executive, came from an entertainment background so had a very good gut instinct about what an audience would or wouldn't like. He'd say to us, 'I've hired all of you because I trust in your talent and your ability. Get on with it.'

   The culture of the channel allowed us to take risks in a way others wouldn't. We didn't have the rights to broadcast the 1990 FIFA World Cup but we could see the interest of the nation and the World Cup fever. So instead we showed the 1990 Subbuteo World Cup. We treated it seriously because it was taken seriously by those playing. And if you work with people like Jane, who had made sports programmes for the BBC, they work out how to make it exciting and entertaining.

S.C. **Steve Carsey, Researcher (Series 1–2)** Jane persuaded Channel 4 this was the sport of tomorrow. I look at my son today playing *Fortnite* and trying to get into competitions with prize money and I think,

Yep, she was right. You can make a career out of being a gamer now. 30 years ago *GamesMaster* recognized that people were playing sports in their bedrooms.

I would have loved my own room to play games, but growing up in seventies Arbroath meant playing videogames in a cupboard under the stairs. Yes. Years before Harry Potter made understairs living fashionable, my siblings and I did it. My mum, bless her, walked into the house one day with what she said was a word processor called the ZX Spectrum that happened to come with two games: *Hungry Horace* and *Penetrator*. The idea of having videogames in your own house was absolutely mental to us kids, because up until that point our favourite thing in life was when Granny Diamond would take us to Pleasureland, which sounds like somewhere up an alley in Amsterdam but was the only indoor fairground on the east coast of Scotland, and it was half a mile from my gran's house. We'd go there when we walked her dog, and while she punted a few coppers on the penny falls she would give us a couple of quid, which I'd promptly sink into *Asteroids*, *Gorf* and *Defender*; this array of impossibly bright and fast-moving pixels would completely mesmerize me, right up until some little local shite would come up and push the hyperspace button in the middle of a game.

I don't know how many novels were ever written on that Spectrum – we shattered Mum's illusion of that almost instantly – but for my two brothers, sister and I that machine was just a life changer; it brought Pleasureland into our homes. We didn't need an endless supply of coins from Granny Diamond. Just a cassette. But with there being four of us we had to share our time equally, so I managed an efficient schedule of one-hour daily gameplay, often sabotaged by R Tape Loading Errors eating up half of that hour. We had names written on a bit of paper on the door with high scores – it was super competitive. *Match Day, Football Manager, Pyjamarama, Kokotoni Wolf, Atic Atac, Daley Thompson's Decathlon* ... We still talk about those games with misty-eyed excitement today.

ALL TOGETHER NOW

J.H. The budget that we were given by Mike for the first series was tiny. In return I agreed to give Channel 4 the first two UK transmissions and beyond that we'd hold all other broadcast rights. It was the best deal I ever made, but I was forced into it because they didn't have the money to fund it in the normal way programmes were.

C.M. Jane never came to terms with spending lots of money doing glossy, high-end productions. But that's part of her ethos. She'd hire people really young, get their ideas and promote them ridiculously. So much so that it was almost impossible to leave because you could never get a job as good. With *GamesMaster*, I was series directing a show at 25. You wouldn't get those opportunities anywhere else.

A.W. **Adam Wood, Series Producer (Series 1–2)** I started working in television fresh out of university as a researcher on a sports show for Jane at London Weekend Television. I later joined 24 Hour Productions, a company that had just been set up by Charlie Parsons, whose live music show *The Word* had just been commissioned by Channel 4. I joined as a researcher but was then bumped up to producer on the first series, tasked with devising stories for the show and booking bands.

I was obsessed with *The Word*. Never missed a minute of it. It was the first show I remember watching where you felt anything could happen. That and *The Last Resort* with Jonathan Ross showed that Channel 4 was the first TV channel in my lifetime where people were shaking things up. Where they were challenging convention and sticking two fingers up at the previous order. It was what I wanted to do with standup comedy. But on a much bigger scale. So I think that's when I started thinking that the standup was a means to an end. And that end was TV presenting.

A.W. I was approached by Jane, who by this point had left LWT to set up her own production company. She told me about this new show she had commissioned by Channel 4 about videogames. I didn't really know a great deal about them but she was offering me my first series-producing job, so I jumped at the chance. There were no plans, so the first thing we had to do was build a team of experts.

J.H. We advertised everywhere trying to get researchers with game experience, but nobody who worked in television wanted to apply. So we started advertising far and wide. It was like the days of *Network 7*, finding yourself with all kinds of incredibly passionate but inexperienced people who'd never worked in TV.

C.M. Young people are easier to control and less set in their ways. The last thing she wanted was a bunch of middle-aged people developing that kind of show.

S.C. I was a manager of a shop in York selling games for the Spectrum, Commodore 64 and Amiga, right through to the NES and Sega Mega Drive. We received the industry magazine *Computer Trade Weekly* and while flicking through it one day I spotted an advert which said, 'Computer games experts wanted to work on a new Channel 4 show. Passion and expertise in videogames essential. Prior experience in television not essential.' So I applied for the job and received a letter saying to come for an interview. A few days later I received a phone call from Jane offering me a job. It was fantastic, but I became very quickly aware in the conversation I wasn't being paid a lot and that it was only going to be an eight- or ten-week contract.

J.H. I said that's how television works. It's how a long a television programme will take to produce, but if the programme's any good it'll
get a repeat and then it'll get renewed and then you'll get rehired.
But he didn't want to take that gamble at first.

S.C. She was very persuasive. I slept on it and she rang back the next day
where I accepted the job. I was forever grateful to her for ringing me
back up.

I liked Steve because he was northern and he looked like Jesus. He
probably had the best hair and facial topiary of anyone in that
first series.

D.P. Dave Perry, Researcher (Series 1) I was hired as a researcher and took
what was a sizeable pay cut for the opportunity. At one point I was
living in my Mini and eating baked beans because I couldn't afford
accommodation. My father said to me at the time, 'Why do you want
to risk your job as publishing manager for a job that's on contract?'
But I'd have crawled across glass for that job. Maybe that's why the
whole show and everything about it in later years meant so much
to me, because of what I'd sacrificed and what I'd risked in the early
days of my career. I could see the potential of it as the only way to
reach out to people and get into their front rooms.

The Hewland International office was based in the Docklands and
was this totally modern glass unit. Inside, though, the tables were
very rudimentary, almost like school desks. Jane had her glass office
at the far end. And we were just sat there. What were we supposed
to do? We had nothing. Absolutely no blueprint or idea what to do.
I was thinking, *This is my job. I've got to find something to do or they're
going to work out I'm doing nothing.* I wanted to be useful but I didn't
know how. So I got on the phone and started phoning all the software
companies and my contacts, selling the idea of this TV show and getting them involved.

A.W. Jane gave us a huge amount of creative freedom. Basically, this
was a show about videogames but apart from that there was nothing. No plans. We didn't know any better and we absolutely had no
fear of failure.

C.M. We knew the very worst thing we could do would be to try and be
cool. We would fail because we were inherently uncool. Jane left us
to it, though she would come in and change everything if she thought
it was going wrong.

There was always that time during filming – every series, first or second day usually – when Jane would visit the set. We would be terrified
because we would have done all this work on these crazy ideas on our
own and then she would turn up and say, 'What the fuck is this? You
can't do that.' And she would suggest something different, which would
put us behind schedule for filming and stress us out. But she was always
right. In retrospect it was a great way to manage us.

THE ONE
AND ONLY

A.W. We didn't want to use an established host and we probably couldn't afford one. We needed someone who had an affinity with videogames, which the audience would recognize. So we set out to find someone completely new.

The best thing about TV presenting is that it is a billion times easier than standup comedy. Standup is the hardest job in the world. Especially if you want to do angry, dangerous, anti-establishment comedy in the mode of Bill Hicks or Ben Elton when you wear little round glasses, have smooth alabaster skin and look about 17. I would leap on stage with way too much anger and shout, 'Hands up who hates Maggie Thatcher?' And big hairy-arsed men who worked on building sites would shout back, 'Fuck off you speccy twat!' You know you are not the best standup in the world when another act is dying on the bill and they get their biggest laugh by saying, 'Oh, would you rather we brought the little Scottish kid back?'

I couldn't handle it, basically. Dying a death on stage in a comedy club was the worst, loneliest feeling in the world. If making people laugh means you are making them happy so you know they like you? Then the opposite is also true. If they don't laugh? You are not making them happy and therefore you feel they hate you. It is crushingly, depressingly lonely. So within three months of graduating I had moved back to my mum's in Milton Keynes, where I shared a bedroom with my 17-year-old brother Michael and started doing temping office jobs. Anything that came up. One week I would be a receptionist. The next week a security guard. One week I had to sit in an office for eight hours a day licking stamps and envelopes for a marketing leaflet company. At the end of it the boss said, 'Did you not know there are moistening pads in the stationary cupboard?'

And then I saw on Channel 4 that they were holding open auditions for *The Word*, and I thought, *OK, let's give this a shot*. One final attempt to make it in entertainment. I mean, it couldn't be worse than standup. It couldn't be worse than licking stamps and putting them on envelopes. So I wrote a funny letter and made an audition tape along with 20,000 other people and found myself in room with 49 of them who were all super trendy and good-looking. It was a horrifyingly nervous audition process with numbers being cut every hour or so. I just tried to throw gag after gag at the process and survived cull after cull until I made it to the last 12. I left the audition convinced I was going to get it. I felt it was pre-ordained. I was going to be a massive TV star, just like I told everyone when I was a child.

I watched the mail every day. I asked my mum if anyone had called from *The Word*. Nothing. And then one day I got an envelope with the super-cool 24 Hour Productions logo on it. I just stared at it. Like I was Charlie with that Willy Wonka bar, hoping to find that golden ticket inside. I opened the envelope. The first word was 'Sorry'. I didn't need to read the rest. I hadn't got the show and it broke my heart. I thought I had nailed the audition. I thought I was certainly smart enough, funny enough. So I assumed they just felt I wasn't cool or good-looking or posh or English enough. And that stuck with me, that was a chip on my shoulder for a long time. Because I loved *The Word* so much. It was like being in love with that girl at school who doesn't fancy you back. So, much like a spurned lover, I had this instant wave of anger against *The Word* and anyone who had anything to do with the show. Which was ironic given what happened next.

> M.B. **Matthew Bowes, Researcher, *The Word*** I auditioned Dominik as part of the search for a new presenter. Lots of people auditioned who then became really well known, like Stewart Lee, Patrick Marber and Caroline Aherne. None of them really fit what we were looking for. Adam contacted me as he knew we'd just gone through this huge exercise, saying they were looking for a presenter for a new show they were developing and asking if there was anyone I thought worth meeting. I sent him some tapes and Dominik was one of them.

I had plummeted into a depressing, angry spiral because I thought my chance was blown. I had lurched from being convinced that TV was my destiny to feeling that nobody from my background really gets a TV show, and I was an arrogant idiot for daring to dream. I should resign myself to a career involving my tongue and envelopes. And then a week later I got the call from this posh fellow called Adam who said I had been recommended by someone from *The Word* for a show they were doing and I said, 'Someone from *The Word*? I *love* that show! I *love* those people!'

And then he told me it was a show about videogames. I didn't really listen to anything else he said after that because I was too busy wetting my pants. Not just because I loved games, but because I immediately realized that – in contrast to *The Word* – looking like a fresh-faced little geek with round glasses wouldn't count against me this time. It really was the most ridiculous turn of events.

So this emotional rollercoaster skyrocketed upwards once again. In the days between the call from Adam and the actual audition I was working as an overnight security guard at Abbey National, which meant sitting in front of a camera monitor all night and occasionally walking around with a big heavy torch. I would sit in front of that screen 'seeing' myself on TV. I would walk around the deserted offices pretending I was presenting a TV show, getting more and more pumped up with excitement every day. If anyone had attempted to break into the place they would have thought I was quite mad.

A.W. We auditioned Dominik in a church, along with many other people. Walking in, he immediately came across as a mischievous choirboy with his centre parting and glasses. There was an energy and innate confidence in him for a guy who'd never presented on TV before. He was cocky, but the clincher was he loved videogames. He played them and he understood this world.

C.M. He had a lot of cheeky charm and he was funny. We were looking for the tone to match who we were: naughty, geeky schoolboys. Dominik was the perfect fit.

My first impressions of Cameron were that he was very clever and eloquent but a bit mad. He had that slightly-too-intense look. Adam was like a slightly older version of the good-looking kids from *The Word*, which I found initially intimidating. But whereas that audition process had been like *The Hunger Games*, this one was completely different. They were so friendly and supportive and encouraging from the off. It gave me a lot of confidence. They gave me some lines to say introducing the show, and for some reason I completely changed them on the fly to feature nob gags. These guys laughed. So I threw in some more. They laughed again. I thought: *Hmmm, I might be on to something here ...*

Then they got me to commentate on a videogame. Cameron filmed it, Adam played it, and this guy called Dave Perry commentated on it with me. He seemed much more down to earth and had really interesting close-cropped hair. I remember thinking, *As long as you never cover that great hair up with something silly like a bandana, we will get on great!*

When they said the game was *Nintendo World Cup* I nearly peed myself again. It was perfect for me. When I used to play *Match Day* in the games cupboard on the Spectrum I would always commentate aloud on my own games – this was like doing that. With added nob gags. I felt there and then I had this job. I was going to work with these lovely people. I was going to be famous after all!

And then I heard nothing. Not a thing. For bloody ages.

J.H. I knew he was Cameron and Adam's favourite but I didn't know what to make of him, so I showed his tape to Harry. One of the many great things about Harry was that he was audience research in my own house.

H.H. She would always include me in her work. I loved that she cared and valued my opinion and built these shows around my interests.

J.H. He was falling about, laughing at this tape, which I took as a good sign. Dominik was hired on that basically.

So I was back temping when Adam called, working for an absolute arsehole of a boss in some financial company who had me doing VDU data entry in a room on my own. I remember he wouldn't even let me listen to my Walkman, and would moan at me whenever I went for a cigarette break. A total control freak. All Adam literally

said was, 'Hi Dominik, it's Adam Wood here and we'd like to offer you *GamesMaster*', and I cut him off and said, 'Adam, can I call you back in 30 minutes please?' I packed my things and walked out the door. I hated it so much I couldn't wait to get out. The boss shouted after me, 'Where do you think you're going?' 'To be on the fucking telly!' I shouted. 'Fuck you!' And I raised my fist like Judd Nelson at the end of *The Breakfast Club*. No word of a lie.

I got home and called Adam back. I thought I was in a dream. This was going to be it. Finally, I would be rich! Then he said how much money they were offering me ... £1,000. In total. For the whole series. That was all. So I did what was the most stupid thing you could do in that situation: I turned them down. Well, not the job. But the money. I asked for double. I have no idea why I did that. I think it was possibly a foreshadowing of the self-destructive streak that took over a lot of my life for the rest of the nineties. Anyway, they came back at £1,650. Thank fuck for that, eh? And then I had some champagne with my mum. She still has the cork.

> **A.W.** It was a big risk from Jane and Channel 4 that we went for a complete unknown. There was a lot resting on him.

Looking back on how I prepared for that first lot of filming, I see it as a *Rocky* movie training montage. Set in Milton Keynes. I moved out of my mum's house into my brother Konrad's place so I could actually have my own room, albeit one I had to share with his cat's litterbox. This was pretty gross, but cut down on bathroom breaks. I stopped drinking. I stopped smoking. I stopped eating chocolate. I wanted to be as mentally and physically fit as I could be. I rigorously researched all the games that were coming up on the show, I wrote and rewrote scripts, I ate bags and bags of carrots. Seriously. That is the best tip I can give you if you want to stop smoking. Every time you want a cigarette? Have a carrot. In fact, I cannot stress enough how important carrots were to the success of *GamesMaster*.

> **C.M.** Dominik wasn't just the presenter. He became increasingly involved in defining the show with us. Sometimes, though, he could be a little over-confident and cocky when talking on the phone to the managing director of Sega. Then we'd have to go and repair whatever damage he'd done. [Laughs.]

LOSING MY RELIGION

C.M.   The vital elements to the show were the games challenges, filmed with a studio audience, fulfilling its remit as a sport. We thrashed out the rest of the format to include reviews, features and tips, but the first thing we had to do was find the look. This was my task, so I was thinking about a world and a precinct to set it in.

A.W.   We weren't very excited about putting it in a studio, not that we could afford one anyway. We thought: is there a space outside of a studio we could use which will give the show atmosphere and make it feel like it's from the world of videogames? We experimented with a few things but quite quickly we liked the idea of a church. They're very atmospheric and there's always a sort of gothic level in platform games. Knowing we were filming challenges, a church has audience seating and a natural entry point for contestants, so there's a focal point at the front. Once you throw a few lights on that and a bit of smoke, you have atmosphere.

C.M.   All the other stuff naturally followed. So then you start thinking, *Right, we need a monk.* So we got Dave Perry coming on as a little monk carrying the Golden Joysticks. Then to make it feel somewhat modern and futuristic, we put lasers in so the contestants would walk through a smoky 'time tunnel' and down the aisle.

I was in two minds about the church setting because I was, and still am, a very religious person. So there was a bit of a moral conflict within me about using a House of God to make penis jokes. However, once we started filming, with all the lighting and lasers and dry ice, it wasn't really like a church any more. It was more like the Pleasureland fairground I had spent so much time in as a kid. Or at least that's how my inner Catholic justified it to me. And it is amazing how much all that extra stuff helps your energy levels. In later years when I did shows that were in dry, bare, standard studios it was much harder to get excited about things.

D.P.   The idea of filming inside a church seemed appropriately rebellious and anarchic. It fitted everything we wanted to do with the show. While Cameron and Adam discussed swooping camera shots and lighting, we arranged for arcade machines to be delivered and placed around the perimeter and for Sony to provide monitors so the crowd could watch the action from the pews. To this day I remember the way I felt when I walked into the old church on the first day of filming. I was so proud seeing it all come together, and knowing that we had made all the right decisions. My God, we built an arcade in a church.

SERIES ONE

C.M. The most important thing was to try and not do what people expected. That we'd set it in some kind of high-tech spaceship or something. We just wanted to do something really visually distinctive and slightly unexpected. So let's take a young 21-year-old and dress him up in a cravat and waistcoat. It was a piss-take in the best possible way.

If I remember correctly the costume consisted of clothes I already had. I was given £20 and I bought the waistcoat or the cravat. One of the two.

It's weird watching those shows back now because that really isn't me on screen. I mean, I am saying my words, but the delivery? The style? It's all so sickeningly nice and twee. I was not, I am not, like that at all. I am cynical and grumpy and angry and aggressive. And my voice on those shows is so high!

All that stuff is down to Cameron. He was the one who came up with that brilliant idea of me putting on the smoking jacket and having a different kind of tea at the end of every show. Because that is the kind of thing Cameron does at the end of work each day. He was 25 going on 65. I actually think that in series one, Cameron was directing me to be ... him, basically. Yeah, I was playing the part of Cameron McAllister in that series. And it worked because along with the church setting it was such a contrast with the videogames themselves.

OUT OF SPACE

A.W. We loved the idea of a videogames figure as the ultimate deity.

S.C. There was a meeting with Adam and Jane about bringing in a left-field, older, establishment personality who would be this central figure, setting games challenges. They were looking at various videos, including Nicholas Parsons, and there was a final semi-democratic vote in the team between Patrick Moore and Jim Bowen from *Bullseye*. Patrick walked that vote. Not that we didn't like Jim Bowen, but Patrick just felt right for the role.

A.W. I liked Patrick Moore just because he was this eccentric old astronomer who in many ways was very incongruous for a show like this.

C.M. We rang up his agent and we met him for lunch to talk him through the show. He seemed keen so we said, 'Look, Patrick, what should we pay you?' And he replied, 'Oh yes, I did a project before. Some nice young men came to me and they said, "Patrick, what should we pay you?" So I told them and we drank it.'

A.W. He didn't know what the hell the show was about but he was up for it. He was pretty much top of my list and he accepted straight away. It was remarkably easy.

> I became involved because the TV company said that if I would do it for them they would give a substantial donation to the Cystic Fibrosis Research Trust. Obviously I couldn't turn them down, and anyway it was quite pleasant and harmless.
> Patrick Moore, *GamesMaster*, 2003

C.M.   His madness was very charming. It just felt right for the crazy boffin role. And it gave him that chance to expand his remit. I mean, with *GamesMaster* he became known to a whole generation of kids, almost overnight, becoming this cult figure linked to videogames.

A.W.   We got him in to do the recording sessions, which were quite quick. We basically had all the lines prepared on an autocue and recorded him against a blue screen to add all the graphics on afterwards.

> I acted as the presiding genius, and it was my role to guide the contestants, explaining how they had to dodge the hideous traps for them in the shape of demons, dragons and assorted ghouls. I dutifully read out what appeared on the autocue. What it was all about I had not the slightest idea, but for a long time afterwards I was besieged by young enthusiasts who wanted to know how they could escape from level six, et cetera. Rather lamely I explained that this was secret, classified information and that they would have to work it out for themselves.
> Patrick Moore, *GamesMaster*, 2003

It took me a long time to find my genuine groove on *GamesMaster*, but Patrick just flew out of the traps. He was perfect. You look back on his clips and you just would not change one word or nuance of what he did. Even the Consoletation Zone, which I never liked as a concept because it wasn't remotely genuine. These kids didn't really write in wanting to know these cheats. The team decided on what clips and cheats we were going to use and then got some kid to say what we told them to. I don't think anyone ever tuned in to the show to get tips for games. And in series two where we were trying to crunch so much content into 24 minutes I felt that time could have been spent on better things. But Patrick made it bearable. And some of the stuff they did with him in that section can stand against any other bit of comedy from the nineties. And that is down to him. He was a comic genius. And he spent a lot of time looking at Uranus.

Sorry.

C.M.   Once we hired Patrick and we had the church, the design iconography followed. We met with some young graphic animators who'd done bits of TV and hired them.

S.D.   Simon Dunstan, Graphic Designer (Series 1–3) I'd previously worked in an advertising agency where I made friends with George Stone, who was a charismatic writer interested in computer games. George came up with the TV series *Max Headroom* and clocked that Amiga computers could work really well on TV. I learnt from him and began experimenting with the technology, placing images on other images in real time. When we were approached to pitch to Hewland International we used some of those early experiments to show how to make cheap film look better with video graphics.

C.M. **Chris Mills, Graphic Designer (Series 1–3)** Simon and I had worked on animations for *Network 7* so we knew Jane already. From this, we then got approached to work on another Channel 4 show, *Star Test*, which would have been around 1987. We set to and created our own company, Real Time Graphics, so we started building up experience and experimenting with the available technology.

When we met Cameron and Adam early on, they knew *Games-Master* was going to be a graphically heavy show. They really liked the idea of it coming out of an Amiga because games at that time were very pixelated. They wanted a strong visual look and I suppose we had the most sophisticated solution. We knew the Amiga inside out and we'd done a bit of broadcast with them already so we knew a lot of the technical answers and capabilities.

S.D. There was a certain creative tension to begin with. There always is when you have two creative designers in a room with a television producer and a director. We had ownership of the look but I can remember being quite upset with Cameron pushing that all we'd see would be the bulbous head of Patrick Moore, which I just wasn't up for. Now I think it's absolutely brilliant. At the time it wasn't how I'd seen it in my head.

> It's a good job I'm not a vain man. I had no idea you were going to do all that to me.
> Patrick Moore, *GamesMaster* Fan Club, 1992

C.M. We had a lot of creative input in those early meetings. For people to listen to our ideas and go, 'Wow, that's really cool' felt pretty good. We spent a lot of time not just on title sequences and in-show graphics but all the stuff around it. I'm pretty sure we had multiple computers in the edit suite running different parts of the background and the animations that come over the top with a bit of blue screen stuff and running mattes on various computers for Patrick's face so it had rippled distortion to it.

A.W. They were very talented. We devised the logo together and went for that big dominant central 'M', which fit the slightly gothic graphics. We developed the title sequence together too, which I was really pleased with. That sense of loading the show and everything taking shape.

C.M. **Cameron McAllister, Series Director (Series 1–2)** They immediately grabbed hold of it all and said, 'Right, we'll build the GamesMaster's world' with a kind of computer blueprint which felt completely new and was very exciting. We had all kinds of problems getting Patrick's head to fit it into this dome thing, but they bent and twisted his head, which made it look all the weirder and better.

A.W. They got it and understood what we were doing. It was the same with the music. The composers, Julian and Daemion, did a terrific job. You listen to the first draft of a piece of music and you're often a little disappointed, but the guys pretty close to nailed the music straight away. We got them to fit it to the rough graphics sequence we had for the titles. It's quite hard getting a memorable hook into a piece of music when it's only 30 seconds long, but they gave us a range of different music beds that we used for the titles, stings and features.

I think the best compliment I can give to the graphics – and music – of *GamesMaster*, especially series one? Try and imagine the show without them. You can't.

I remember when I first saw them all put together when I went in to do some voiceover work just before we aired. I sat in a dark edit suite in central London and watched this brand new world explode in front of my eyes. I actually got a bit scared because I think that is when I realized this show was going to be a big deal and my life was probably going to change.

GET READY FOR THIS

S.C. Jane would always say to me the show is about the challenges and what we're making is an entertainment show, so don't worry about the gamers watching the show because this is the only show of its type on TV. It taught me a lot in understanding how sport can be entertainment and entertainment can be sport.

D.P. We knew through years and years of playing videogames and writing for fanzines what the best games were, but we didn't know which ones would be best for TV. Cameron and Adam told us that each challenge had to last a maximum of two and a half minutes, which suddenly presented us with a problem. It took us ages to figure out what games were viable, and there was a lot of goofing around figuring that out. The lucky thing was having Adam and Cameron being totally naive to videogames. They'd join us in sessions as new gamers with all this interest and enthusiasm. Through these new eyes we were able to see what games had the wow factor and which didn't. Sometimes the shit games were good on TV and sometimes the good games weren't.

S.C. Even though I came from the games world I wanted to work in television. I had no desire to be a games journalist or work in the games industry long term. So I leaned more into general TV research work like celebrity bookings and coordinating audiences because I wanted to learn how to be a TV producer. A lot of the grunt work was left to me to pick up the phone and make contact within the games industry to let them know what we were doing and get their support.

D.W. **Danielle Woodyatt, Head of Global Communications, Virgin Games** It was a match made in heaven. At the time Virgin Games were turning a corner. We had a strong portfolio of games developed in-house with our offices all across the world but we also had an incredible portfolio of affiliate labels to publish games from Capcom, Lucasarts and Westwood Studios.

I met up with Hewland and Dominik and we just immediately clicked. This was a show where we could showcase our games to consumers in a much more mainstream way than we ever could simply advertising in print. The show hit the industry at the right time and we were ready for it.

S.C. The whole show depended on challenges working by not being too easy or too hard. It took us a while to distance ourselves from the fact we were gamers, so getting the balance right between contestants walking the challenge and making a mockery of the whole show and equally never being able to complete a challenge while all making it entertaining was always in mind. There's nothing more boring than watching someone else playing a videogame and having fun. I very quickly came to understand it was about creating challenges that were entertaining for people who were not necessarily gamers and sitting at home trying to follow something on screen that by its definition was quite hard to follow. I took a lot of those lessons to other shows I developed, like *Robot Wars*. It would have been very easy for us to overcomplicate the gameplay because in our heads we wanted to showcase these amazing games.

J.R. **Julian Rignall, Co-Commentator (Series 1)** I was working at the EMAP offices and answered a call asking me whether or not I was interested in doing reviews and games commentary for a new TV show that was being put together. I thought it might be entertaining, and a good way to promote the magazines I was working on at the time – *Mean Machines* and *Computer and Videogames* – so I said yes.

The games commentary was the only part of the filming that made me nervous. Because it was the closest I had got to what I imagined it was like on a movie set. All these talented technical people had spent ages setting up the games and the monitors and the cables and the sound and the cameras and the lighting and the bloody dry ice. You wouldn't believe the number of times Cameron shouted 'Action!' only to then immediately say, 'Cut! We need a touch more smoke.'

So all this stuff was set up and then I had to really nail it perfectly. In my first ever television job. Added to that were the nerves of appearing with the co-commentators. The likes of Neil West and Julian Rignall were proper hardcore gaming gurus from the magazines. I felt like I was an interloper and they resented me because they had devoted their lives to games and I was just coming in one day to get the glory. Those twin prongs of nervous anxiety I think really helped the enthusiasm and energy of the games challenges. That, and it made such a nice contrast with the more laconic delivery of Patrick and my other bits about cups of lapsang souchong and whatnot.

J.R. There was never a feeling that he was some kind of a fraud. The only challenge we faced came from the both of us essentially being thrown together to produce commentary with no rehearsal or prior discussion. We just went up to the pulpit, players started playing, and we began to commentate. It was all ad hoc, and I think those early series commentaries were pretty rough, with both of us talking over one another. Still, it set an enthusiastic tone for what was to follow, and later commentaries improved as the series evolved.

N.W. Neil West, Co-Commentator (Series 1–3) We all felt like interlopers. What Dominik maybe saw as frostiness was actually pure terror. To me, he seemed a bit cocky but was basically a nice guy successfully winging it. A group of us from the Future Publishing crew drove up from Bath, not quite believing what we were going to. We were all so young and somehow we had all found ourselves working on videogame magazines, which was brilliant enough, and then with one phone call somehow we all found ourselves appearing on national TV. Spawny bastards, I believe is the correct term.

F.O. Frank O'Connor, Reviewer (Series 1) Everyone at work made fun of everyone else, but being on the show allowed them to focus on whatever we were wearing, how much make up we had on, and nonstop cries of 'GamesMastaaah'. Neil had a kind of attainably plain TV look, so he ended up as an on-screen co-commentator. They had me as a talking head opining, reviewing games. I was bemused when first asked as I had no public speaking or media expertise. Or personality, charm or looks, and I rambled on about games in a droning yet chirpy sing-song cadence, so in my own way, I like to think I invented YouTubers.

S.C. There was a genius notion discussed in an early meeting of getting celebrities to play videogame challenges. It was probably one of the first shows that took celebrities and put them in a fish-out-of-water scenario. Pretty much all reality and entertainment TV shows now contain celebrities doing things they're not used to doing. So the idea of getting celebrities to play videogames – and at its best videogames that had some relevancy to who they were – that made editorial sense.

D.P. Meanwhile, I was negotiating with a number of software companies to arrange a selection of high-value prizes for the contestants to win. These included arcade machines, foreign holidays, cup final tickets and so on. However, due to the time slot of the show and the strict rules surrounding prize values on Channel 4, it quickly became apparent that none of these prizes would be suitable and that something far more symbolic was required.

SERIES ONE

At around the same time, I had been having a conversation with a contact of mine at joystick manufacturer Spectravideo, called Richard Sekula. I mentioned in passing the problems we were having complying with broadcasting rules and regulations and needing a suitable prize for our competitors. I couldn't have picked a better person to call. Richard told me that they had devised the idea of Golden Joysticks housed in plastic cases as awards to store managers in recognition of particularly impressive retail sales, and that they still had 20 of these awards sat in a warehouse gathering dust. It was like a bolt from the blue. It was arranged that Richard would send me one of these sticks to have a look at and that if we wanted them then they were ours. They were perfect. I took the idea to Adam and Cameron and bingo, that is how the *GamesMaster* Golden Joystick was born.

I have been doing TV, radio shows, newspaper columns, magazine features and books for 30 years now, on both sides of the Atlantic, and 95% of the people I meet ask the same question sooner or later: 'So, do you have a *GamesMaster* Golden Joystick?' It's up there with the *Blankety Blank* Chequebook and Pen, and the *Bullseye* Tankard as a TV prize icon. It was a truly brilliant idea.

RUN TO YOU

Contestant: **Alex Verrey**
Game: **Sonic the Hedgehog (Sega Mega Drive)**
Challenge **Collect 150 rings on Green Hill Zone, Act 2 within 2 minutes**

A.V. **Alex Verrey, Contestant** I used to rely on Teletext to get my daily hit of gaming news. One day there was news of a new TV show in production with details of how to apply to be in the audience. I was around 15 at the time and a huge gamer, so myself and my mate Martin applied. They ended up throwing tickets at us, as many we wanted, because they were filming in term time and they couldn't get audience members. They were also looking for contestants, so when they asked if we were interested in being on the show we jumped at the chance.

We were invited for a chat and bunked off school to head down to the Hewland International office where they decided on our challenges. Mart was given *Terminator 2* and I would be playing *Sonic the Hedgehog*, where I had to collect 150 rings within a time limit. I practised day and night and a few days before the show was filmed, Steve phoned me and asked how I was doing. I said, 'No problem, I can get like 160.' Genuinely, they didn't tell me until we got there on the day and Dominik interviewed me on camera that they were going to set the challenge higher. I started the challenge, but in order for me to get all the rings in the allocated time I had to start with a spin. And if you mess it up you die on the very first enemy of the Green Hill Zone. I died in under two seconds. It was soul-crushing. I must have played through it thousands of times at home and never died but, of course, I was hit with the pressures of being in this very unnatural experience with all the cameras pointed at me. In what I refer to as my *Sliding Doors* moment, they gave me one extra go and I won. My life unfolded in accordance with what happened that day. It set me on the path towards videogames being an industry that I still find myself working in today.

It was an exciting day. I'd never seen anything quite like it, and there we were, these two kids bunking off school and going to this filming day. We didn't really know what the hell was going to hit us. We stuck around the entire day after the challenge was finished and I walked away with my Golden Joystick. So it was thrilling to be there and to watch it all being filmed, but it was also extremely laborious and very slow. They were in their first filming block so they were still finding their feet. Dominik was still finding his feet too, so shots would take a long time, and you'd also have all the technical issues of consoles crashing.

Whoa there, Alex! I *never* fluffed a single take. Ask Cameron or Adam. The shots took a long time because of the bloody dry ice!

RHYTHM IS A DANCER

Contestant:	Danny Curley
Game:	Shadow Dancer: The Secret of Shinobi (Sega Mega Drive)
Challenge:	Guide the warrior through the second and third levels within 2 minutes 30 seconds

D.C. **Danny Curley, Contestant** I became Sega European champion in May 1991. Through winning that, I was flown all over the world First Class, staying in five-star hotels and living the life of Riley. One of the researchers at *GamesMaster* got in touch with me because by that point I was all over the TV and the papers. I was living in Manchester at the time, so when they asked me to take part, I said to them, 'OK, so how are you paying for my expenses?' and they replied, 'Well, normally our contestants pay their own way.' And I just went, 'I'm the European Sega champ. If you think I'm paying to come on to your show, you're off your head, man.' Obviously, *GamesMaster* became massive, but at the time nobody knew what it was. Tiertex, a games studio that I was working for as a tester, thought that it might be a bit of good publicity having me on there, so they paid for the train ticket in the end.

The researcher told me a week before I went down to film that I was going to play *Shadow Dancer*. I had a Mega Drive and I already had the game but when I got down for filming, they took me into the back room and said, 'Look, we're going to make it look like you've never played it.' And I said, 'Well, that's ridiculous. You can tell that I've played it. Anyone will be able to tell that I've played it.' It was bizarre. So having made a big thing of not doing that, I started my challenge and within two seconds I got distracted and killed. [Laughs.] They said I could have one more go and thankfully that was more successful.

Danny Curley was the first games-playing legend we ever had on the show. I obviously liked the kid because he was from Manchester and we didn't have enough of us on the show from north of Watford. But the best thing about Danny – and he is someone I have remained in contact with to this very day – is that he looks like an angel but he is without doubt the foulest-mouthed, most reprobate kid we ever had on the show. I mean, that first challenge in series one he was like 15. And as soon as he finished it he was outside the church smoking a cigarette asking, 'Can someone get me a fookin' can?'

It's completely fitting that he ended the nineties writing crazy features for *Loaded* magazine. But he was the genuine article when it came to games playing. He was to gaming what *Rain Man* is to counting.

D.C. I don't have the Joystick now. In 2000, I was living in London and I decided I wanted to live in Ibiza for the rest of the summer and just get a job out there handing out flyers and living a much simpler life. So I took all my stuff, which included a *You Bet!* trophy and the *GamesMaster* Golden Joystick, and I flung it all into a skip, went down to Gatwick and flew off to Ibiza. They're all in landfill now somewhere.

ICE ICE BABY

Contestant:	Pat Sharp vs. Mick Brown
Game:	Ski or Die (Commodore Amiga)
Challenge:	Beat the opponent with the highest combined score

P.S. Pat Sharp, Contestant I wasn't big on videogames but my kids loved them. We were booked because we had the Pat and Mick records out at the time and we probably thought it was good promotion for the brand and double-heading DJ act. We just said yes to everything. Often we would pay for our own parking or train and never got the money back. We probably didn't get paid for *GamesMaster*. We just turned up and said, 'Here we are, what do you want us to sing?' And they said, 'No, you're here to play a videogame.'

It was a bit of a wacky, cold and miserable day, hence why I was wearing a big ugly jumper. What I remember most about the whole day was sitting playing that skiing game in a head to head and looking down to see my controller wasn't even plugged in. I just remember twiddling and nothing was happening. The Golden Joystick is probably pride of place on Mick's mantelpiece. It was one of the few awards we won as Pat and Mick, let alone Pat or Mick.

Pat and Mick were lovely. Kendo Nagasaki less so, but he was still my favourite guest from series one. As a working-class kid I was used to always having sport on terrestrial telly: snooker, darts, boxing, football, you name it. So to suddenly one day have Jimmy White, Eric Bristow, Barry McGuigan and Emlyn Hughes standing beside me and, like, chatting to me? It was bizarre. It was a dream.

Wrestling was a religion in our house. Every Saturday without fail us kids huddled around the box, cheering on Big Daddy against Giant Haystacks. But Kendo Nagasaki was the scariest entity of my childhood because he never took the mask off. And when he came on the show, he still never took it off. Not even when I tried to chat with him backstage. I literally said, 'Kendo, I am so happy you came on the show, I have watched wrestling all my life.' And he remained in character and said nothing. Just stared. Into my soul. Darth Vader in Lycra. It was brilliant. If he had turned out to be some smiley bloke who sat backstage, mask off, sipping a mint julep, I would have been crushed.

I think it is also my favourite line from series one.

Me: You're playing against Kendo. Or can I call you Ken?

Kendo Nagasaki: [Says nothing.]

Superb!

UNBELIEVABLE

Contestant	Archer Maclean vs. opponent
Game	Jimmy White's 'Whirlwind' Snooker (Commodore Amiga)
Challenge	Beat the opponent with the highest score within I minute 30 seconds

A.M. Archer Maclean, Contestant I went on the show with Jimmy White to promote my game, *Jimmy White's 'Whirlwind' Snooker*. I was booked to play this kid who spent months winning his way up a national computer snooker championship organized by Virgin in the PR run-up. He was supposed to be the UK's best computer snooker player, yet the director still came up to me and said, 'Let the kid win but make it look real close.' No kidding. Anyway, I was actually quite worried that I was going to be completely thrashed at my own game, so I put some practice in beforehand. On the day, it turned out the young champ

was good but not mega supreme, so I was in with a chance of having a respectable score. We filmed it all in one continuous take, and sure enough the scores were almost level, but I embarrassingly went and actually won the match by one pink ball and promptly won the award that was really supposed to be for my competitor. It was so embarrassing and the kid and his family were visibly upset about the whole thing. I got a good slagging off afterwards for that. [Laughs.]

D.W.   I gave him an earful for that. He was so competitive. I'd been with Archer on other press trips presenting *Whirlwind* to journalists and seriously, he wouldn't give up. He wouldn't even let the journalists have a go. [Laughs.] We took it to EMAP and I was pleading with him to just let them play it for themselves but he was like, 'No, I just need to show them this bit. Oh, and then I'll just take this shot.'

A.M.   What wasn't shown was me giving the kid the nice Golden Joystick trophy because I thought he deserved it and he should have won it after all those months of local snooker events. We made a bit of a song and dance over it but because that bit wasn't shown, I got a real dressing down from loads of games journos for beating him in a contest which wasn't supposed to be about me.

The most upset kids ever got with me was on the first day when we finished a challenge and I went backstage and said to Adam, 'Oh for fuck's sake, that last kid was a bit of a bedwetting wee twat, eh?' Adam's face went white. And I heard, after a second's delay, my voice booming those words out in the church. To the whole audience. And this kid and his parents. That's how I learnt to always unplug your microphone between takes.

Paul Gannon, Contestant As a child all I wanted was to be on TV. I auditioned and was invited to play *Duck Hunt* but I didn't own the game to practice at home, so my first time playing was during the technical run. I won the first two rounds and thought, *This is easy.* [Laughs.] I wasn't stressing during filming, concentrating more on looking like an action hero. Shooting ducks was fine but the clay shooting stage was a completely different game and I lost.

If you pause it you can see the moment my heart breaks. I'm inches away from crying. Distraught, Dominik comes over and says, 'You just got a bit trigger happy, didn't you?' My overriding memory is then getting locked into repeating the phrase 'trigger happy' back to him. If I have a tombstone it will read, 'I just got a bit trigger happy' with a picture of my face and teary eyes. That said, if my small footprint is that I appeared on *GamesMaster* then I'm happy. Years later, in an act of confrontational therapy on *Digitiser: The Show*, Mr Biffo dressed me up as the duck and had his guests hunt me. Mentally speaking it didn't help. [Laughs.]

A

B

A
Manic minor
How it all began. Me with the rubber-keyboarded wonder of the ZX Spectrum.

B
The dashing troubadour
Me in *Magpie On The Gallows*, some medieval theatre bollocks at Bristol University. But in it I got to snog Anneka Rice's sister.

A
Lighten up
A 1991 publicity shot for my standup comedy show.

B
Kicking butt
Me, Simon Pegg and David Walliams in a production of *The Rover*, an extremely dull medieval play at Bristol University we bravely smoked our way through.

B

A

B

ARCHIVE I

A

A
Totally made up
Me with the lovely Dolat, who was also one of the three contestants I called PLANK on the wittiest bit of series one.

B
Motley trio
Barry McGuigan gets between Dave and me. The next man to dare try that was called Mario.

C
Aces
Annabel Croft, lovely lady. More importantly, though, standing beside Dave is Chris Kelly, without whom I would never have got an agent. And money. Proper money.

D
Good neighbours
Ashley Paske with Dave and I. He was a lovely bloke – Ashley, that is. Oh OK, so was Dave.

B

C

D

ARCHIVE I

Wired audience
Someone's mum doing a spot check for drugs and weapons on set. Possibly. Actually, on the far right of the photo, that is my sister. For real.

Testosteronetastic
Curry. Lager. Arm wrestling. What more could you want? Adam Wood, who is wrestling me in the top-left pic, was insanely strong. Probably ripped my arm off that night. The bottom-right pic is Cameron, who came up with amazing ideas. And a red jacket outfit.

ARCHIVE I

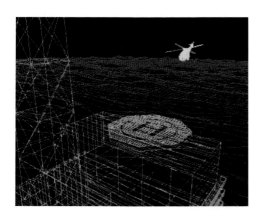

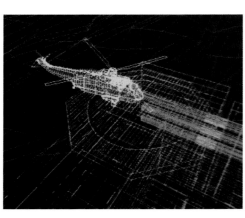

'Pixel by bloody pixel'
It took two Amiga 2000s for designers
Chris and Simon to create animated maps
of Patrick's distorted face, purposely run
slightly out of phase to create a
time-lapse effect. Though you can
probably do it on an app now.

House of Love

'We'd been, I'd like to think, pretty solid pals in the early days. We were there right at the start as I co-presented with him on the day of his screen test. We'd go out for drinks and escapades at parties, like locking the directors of Hewland International in the toilets.' Dave Perry

ARCHIVE I

Suits you, sir
But it didn't, did it? The worst outfit any
TV presenter was ever told to wear and
was too distracted by being newly famous
to think about it until it was too late.

CAN'T STOP THIS THING WE STARTED

> After two weeks of 'TV's only show devoted to videogames', it's hard to avoid the conclusion that the imagery is almost exclusively masturbatory ... *GamesMaster* does nothing to make you revise that opinion, although it tinges it with self-contempt: after all, the only thing dumber than pointing your throbbing joystick at *Sonic the Hedgehog* for hours on end is watching someone else do it through a TV set.
> Mark Steyn, *Evening Standard*, 1992

I watched the first episode down in Bristol with my girlfriend Myfanwy, who was still in her final year there, and a bunch of our closest mates: David Walliams, Jason Bradbury, Katy Carmichael and Callum Greene. We'd all done plays and comedy stuff together as students and they had all been such a big supportive, collaborative part of my development as a funny guy when I was starting out as a comedian at uni, I wanted to be around them for the climax of it. We didn't know then that everyone else in that room would go on to do much bigger things than I in TV and movies.

It was a weird experience watching and getting friends and family saying how much they loved that first episode, because while I thought the show itself was great and original and groundbreaking, there was still that nagging voice in my head saying that it wasn't really me being me. I didn't really enjoy watching my bits at all. I wanted to be a bit less twee and a bit more dangerous. Obviously, I see now a lot of that was from this hang-up I had about me not being 'cool' enough for *The Word*. Luckily, the reactions to the show from some quarters took care of that.

C.M.   We knew that we had to try and create a little noise by being naughty. We didn't have to try too hard. Dominik just had to write in links like, 'Here's a game that's going to make you steal from your parents', and parents would write in to say, 'This is disgusting.'

One of the things we had to defend was the game *Heimdall*, where you had this girl in stocks with her hair in plaits, pinned to a board. You had to threw the axe to chop the plaits to release her and, of course, if you weren't very accurate the axe would just split her head open. There was one contestant who just threw it right on her head and Dominik said, 'Oh, one in the head, just to show her who's boss.' Parents were straight on *Right to Reply* for that one.

J.H.   There were so many complaints to Channel 4, but if we didn't make

Right to Reply with complaints at least once a series we weren't doing our job. *GamesMaster* was a show parents hated, but it wasn't a kids' show. We pitched it as quite radical and bad, which reflected its underground culture.

Going on *Right to Reply* was my first TV achievement. It was like a badge of honour. Even though I felt I was this twee character on the show, the words I was saying were getting us into trouble, which felt a bit more in line with what I wanted from my life and who I really was. That said? While I will defend a lot of the *GamesMaster* content to this day, the *Heimdall* comments that popped our *Right to Reply* cherry were actually pretty bad.

> A.W. Despite the inevitable noise that the show and videogames in general were a bad influence, the first rating for Channel 4 was around 2.6 million, which is a number now that would constitute one of their biggest hit shows. So for a little show that went out at 6.30 p.m. it was amazing. Of course, to us, I remember the ratings didn't really mean anything other than it was great that everyone and the channel seemed happy. We had no real realization how successful it was because we didn't really know the reference points at that time.

I didn't appreciate how big the ratings were, I just knew that after the first week I was utterly inundated with requests from newspapers for interviews about what they were calling the hottest new show on TV. I think I spent what felt like a solid month doing interviews and photoshoots for everything from the *Telegraph* to the *Mirror*. We received great reviews in the *Sun* and the *London Evening Standard*.

It was great for all my family. Everybody gets a piece of that success, don't they? My siblings were kids themselves so they became little celebrities at their schools. My youngest sister went to Sylvia Young Theatre Academy in London. One of her friends was at the house and was so excited she wanted a photo taken in my room. That girl was future Spice Girl Emma Bunton.

I was most happy for my mum. She was the one who had put me in youth drama groups. She was the one who made me sit a scholarship exam for a posh boarding school when I was ten, which basically gave me the kind of education people from my background don't normally get. That's where I learnt words and how to use them, but she had to make the sacrifice of me being away from home. Now I was so happy that she had a famous son. She had worked as hard as I had for it.

The only thing that I felt iffy about were the newspapers that pointed out our show was getting more ratings than Jonathan Ross. He was my TV hero. I remember meeting him for the first time at a media function and a videogames PR person said to him, 'Ah Jonathan, here's your big rival!' And I just went bright red. I wasn't a rival to him at all. He was operating at a different level of entertainment. He was totally cool about it, but I was a bit embarrassed.

A.W. I was quite surprised by the reactions of the editors and techni-
cians working on it. I was putting an online edit together for the
first show and the editor was like, 'Jesus, you've put together a great
show here. It really works. It's really original.' I thought he was just
being polite but I started getting that response from others. Charlie
Parsons, my old boss at 24 Hour Productions, was incredibly compli-
mentary and quite covetous of it. You often don't get that kind of a
response from people in the industry. Maybe there was a sense that
we'd taken a few risks and that made it feel fresh. And people were
probably reacting to the ratings, so they noticed it in a way we didn't.
It became clear quite quickly that this was going to be something
that would hang around for a bit and be a returning business for
Jane. The only negative comment was from a producer, who said, 'I
love the show but I don't like your host.' This was a Scottish producer.
Bizarrely, he said the host had adopted a fake Scottish accent.

I have to say this is my favourite fact about series one that I did not
know about before this book. Scottish people, eh? Whit're they like?

A.W. There was part of me that was a little embarrassed by the positive
reaction. I loved doing the show but it was, in all honesty, a little show
about videogames. It wasn't like I was a passionate games player. My
interest was in the challenge of trying to produce a mainstream show
about videogames.

D.P. We were part of a phenomenon that was about to explode and take
over. Videogames were bringing a third unit into youth culture after
films and music. Thanks to *GamesMaster* we had the potential to be
at the forefront of it. To be the rock stars of the games industry.

What you must realize is that – as opposed to Jane and the team who
had devised this show and worked on it for months, or even years in
Jane's case – for me, it all happened so fast. I was the last person to
join the team. I auditioned at the end of September. And by the end of
January I was the host of the biggest new show on TV, basically. That is
just four months; 120 days. And it felt even quicker than that because
of the adrenalin of filming and doing voiceovers and whatnot. That is
a ridiculously short time for your life to turn around from the bottom
to the top. And I had only just turned 22.

I was still utterly penniless. After the actual filming I went back to
sharing a room with my little brother Michael at my mum's house. I
couldn't afford to move out. It's like those boy bands who have a
number one single but the record company gets all the money. I think
it was one of the twins from Bros who said there is no greater curse
than being famous and skint. So while viewers saw this new TV star
and probably thought I lived in a mansion, in reality I was a 22-year-
old guy lying at night next to his snoring wee brother thinking, 'What
the hell has just happened here? And how do I make some proper
money from it?'

SERIES
TWO

OCTOBER 1942

o host of TV's hottest new show should really be staying in a room with his brother's cat. Or living with his mum, sharing a room with his other brother. I needed to move to London to become a proper, grown-up celebrity. I didn't have any money. But I did have my lovely girlfriend Myf, who had lovely parents with a lovely house in Putney. So I moved in there for what was a truly wonderful summer of 1992. I was very close to her parents: her dad made environmental documentaries for TV, Myf was making TV as well, so it was all very lovely and middle class and media. My childhood was pretty chaotic, with lots of rows between parents. My dad was one of those stereotypical working-class Scottish dads who had a great singing voice, great patter and an even greater temper. He walked out on us when I was 17 for someone the same age as me, so my home life was a big drama. Myf's family were a total contrast: much quieter and more stable, and I felt I needed that, what with the way I had been catapulted into fame, for want of a better phrase. I needed a clear head.

I had very quickly achieved the most difficult thing in a media career: the hit show. I didn't have to spend years clawing my way up a ladder. So I was able, at 22, to sit and think, OK what can I do now?

Chris Kelly was the *GamesMaster* researcher I was closest to, and he said I needed to get an agent to help with my career development and, more importantly, to help me cash in on the success of the show. He recommended this guy Tony Fox, an old Radio Luxembourg DJ, who had that classic Smashie and Nicey radio voice. He repped the likes of Nicky Campbell, Bruno Brookes, Janice Long – lots of radio announcers. As much as I loved video-games as a kid, music was my obsession. Listening to it, singing it, recording little radio shows on cassettes. All that stuff. Then I saw Eric Bogosian's *Talk Radio*, which just blew me away, so radio was definitely on that list of ultimate goals. Tony was a good fit for that.

He was also a bit of a wheeler dealer when it came to money. He literally left no stone unturned when it came to financial opportunities for me. Jane's business partner Hilary Goldman hated him because he knew how much money I should be making, not just from the show but from cashing in on everything else. And Hilary wanted to cash in on everything else as well, and this led to some real conflict by the end of series two, with poor Jane stuck in the middle.

I will say this, though. As much as we hated each other, Hilary Goldman's role in the success of *GamesMaster* should not be underestimated. No one talks about her. Mostly because she was scary. Hard as nails. But the *GamesMaster* Fan Club? *GamesMaster Live*? All those things that sprung up after series one? Were down to her. She turned *GamesMaster* from a show into a commercial entity. I hated her at the time but looking back I realize she was brilliant. Jane is a genius, but Jane is the creative force. All great TV companies need that financial rottweiler as well. Hat Trick had it. Jimmy Mulville was the creative guy, Denise O'Donoghue was the money. That's how it works. You can't go from a 10-episode series to a 26-episode series without a Hilary Goldman.

It's a ludicrously huge leap for a production, and a ludicrously huge leap for someone like me who had been completely skint and unknown a couple of months before. The biggest difference was when it came to meals. I was now taken out for them. You have to understand that my family were working class and I don't remember a single time we ever went out for dinner to a restaurant. When I went to boarding school I got taken out with rich friends and their parents sometimes, and I was like a character in those *Trading Places*-style movies who doesn't know what cutlery to use. I remember being laughed at by a waiter because I pronounced 'escalope' wrongly when I was about 14. I felt humiliated. But after the universe-expanding success of *GamesMaster* series one, I was living in escalope heaven. Escalopalooza. And I wasn't even paying for it!

Every day of the week a different videogame company would take me to one of London's finest eateries. That was incredible. You can get addicted to restaurants very quickly and I don't think that's necessarily a good thing. Because you're waited on, aren't you? You are called 'Sir'. You can complain about anything and you will always be right even when you are wrong. And if you have that every day? Especially at just 22? It's easy to believe that you are something really special. I wasn't aware of all this at the time. I was too busy having fun. So were the people taking me out. A lot of them weren't much older than me and were going through the same thing. One minute sitting in their bedrooms playing *Manic Miner*, and then the next they have an Ocean Software expense account at Quaglino's. And they were all such lovely people. I can say hand on heart that while the media is at least 50% shitbag (in Canada as much as the UK), I can't really think of anyone I knew in the games industry in the nineties who wasn't totally ace. But our universes expanded a little too quickly.

So there is a lot going on there at the beginning of that series. And as a result everything changed during series two. Everything. The show changed. I changed. The levels of ambition changed and the amount of money changed. When you go from 10 episodes to 26 you aren't just a TV show – you are a franchise.

SOMETHING GOOD

J.H.   Jane Hewland, Executive Producer The first series was only 10 episodes but when Channel 4 saw the ratings they recommissioned it to 26 episodes – a huge commission. One that's almost unheard of nowadays. When you're dealing with those sorts of numbers … we negotiated a much bigger budget.

M.M.   Mike Miller, Head of Sport, Channel 4 The fact that we had a good time slot for the show and kept it shows what the channel felt about the programme. The nature of television changed from when I joined Channel 4 to when I left 10 years later. In the beginning, you'd have a programme and you'd say to a scheduler, 'Can you find a good place for it?'. By the time I left, the scheduler would be telling me, 'We've got this slot, we need X million ABC1s. If you can give me a programme that you think can hit the demographic target then we'll slot it in there'. So the whole thing flipped on its head. If a programme didn't work in that slot, they'd put it in a later slot or an earlier slot where you have fewer potential viewers, so the ratings would go down and they'd go, 'Oh it's not doing very well', and it was a self-fulfilling prophecy. So the channel had faith in *GamesMaster* and could see that it worked. And also we allowed all the spin-offs to happen, like the magazine and the live shows. If it wasn't a success, or if it wasn't good for the brand image of the channel, none of that stuff would have happened.

J.H.   When you have a kids' craze, the stronger the craze the quicker it will burn out. At this point we were at its peak but there was a period in the mid-nineties where we were in between markets waiting for the new machines to launch and we suffered for it. Once the PlayStation took off, it revived the craze again and it became a much more mainstream, popular thing.

> I did read an article in the *Daily Mail* recently about games causing harm, but this was news to me. The trouble is, whenever these fads come into fashion people can get addicted. That will always happen. I remember when I became obsessed with chess and I was making chess moves in my sleep. I don't think parents with young people who have serious hobbies have anything to worry about. If it were not computer games, then it would be something else like yo-yos.
> Patrick Moore, *GamesMaster*, 1993

H.H.   Harry Hewland Nintendo, Sega and SNK started sending all these consoles and games to my mum. I felt like a king at school. The buzz was palpable. People were like, 'Get me on that show'. The flip side to it was getting a bit of grief, but generally it was just real interest that this gameshow was on TV and all the rage that the son of the woman who ran the thing was at school. I almost felt a little bit embarrassed about it at times, because there was so much attention.

A.W. Adam Wood, Series Producer (Series 1–2) When we started in the church we weren't sure whether we'd go beyond a series, but when we were recommissioned it seemed to make sense to change the level, as it were, and that obviously became the theme going forward.

J.H. We also weren't allowed back into the church after series one due to the number of complaints about the show to Channel 4.

A.W. It was the right decision. It would have got really stale just being in the same setting. Videogames are so varied in their worlds, we thought we should be creating a new one each time.

C.M. Cameron McAllister, Series Director (Series 1–2) I loved developing each series and creating a world for it. I was really excited by the idea of a gaming platform out at sea, so I thought it would be great if we could create a kind of converted oil rig.

A.W. I did a recce of a few places, one of which was this old Victorian pumping station. There's a few of them around London. I went inside and thought, *Wow.* It felt quite square so it could be the inside of an oil rig with tiers upon tiers of platforms as an obvious place to put an audience peeking over, and these huge steps leading down to the games playing area as both an entrance and a focal point for contestants. It just had a lovely symmetry to it, with these banks of machinery, pistons and pumps.

S.C. Steve Carsey, Researcher I remember seeing that location myself before we decided to use it and looking at it and going, *Blimey, this is going to take some lighting and smoke machines to fill,* because it was just vast. It created this gladiatorial feel that was really perfect for competitive games playing. It was a great find and visually stunning.

D.J. Doug Johns, Researcher (Series 2) We were filming in summer during a heatwave and it would get so hot inside. Obviously we had a lot of lights in and people don't realize how much heat they put out. I was down on the ground with Dominik setting up a challenge and looked up to see one kid just swaying back and forth near the railing. They looked like they were going to collapse in the heat, so a load of us sprinted up the stairs as quickly as we could to get to them before they fell over the edge. They hadn't realized themselves how close they'd been to falling over, but we gave them water and calmed them down. Considering we then filmed those same kids literally running up and down stairs we were very lucky nothing happened. Not in a month of Sundays would an audience be allowed up there like that now.

C.M. So we had a location and then we started thinking about what else we would need for our new world. We brought in Sarah, a model, to be the diver who would bring up the Golden Joysticks from a misty pit.

D.P. Dave Perry, Co-Commentator (Series 1–6) I'd been the monk handing out the Golden Joysticks in the first series so I was interested as to who was going to be doing that in the second series. And when it was

Sarah, I thought, *That's a shrewd move. Sarah in a wetsuit, looking straight out of James Bond.* That just made sense to me. Yet they stuck her in a fucking full-length diving suit and mask. [Laughs.]

C.M. We loved the idea that the audience had no idea who was behind the mask. It was kind of like The Stig from *Top Gear*, except we did it 10 years earlier.

S.C. They were also looking at bringing in a character called Auntie Marisia to serve refreshments to the audience and guests. With budgets being tight, Jane asked if we knew of anyone and I said I think my grandma might be up for it. So down she came on the train from Yorkshire. She put on her pinnie, wheeled out her tea trolley and became a recurring character. She didn't get paid and only did it because I asked her to. You can imagine it definitely made for a talking point in the family at Scarborough. My mum and dad never had a chance to come down to see the show being recorded so I love the fact someone in my family saw me at work in such a bizarre, surreal way.

I do actually have an Auntie Marisia. She was the one member of my mum's family who did manage to leave town. She is my favourite of my mum's sisters because she lived in Saudi Arabia and then America and her husbands were always loaded. She would come back to Arbroath at Christmas wearing designer clothes and with the most beautiful exotic perfume: Fendi and Oscar de la Renta were two I remember. She was loud, funny, had an American accent and was the most glamourous person in my childhood. I literally mentioned her once to Cameron and he fell in love with the name more than anything else and before you knew it she was a character on the show. That is classic Cameron. But it was a bit bizarre to have her 'character' played by Steve's granny. She actually looked, sounded and acted the complete opposite of her real-life counterpart.

A.W. Given we'd decided to go industrial with this idea of a converted oil rig, Cameron naturally thought it should be a holiday camp. [Laughs.] Hence Dominik's costume.

Biggest mistake of my career was not paying attention when they were setting up series two. With the exception of two holidays with Myfanwy to Thailand and New York I didn't have a day off from the moment series one finished. I was too busy opening every single video-game shop that appeared, and then negotiating deals for games columns in *Smash Hits* and regular game slots on the *Steve Wright Show* on BBC Radio I. So I don't remember having many conversations about sets or clothing. I was told we were going to set it on an oil rig. *OK, fair enough*, I thought. And the location was this giant pumping station. 'OK, fine', I would say, on my way to some paid appearance. And then at some point they said it was going to be a holiday camp and I thought: *Hmm, that sounds a bit weird but, you know, that's Cameron just being Cameron. Trust him.* And I really took my eye off the ball. And then before you know it, I have this Butlin's Redcoat outfit that is just utterly ghastly. Horrible.

I spoke to Cameron and Jane about it but they told me it was part of the overall vision for the series. It was all going to work within the world Cameron had created. And that was the last time anybody ever told me what to wear on a TV show. That was why I then became an associate producer on the show. Because I had to have more creative control so no one would make me look like an arsehole. I have had a reputation at times in my subsequent career as someone who can be a bit less than flexible, though I prefer the phrase 'passionately committed to a vision' myself. My Canadian radio bosses in particular will tell you that if something doesn't feel right to me, I don't do it. That's what the red jacket taught me.

> C.M. Unbeknown to me, Dominik hit rock bottom with that. I didn't realize it at the time but apparently I put him into therapy for several years because I made him wear that Butlin's red coat. Somebody told me ages afterwards that I had really fucked with his head making him wear it. But I thought it was brilliant because it was tongue-in-cheek. The idea of a futuristic Butlin's and a gaming rig I thought was a strong visual look. But I didn't realize how humiliated he was by wearing it. He was really cross with me for years.

I am insecure about how I look. I had bad eczema around my eyes as a kid. I literally had to pour a million tons of hydrocortisone ointment on them. I was very aware of that. And so to take that insecurity and put it on TV is a challenge. And then I developed the massive chip on my shoulder about how I hadn't got *The Word* because I wasn't cool or trendy or good-looking enough. Cameron made this insecurity a million times worse by dressing me like a total twat. I was the public face of the show. Not Cameron. But his decisions impacted my public persona and thereby my life and my success. I would turn up to games shop openings and the owners would say, 'Where's your red jacket?' And they would be genuinely shocked when I told them I did not dress like that. But that is the persona others create for you if you let them. And as the face of a show you carry that can.

There were so many things I wanted to do with my TV career with music and movies and comedy and other aspects of culture. And I felt the red jacket ruined it. It portrayed me as this camp, effete, wimpy dweeb. It destroyed my confidence. It removed any fun from series two for me. I literally hated every day of filming on set. To be meeting the likes of Robbie Williams, Vic Reeves, Tony Slattery – people you really want to meet? And to feel you look like a total twat? That is heartbreaking.

Now, obviously Cameron's vision worked. The popularity of that series proves that. But while it worked for the show? It didn't work for me. As a result I think my performance is almost as bad as it was

SERIES TWO

in series one. Because at the back of my head, in every single shot, in every sentence and word I say? I was thinking how awful I looked. And I think it shows. It's not a very natural performance or delivery. I just wanted to get the filming done and put my real clothes back on. Hipster jacket and jeans and a band t-shirt. And forget the teetotal fitness regime of series one. At the end of each day of filming I just wanted a very big drink.

And that was the first seeds sown of my leaving the show. I remember in the gap between the two filming blocks I thought, *Shit. If I stay with this show what the fuck will they make me look like next?* So I stopped caring as much. I thought, *Fuck it. Let's just get through it. I can quit after this.* And what is interesting is I think that made my performance in the second half of the series a bit better. It's quite liberating to not care. You push the boundaries a bit more. And I think that side of me that gave no fucks grew on and off the show as the decade progressed.

> A.W. We would write a sort of script for the show but then Dom would put it in his own words. All that innuendo and double-entendre was him.
>
> C.M. Sometimes we had the odd run-in. He was very, very funny but occasionally we would have to rewrite and just slightly rein in some of his links. Not because they were too rude – in fact, we always pushed for more – but because he loved throwing in these highly pretentious movie or literature references. We'd go, 'Oh Dominik, for God's sake.' He used to get so upset if we touched his work.
>
> A.W. Dominik could fall out with people. He could be quite outspoken and he loved a little bit of a barney sometimes. So if he rubbed up against someone things would need smoothed over. Or someone would say something and Dom wouldn't let it go.

I think that comes from being a standup comedian. You work on your words so much – they are precious to you. You live and die by those words on stage. So you don't really like anyone else telling you they don't work. And it was so weird to suggest all these things about shoving throbbing joysticks where the sun didn't shine with Adam and Cameron going, 'Yeah, that's fantastic.' And then the minute I slipped in a mention of a philosopher they were shocked and appalled. It was like, penises? Good. Plato? Bad. I felt we could do both. What can I say? I had just graduated. I love philosophy. If you think Adam and Cameron reacted against it in *GamesMaster* scripts? You should have seen some of the responses from editors when I did it as a columnist at the *Daily Star*.

C.M.   As we were given a bit more money by Channel 4, I was able to shoot a proper title sequence. I flew up to an oil rig near Aberdeen, filming in and out the side of a helicopter swooping in from all angles. I was really pleased with myself for what I'd shot, but when I brought the footage back, everyone was a bit like, 'Yeah, it's all slightly shit.' Russell, the editor, added some spark to it and some effects and then the graphic designers took that footage and made it look a million times better.

Cameron was so excited on that title shoot. He was like a wee boy at Christmas. I was the opposite. My dad worked on the oil rigs. I had been to them before. They are boring and freezing cold. I had been on helicopters before. They are terrifying things that make no mechanical sense to me. I still don't know how they stay in the air, even though my dad used to dangle outside them on bits of rope rescuing people. So a whole day making flybys of oil rigs with the doors open and then standing on the freezing platform welcoming people on board was just bah humbug to me. Now, I know what you're thinking: 'But Dominik, you don't actually appear in the opening titles.' Exactly! After all that palaver Cameron didn't even use those shots of me. He really was not my favourite person back then.

C.M.   Chris Mills, Graphic Designer (Series 1–3) I had a lot of fun doing the changeover sequence from the first series crashing and rebooting into the second series. We were in the edit suite and found a picture of some sheep in a field as a photograph and we just stuck that under a fixed rostrum camera pointed down at a desk and that picture was the 'normal play will be resumed' shot. The guys were right up for that. Adam thought it was hilarious. They were very indulgent of us but very much on the same wavelength.

A.W.   That rebooting and the idea of progressing to a new, higher level, I thought what was produced looked incredible.

S.D.   Simon Dunstan, Graphic Designer (Series 1–3) Although it may seem a bit arrogant, we were the only people doing stuff like that. It's not like they could go to another boutique and find someone else to do it. It was very innovative for its time. The edit suite was quite an open, creative space. It wasn't very regulated. There was a lot of play going on.

R.T.   Russell Thomas, Editor (Series 1–2) Dominik was always coming into the edit suite too, as this young, enthusiastic person, interested in what we were doing.

Once I was an associate producer I started filming features for the show, and putting together the review sections with the utterly adorable Russell Thomas. It was really fascinating to see the show from the other end. And it was complicated to do. It took a whole day to edit a review section. You had to edit the real shots with the graphics added a layer at a time, putting each layer down on to different tapes. You could probably do that thing in seconds these days, but this was using proper old-fashioned analogue tapes. Editing suites were fantastic places to be in the nineties. This one was in Covent Garden and at lunch you could literally order anything from anywhere. There is also a rumour that certain editing suites sent out for cocaine and put it down on the invoice as 'fruit and flowers', but I couldn't possibly comment.

C.M. Chris Mills About 10 years ago, I was watching Australian Football League and all the graphics on the stadium screens were vaguely familiar. They had little screens coming down with metallic suspension and cables either side, coming down and in and out of frame, and I just looked at it and thought someone's been watching *GamesMaster*. Someone's found it somewhere and thought, 'Oh that looks pretty cool.' It was just awkward and silly with no rationale for it.

JUMP AROUND

Heavily ring-modulated and without his nine-inch refractor, Patrick Moore resembles a septuagenarian Max Headroom on an ECT machine, and reads a script containing some pretty heavy street jive, none of which (I suspect) he understands.
Victor Lewis-Smith, *Evening Standard*, 1992

S.C. We recorded the Consoletation Zone scripts with Patrick at a small blue-screen studio in Soho. We'd sit Patrick on his chair and bang out these consoletations with an autocue. We knocked out a lot and of course he had no idea what he was saying. To be fair, to anyone not au fait with videogames or cheats on console games it was just like a series of bizarre ramblings. I'm sure the rest of the studio crew must have gone *What the hell is Patrick Moore going on about, left, right, up, right, down and down.* Out of context it must have sounded like gobbledegook.

P.M. Patrick Moore, GamesMaster (speaking in 1993) I know absolutely nothing about computers and videogames. I'm a fake. Whenever people ask me about what to do on level six or whatever, I haven't the foggiest what they are talking about. I can drive a car and fly a plane, but when it comes to Nintendo I am completely lost.

P.S. Peter Scott, Researcher (Series 2–3) I joined production of the series in November 1992. They were just finishing the main filming but I didn't get to go down to the main location as I was working on the Consoletation Zone. Within a month I'd come up with ideas and filmed various features, such as taking gaming grannies to the London Trocadero, as well as writing a gazillion cheats to be read out by disappointed children as they couldn't ask their own questions. It was predetermined but I would place their own questions in a file and get back to them with answers because I was nice like that. I got to write scripts for the King of Stars himself, Patrick Moore, but my proudest moment was filming a chicken asking a question of the GamesMaster. It made Jane spit out her white wine when she saw it. She thought it was the unfunniest thing that had ever happened. But everyone else howled and hooted with laughter.

We should have had more farmyard animals in the Consoletation Zone in series two. Those bits were great. But they were too few and far between. I loathed that part of the show by then because of the real estate it took up. Look at Take That. Biggest guest we could have got. The chat with them is edited down to about three seconds. The challenge itself over in minutes. All so we can have two or three minutes of kids asking for cheats that had already appeared in magazines by the time we aired. But once again, the genius of Patrick Moore, his delivery and his bravery to just go with the flow made it occasionally bearable.

I get that it's important to give your audience the chance to appear on their favourite show – that helps generate a fan base – but I think it would have been a much better format if we'd dumped the Consoletation Zone and spent more time on challenger chats and proper features. Oh hang on ... that's what we *did* do ... in series five ... when my power was immeasurable! [Laughs.] Of course, looking back my feelings on this could purely be that I just selfishly wanted more of me talking to people. That was the most interesting bit of the show for me from very early on. That tiny bit of it where I could be a chat show host. So I guess once again there was that bit of me that was already wanting to do stuff beyond *GamesMaster*.

S.C.   Some of the interactions with Patrick Moore were hysterical. We recorded them in sessions deliberately in an area with nearby restaurants. There was a curry house that Patrick liked and he'd always insist on us going for a curry every lunch. So there'd be me, Doug and Pete sat with Patrick. He was, let's say, a gentleman of his time in regards to his views on life. I was a huge amateur astronomer in my day and I used to watch *The Sky at Night*, so meeting him for the first time was quite memorable.

SERIES TWO

EVERYBODY IN THE PLACE

A.W.   With the show's success we were able to begin booking a higher calibre of celebrity guest. The games industry seemed to be happy with it, too. It felt like we were pushing at an open door. People were happy to get their games on the show and behind the scenes Jane was talking to manufacturers and lining up exclusives.

S.C.   Indeed, by this point we were getting pressure from games publishers wanting us to show this amazing bit of their game and we'd go, 'Yeah, it's great, but it won't make any sense at all to our viewer without any context, background or history of what the game's about.' Once we had the games industry on side, it was easier for us to turn around to them and say, 'We want you to build a challenge into your game for us, or create a special level because then it'll be easier for us to feature your game on our show'. We were all very aware of the fact that having some level of visibility on our show was worth far more to the games industry than having a full-page advert in a videogames magazine, just by virtue of the numbers involved. It was a different scale of exposure.

Even though I was terrified the videogames aspect of the show would pigeonhole a future career for me in other things, the one bit of making series two I really did enjoy was going into the office and trying out the challenges for myself. Steve would have a load of them set up and then I would have a go while Adam made notes and sometimes suggested tweaks that might make them more entertaining. That was fun. Because at heart I was still a gamer, you know? And then fitting the games to celebrities – that was a real skill.

S.C.   I did a few co-commentary appearances at this point and it was a running joke that because I had a goatee beard and long hair Dominik would always introduce me as 'Stephen of Bethlehem' or 'Stephen of Nazareth'. Just this running gag that I was a messiah. [Laughs.] I liked doing commentary but hated doing it at the same time. I wasn't natural at it in front of the camera in the same way that Dominik was. It filled me with a real feeling of sickness.

H.H.   Still to this day, I can say one of the best jobs that I've ever had in my life was filming in the summer holidays. My job was to sit in the games room and teach the celebrities how to play the games. They'd show up about half an hour before filming and invariably wouldn't have any idea what to do. Some of them had never even played a video-game before. I'm not sure I did a very good job but it was incredible.

S.C.   Unbelievably we'd booked Take That to play *Bomberman* as a replacement for a bigger name. Adam said, 'What about these boys? They're on the cover of *Smash Hits* next month and they're going to be big, aren't they?' You could see they were bubbling up, gaining traction with the press. By the time the show broadcast in November, it looked like we were the best celebrity bookers in the world, but it was more luck than design.

Of course, there was five of them so we identified that the only game in existence they could play at that time was *Bomberman* on the Amiga. It had a special dongle that plugged into the back and allowed you to have a fifth joystick. They arrived an hour before film-ing going, 'OK, what are we playing?' So Harry and I sat backstage with them teaching them how to play this game. They all picked it up quite quickly but even then you could tell Robbie was hyper compet-itive. You felt the others were there to just promote their single and have some fun, but Robbie genuinely wanted to win.

Robbie Williams is one of the greatest human beings I have ever met. All of The That were lovely blokes, to be honest, although I did piss off Gary Barlow. I was standing next to Dave in the Portaloo toilets out-side having a wee before they were supposed to arrive and he asked me, 'So which one of Take That's your favourite?' Possibly a strange question to ask another man while you are peeing together, but fair enough. I replied, 'Ken. They're all fucking called Ken, aren't they?' At which point the toilet flushed and out came Gary Barlow. I tried to cover it by saying, 'Hey Gary! I knew you were in there, pal. Nice to meet you.' He just smiled politely. And washed his hands. At least he washed his hands. Dave then hilariously proceeded to call them Red Ken, Blue Ken, etc. during the whole game commentary. It was probably his best bit of commentary on the show ever.

What is bizarre about this story is David Walliams, who I got a job as a runner on that series, tells a version of this tale in his autobi-ography that has him peeing beside me, rather than Dave, and him upsetting Gary instead of me. I can only assume either I have gotten confused with my Daves, or Gary Barlow and I both spent a lot of time in those Portaloos with a multitude of Davids. For whatever reason. The nineties, eh?

But anyway, Rob was my favourite of Take That because he really wanted to win. He loved the show and he was the only one of those lads I ever bumped into again. Something that is great about the guests who appeared on the show is that that it was such a unique, memo-rable experience for them. That's why I can bump into Ant and Dec decades later and they remember being on the show. I can tweet about

Tony Slattery's battles with addiction in 2018 and he then drops me a note saying how much fun he had on the show. To do that after a quarter century and mountains of cocaine – for both of us – is a tribute to the show. And it leads to fantastic situations for me wherever I go.

For example, in 1994 I was at the first T in the Park aftershow party in the Glasgow Hilton with my pals and their wives and this voice boomed out across the room: 'Dominik Diamond from *GamesMaster*, you did not shag my mum!' And that voice belonged to Robbie Williams. Apparently someone had told him that I made a joke in my *Smash Hits* column about having sex with his mum. I told him I hadn't written anything of the sort and asked him if he still had his *GamesMaster* Golden Joystick. A huge smile broke out all over his face and he told me how much he loved it and that it was pride of place in his house. Then, because he really is the most charming man in the world, he insisted on meeting all my pals and their wives, and even got down on one knee to kiss the hands of the ladies. Then he asked me if I wanted to meet Noel Gallagher and go to his room for a party. Obviously, I said yes, so Robbie dragged me over to the other side of the party and there was Noel. I had brought my mate David Wells over with me because he himself was a guitarist in Scottish eighties band H2O and I thought he would dig it. However, when Robbie said 'Noel, this is Dominik Diamond from *GamesMaster* and *Smash Hits*!' Noel gave me a look of utter boredom, as if I was the millionth D-list celeb who had come up to him that night. Which I probably was. I panicked a bit and all I could think of to say was, 'Hi Noel. This is my mate David, he plays guitar too.' I never made it up to Noel's room for that party.

INFORMER

D.T. **Dan Tootill, Reviewer (Series 2)** I'd joined *The GamesMaster* Fan Club when I was 14. I'd watched the first series and was obsessed with the show. The welcome pack came with an application form inviting members to either be on the show as a challenger, submit a cheat for the Consoletation Zone or take part in the reviews section – I thought I'd give it a shot. One of the researchers called for a quick audition over the phone and soon I was invited to film games reviews for the new series. Filming took place at an audio production studio with the tiny sound booth used as a green room and the camera set up where a band would usually record. They had every computer and console in there and it was a squeeze to get everyone in, but that didn't matter given I was so excited to be sat right next to Jaz Rignall.

J.R. **Julian Rignall, Reviewer (Series 2–3)** It always felt like everyone at Hewland was in a rush and stressed out. They shot numerous reviews for different episodes in a single day, and it was a bit of a nightmare just cranking them out one after another. We'd sit around twiddling our thumbs for hours waiting for our turn to shoot our reviews, and when it was time, we were expected to rattle off an interesting and coherent review within a matter of seconds, which was quite a challenge. Despite that, though, it was fun and we tried to make our reviews as interesting as possible, despite us not really being given enough time to go into any meaningful depth.

D.T.   I got a call the next day saying the footage was unusable and the lighting was all wrong. I wouldn't be on TV after all and, worse still, my schoolmates would all insist I had made the whole thing up. Fortunately I was invited back to review mostly strategy games, my least favourite genre. The second time felt stressful and rushed with only 20 minutes or so to figure out *Mega-Lo-Mania*, and I don't think I even played *Utopia* despite reviewing it. I pretty much blagged my way through it, nervous as hell and trying my best to do a decent job. When the episodes aired, I looked so weird and unnatural with my huge wide-open eyes staring into camera. I was mortified. It made me a laughing stock at school and, thanks to YouTube, the snarky comments keep coming to this day. Despite all that, I'm still really proud to have had a small part in the show.

J.R.   I hadn't realized until recently that I appeared in a compilation of the Top 5 Worst Reviewers' Haircuts. It doesn't surprise me that they did that. I and several others were easy targets with the crazy hairstyles we sported in the early nineties. [Laughs.]

COME AS YOU ARE

Contestant	Opponents vs. Danny Curley
Game	Sonic the Hedgehog 2 / Mario Lemieux Hockey / Arch Rivals (Sega Mega Drive)
Challenge	Beat Danny Curley at any challenge on any game

D.C.   I competed in the UK 1992 Sega Championships because to keep hold of my European crown I first had to win the UK tournament. This time I was competing against eight others and I fucking hammered every one of them. They may as well have just sent eight penguins to take on a polar bear. I'd been a games tester for about six months at this point, which Sega knew about but they were hoping that I'd lose because I was just not what they wanted for the brand. They wanted a polite 15-year-old boy they could use to market and instead they got this rough bastard from Manchester who swore and smoked and drank. When they realized that I was also going to win the European Championships, they decided that my being a professional games tester meant I was now disqualified and they took away my UK Champion title. Despite them already knowing what I was doing for a job. They just made up some bullshit rule after I'd won the tournament to get rid of me.

GamesMaster invited me back for series two as the reining Sega Champion. I was asked to come back for three more episodes and take on challenges from the audience. I said, 'All right. You pay my train ticket this time.' [Laughs.] 'And I want a hotel.' They paid my train ticket but they wouldn't stretch to a hotel, so Steve ended up letting me crash in his bed while he slept on the couch. I just looked on, thinking, *This is what it's like to work in TV.*

I went down to film on my first day and they made it look like I was meant to be challenging anyone in the crowd on any random game. That's obviously bollocks. I was a good games player but I wasn't a Jedi. I wasn't Luke Skywalker. I did know ahead of filming the first challenge would be *Sonic 2*, so that was no problem. The second challenge was *Mario Lemieux Hockey*, which I didn't know until an hour before, so they gave me a copy I could practise with. The lad that I played against had played it for two weeks and it was close but we drew so he didn't technically beat me. And the third challenge was *Arch Rivals*. A basketball game I'd never fucking heard of. I said to the guy beside me, 'What fucking button does what?' So on the third game I was beaten.

I was utterly determined that Danny come back on the show. Fuck Sega disqualifying him because they didn't like him being a bad lad. He was the people's champion! And the poor kid had to play these games he had never played before and still did great. Was Danny the best games player to feature on the show? Possibly. Martin Mathers was maybe better, but Danny had more appearances than any other challenger. He got four – *four* – welcome walk-ons with an audience. And his own feature.

D.C. A few months later the team got in touch and said come down to London for the day as we want to do this little feature on the life of Danny Curley. The most fun I had on *GamesMaster* was doing that feature, more so than the challenges. They wanted to film me walking around Soho in London for some reason. One of the researchers, Doug Johns, was running round asking people, 'What do you think of Danny Curley?' One of the guys we bumped into was Mike McShane, the American comedian from *Whose Line is it Anyway?*

> His dexterity, his unflagging ability to play 10 hours on end without food or light qualifies him as a major videogame mushroom.
> Mike McShane, comedian

I directed that feature! I got Danny walking past porno shops in Soho and Doug runs up to me and says, 'Mike McShane is round the corner.' 'No fucking way!' I replied. Then I heard his famous Canadian voice boom out, '*GamesMaster*!' Turns out he was a big fan of the show and was more than happy to wax lyrical about Danny's games-playing brilliance. And at the end Danny tells kids to study hard at school. It really has everything. As a director, it's probably my *Citizen Kane*.

> D.C. I love Dom. I've always loved him. It would be another year before I made a video, *PowerPlay*, with him, which was just us two pissing about on location for two days. Really bizarrely, on the video cover they put me in the foreground, front and centre, while Dominik was much smaller, poking out behind me. It was crazy. To get Dominik Diamond from *GamesMaster* involved and then lessen his profile in the marketing.

I still have *PowerPlay* on VHS! And at least once a month I whip it out, look fondly at the cover and wonder why the fuck Danny is at the front of it and I am in the background. But that is a measure of Danny's standing in the games community. Even I give up centre stage for the legend.

> D.C. As I became older I was getting more into alcohol and weed and trying to get laid. *Alex Kidd* and *Altered Beast* started to lose their appeal. I just wasn't paying as much attention as I used to. I got older and I wanted to go to the pub. That was the end of competitive games playing.

STICK IT OUT

Contestant:	Letty Edwards vs. Auntie Marisia
Game:	King of the Monsters (SNK Neo Geo)
Challenge:	Beat the opponent in a best-of-three fight

> L.L.E. **Lovely Letty Edwards, Contestant** My husband was a chairman of a company in Bristol and one day he brought back a company computer, which was this huge thing, as they were back then. It came with a copy of *Lemmings*, and while he had no interest in games I absolutely adored it. I worked through every single level. Anyway, I was watching the first series of *GamesMaster* when they had a guy come on whose challenge was on an early level of *Lemmings*. He was total rubbish. [Laughs.] I rang the office and mentioned that not only was I 52 and playing computer games, but that I could easily beat him. They immediately wanted me on the next series.
> My son knew I was going on and was thrilled to bits, as were my other children. Very sadly he died in the week I was due to film it. I said to my other son and daughter that I wasn't going to do the show and that I couldn't go through with it but they said, 'Mum, he was so excited for you to go on the show and he wants you to do it.' So I decided to go through with it in his memory.

When I got there the game they wanted me to play was *King of the Monsters*. I was playing against another gaming granny in a best-of-three. I had 10 minutes to practise with a joystick, which I wasn't used to playing with, and lost the first round. I felt my heart and soul just wasn't in it. But all of a sudden, it was like my son nudged me in the back and said, 'C'mon, you can do it, Mum'. And with that I just went mad. I slaughtered her. [Laughs.] And I won the joystick. It was all for him.

WALKING ON BROKEN GLASS

Contestant:	Vic Reeves
Game:	Sleepwalker (Commodore Amiga)
Challenge:	Complete the level without waking Lee

Something I had ~~more~~ input into by this stage was the choice of guests on the show, so for me it was basically comedians, pop stars and athletes. That was my jam. Pop stars because I loved music. Athletes because I watched that stuff with my mum as a kid, it's her favourite sport and I wanted them to say hello to her on telly so she could feel special. Comedians because all I want to do in my life is hang out with funny people.

You can basically throw anything at comedians and they will give good chat. So you have Josie Lawrence talking about wanting a videogame where you go around snogging people, and lovely Tony Slattery saying how much he hated videogames. The absolute master, though, was Vic Reeves playing *Sleepwalker*.

> **V.R.** Vic Reeves, Contestant It was possibly THE highlight of my life.

Vic just has an otherworldly level of comic imagination. Picasso with words. And I didn't even have to ask him anything. He just started going on about the dials behind me, asking which one was my favourite. And what that taught me, as a fledgling comedy presenter, is don't ever feel scared about not having control of chatting to someone on the telly. If they are of the calibre of a Vic Reeves? It's not about you. It's about them. Let them lead the dance and just enjoy it. You can tell that all my reactions and laughs with him are totally genuine. Actually, that was one of the few moments of filming where I forgot about how much a dick I looked in that red jacket. He also has one of my two favourite lines ever from a guest, when he said he didn't like snakes because anything that breathes through their teeth is suspicious. I mean that is just genius.

The *Sleepwalker* game was a great concept which raised tons of money for Comic Relief, but most importantly it got me on *The Big Breakfast*. I shot a filmed feature with Chris Evans at HMV, who was another person you learn so much from working with. I'd just started to direct some of the *GamesMaster* features and to see how he directed the cameraman and the shots when he was on location was inspiring. He could see the whole thing in his head. The whole TV production.

And then to go down to the iconic *Big Breakfast* house itself to talk about the game was just thrilling. It is the most original programme in the history of UK television as far as I am concerned. The way it took a tired format and reinvented it and then kept it fresh with an unending conveyor belt of new features? That was superb, and it was a very special show. To see the energy down there in the house itself, it's so thick it's like you felt totally buzzed from the moment you walk in. Best of all, I was interviewed by Zig and Zag, who were obviously the real stars of the show. I had never filmed with puppets before, and even though you meet the guys behind them, within seconds of the cameras rolling their performance is so good that you don't question they are anything but utterly real.

ZIG We love double D! He knew stuff about stuff and videogames!

ZAG Well, he always said he knew stuff about videogames, but I don't know if he actually did?

ZIG But his name was Diamond so you had to trust him!

ZAG Didn't he once tell us that his brother was in the Beastie Boys?

ZIG Oh yeah, and that wasn't true!

ZAG Anyway, *GamesMaster* was one of our fave shows. Back when videogames were big plastic cartridges you slammed into dusty consoles.

ZIG And the colours were so vivid that my eyes went permanently crossed! That's true!

ZAG Why's Dominik Diamond writing a book about *GamesMaster*, anyway?

ZIG Yeah, he should write a book about a wizard kid who goes to boarding school in a castle.

ZAG It's been done, Zig.

ZIG Aw. Not again!

RUNAWAY TRAIN

There is no bigger example of the bloated commercial behemoth *GamesMaster* had become than *GamesMaster Live*. It was exhausting for me.

When you record a TV show you say a bit. Have a break and a cigarette while they reposition cameras. Then say another little bit. And

if something breaks down with a game then you just go off and smoke more fags until they get it working. With *GamesMaster Live*? No breaks. No stoppages. If a game doesn't work? Or there are any other technical problems? It's me standing there telling jokes until it works. All day. And all of it wearing the fucking red jacket. Which is also mentally draining in another way. I was live, on stage, with a microphone, in front of a thousand people, which is the exact situation I dreamed of as a standup. But this was in front of kids and parents. At a trade show.

I think that was the moment I knew I didn't enjoy being recognized. Don't get me wrong, it is very flattering to have people come up to you in the street and say they rate your work. That is great validation. But to be in a massive hall with thousands of people in there? And not be able to walk 10 feet without being surrounded. That just gave me panic attacks, especially as someone uncomfortable with their appearance. And you have to be constantly upbeat and smiley and funny, otherwise you worry that you'll disappoint fans. That takes a lot of effort if you are tired or whatever. And that, sadly, is when eventually you look to things like alcohol and drugs that will make you feel more confident and less tired. Which is not good. But back then I just did what I was told.

H.H.   I was behind the stall selling posters and collecting the money thinking, 'Wow, this is fun.' I had no idea until then that my mum and the show was generating this huge excitement around the country about videogames. Being caught up in all of that and feeling like you were part of the royal videogame family was exciting. It was just snowballing. The craze was massive. It was a time when the world wasn't so disparate and before everyone had their own niche interests and private corner of the internet. Everybody got caught up in the hysteria around something and it felt like a shared cultural experience.

D.J.   We ran *GamesMaster Live* like the TV show and had challengers up on stage. I remember Dominik getting me up to co-host for some of the challenges. There was this one blind kid that could play *Streetfighter II* and, awesome, good on him. So Dominik asks me, 'How do you think this guy's going to do? Pretty well?' and I said, 'Oh I can't see it myself.' Dominik just looked at me like I'm a total moron, which I was. I hadn't said it to be a smart arse, I was just an idiot blurting out words. So I was shuffled off stage quickly.

At the end of the day we lumped a load of show merchandise, posters and T-shirts, in the hire van, which Steve drove back to London. He parked it at some hotel so we could get some food before we headed off back to London. Didn't bother to bloody lock it. Our van was nicked, including our bags, clothes and everything. We didn't have a lot of money back then so that loss was felt. Typical Steve. Worse still, when we got back to the office, we found out the van hadn't been insured. We were like, 'You have to replace our stuff.' The accountant Hilary was like, 'Well that's a games T-shirt you were given, so that's worth nothing'. And we were just like, 'We're people on about £16,000 living in London, just cough up for our clothes.' She was pretty tight-fisted.

I remember hanging out with Doug Johns a lot. He made the experience slightly less horrific because he was a lot of fun to be around. Simultaneously one of the most wonderfully kind and most wonderfully sick-humoured people on the planet. And I supposed if I hadn't done *GamesMaster Live* I would never had met Kirk. And Kirk makes Doug look like Mother Teresa.

> **K.E.** **Kirk Ewing, Co-Commentator (Series 5–7)** I'd been watching *GamesMaster* and felt Dominik was somebody I should know given we had a Scottish connection. Given we had a videogame connection. I went to *GamesMaster Live* to meet Dominik. I had no links to him whatsoever but I basically just doorstepped him and said, 'Right, you and I should be mates.' He was like, 'What? Fuck off, who are you?'
>
> Dominik was in his element. He was fucking *GamesMaster* and he'd just finished a live set. I must have caught one of the crew to give me an introduction and we all ended up going out for a curry together that same night.

I did not like Kirk to begin with. Partly because he came on like such a fanboy, which even 30 years on he still does, to be honest, but now I really like that about him. He finagled his way in by playing the Scottish card via our lovely Scottish receptionist Yvonne. The Scottish card always works, because no matter where you are in the world a Scottish person is legally bound to accept chat from another Scottish person.

> **K.E.** I had this ulterior motive in wanting to speak with him, which was that I was working on a documentary idea so specifically I was going to ask Dominik if he'd be the presenter. And then, I guess, be friends with him afterwards. Careful what you wish for, right? [Laughs.]
>
> Neither of us really liked each other at that first encounter. If you ask Dominik I'm sure he'd say the same. Anyway, he was in a bilious Dominik mood that night. When I presented the idea of the documentary to him he said, 'Yeah, OK, I'll definitely look at that.'

He said he wanted me to do some documentary about videogames in Scotland, which sounded really boring, so I tried to just palm him off with my agent's number. But he wouldn't go away. He just kept lingering around. I would come off stage, and there he was again, this bizarre, giant, hairy man. I would go into a random pub in Birmingham, and he would also be there. I would go into the toilet, and he would be there. That last one is another recurring theme of our relationship. So eventually I said yes to this documentary just to get rid of him.

> **K.E.** The documentary was called *Fair Game* and the objective was to expose the world of computer game piracy. I'd been a pirate in terms of copying and distributing videogames for quite a while before, so I had these various contacts from market stallholders up the tree to the guys that cracked the games. So Dominik and I embarked on this

SERIES TWO

documentary, which was also the first time that I met Dave Jones from DMA Design, as we used them as the example of the developer losing money on these videogames contrasted with the stallholders who were making all this other money, dark money, off of the games.

Dominik and I, over the period of what I guess was about three weeks filming, just had an absolute ball. We had a complete hoot. We got him stoned for the first time. My cameraman at the time was a massive marijuana blazer. He was just insistent that everyone just sort of got stoned all the time. So Dominik was probably in ill shape to go and present anything by the time we started in the morning. But we had a ball all over Scotland and that was really the beginning of our friendship sealed from that point. And off we went.

In retrospect I am so glad Kirk was a borderline psychotic stalker, because he did become my best friend. There is nobody like Kirk Ewing on the planet. He is a fascinating man. I can honestly say I have laughed more in the company of that man than in the company of any other human being. And *Fair Game* was a really good bit of investigative journalism and also just a total giggle from start to finish. Literally, a giggle because Kirk and our wonderful cameraman Paul Gavin set out to get me stoned for the first time in my life. Every night after filming. Totally wrecked. Wrecked at night but producing magic the next day. And that set the template for our beautiful, hilarious, dangerous but never dull, friendship since.

J.D. **Jim Douglas, Editor, *GamesMaster* magazine** We launched the official magazine at *GamesMaster Live*, which I only have very faint memories of because by that point we were operating on fumes to meet a very compressed launch schedule.

I was really lucky because we were kind of given all the resources we could possibly want. The launch editorial team had 10 people on it, which was just amazing. Normally a mag of that size would have maybe five or six, so Future obviously needed it to work. It was a big high-profile launch and it was really exciting but we had to go through the creative process ourselves and obviously had to get Hewland and Channel 4 to sign off on all kinds of stuff. So, for example, they had to approve the change in logo. The original TV logo had the 'M' in the middle and it was really distinctive but kind of a bit useless as a magazine logo, because it just didn't really look very good. We had all sorts of conversations and were trying to get them comfortable with how we would represent the brand and the show well but in a way that would still make it a successful magazine.

We didn't have a massive amount of time to work out how we were going to try and reimagine the TV show in print form, but we tried to bring as much of the show as possible into the magazine. I had a brilliant design team led by an art director called Wayne Allen. He decided early on he wanted to make the magazine feel as if you were watching it on a screen. So we did things like lay out the contents page as if it was based on the oil rig itself. We had this idea that rather than just turn to the tips on page 66 or whatever we'd present you with the Consoletation Zone. Wherever possible we'd try to take ideas from the show that would work.

One of the biggest challenges was bringing in Dominik's presenting style, as so much of the TV show was built around that. He was doing such a fantastic job presenting the show and running the challenges. That was one of the most difficult parts to bring into the mag because you just can't recreate that experience, but Dominik ended up doing a column for us and that was one way we brought some of his personality into the mag.

My 'Big Purple Column' was wonderfully self-indulgent. There was no point in me writing about games really, because Jim assembled the most ludicrously talented staff who would do that more than ably. So I just wrote about me. There were some bits of lifting the curtain to reveal what happens on the show but it was mostly about all the weird and wonderful things I was doing in my crazy life. So one week it would be about me nearly dying in a flight to Vegas, the next week would be about me hanging out with the Manic Street Preachers or trying to surf in California. As funny as the columns were, there is definitely an angry, grumpy edge to some bits. And that is me trying to distance myself from this ghastly fake persona I had on the show. And that in retrospect is the origin of the Dominik we saw in series four onwards.

Most of the time I only wrote about games to settle scores with publishers who had pissed me off. I remember doing it with Sega once. They sent me a review game and it had an address on the back I had to return it to within a week. So I kept it and wrote in the magazine about how much money they had made out of me and my show so I was keeping it. And fuck them. So yeah, I didn't fuck around with the little companies. I went for the big boys. What a dick I was.

> J.D. Looking back, I was working with a great launch publisher who did a brilliant job of insulating us from the pressure. They weren't in the business of micro-managing. We were kind of left, if not to our own devices, then with certainly enough freedom to operate. I'm sure it would have been a different story if the sales had been terrible, but we sold massive numbers, like 232,000 copies of issue one. Once you get beyond that launch phase and the sales start settling down, you start to think, *Oh it was all a flash in the pan. We've had a great first issue and now it's all over.* But the fact that the magazine went on for decades means that it was a success. I was only editor for less than a year so there was a whole raft of other fantastic editors who took it on and developed it and moved it forward through countless re-designs. That was one of the other things that was so good about it: that other people wanted to do different things with the magazine and keep it fresh. If we were just slavishly locked into the issue one template then it would have got stale.

I clicked with Jim immediately. He is a very special person. He was terrific company: very smart, very knowledgeable and very funny. We
had a lot of laughs. I still have my Filofax from 1993 and it is incredible
to see how many times I have 'drinks with Jim Douglas' written in as
appointments. So it was only natural that we got him on the show as
a co-commentator.

J.D. I did bits of co-commentary of challenges with Dominik on the show
and at *GamesMaster Live*. It's really only after the event you realize
what a tricky presenting job that is, because he was trying to make a
videogames show make sense to people, which was already difficult,
while trying to inject it with humour and personality. That's not easy
without coming across as naff. He was also having to deal with loads
of people who were supposed experts in videogames who weren't TV
trained at all. Some of us better than others, and I definitely count
myself in the list of the latter. I'd struggle through games commentary
and he kept it all together and moving.

One of my TV appearances saw me commentating on a tennis
game for the SNES. Dominik was keeping the match commentary
going and building the sense of tension. My job was to step in and
try and add a bit of expert commentary and colour to the challenge.
Because of the nerves, though, I just could not get the scoring right at
all. So there'd be a rally where somebody would score a point and I'd
confidently jump in with, 'And that's deuce!' where obviously it wasn't
deuce at all. So they'd have to go back and restart the challenge and
I could hear the director in Domink's earpiece going, 'Jesus Christ.'

END OF
THE ROAD

GamesMaster **is claiming success in the ratings war, having**
announced that the viewing figures for its Christmas show were in
excess of 3.1 million. This equalled their all time viewing record. The
figure made it the most popular show on Channel 4 that day.
Sega Pro, **1993**

C.M. It's funny, as I thought series one was going to be such a tricky world
to build on visually, but I was really chuffed how well the second
series worked, as it had developed such a strong identity and brand
by this point. Part of the joy of making the show was that the budget
wasn't huge. If it was it would have lost some of its rough-and-ready
cheekiness. Everything was done was on a bit of a wing and a prayer
and it was all the better for it.

I don't like series two. Apart from my outfit ruining any joy I had watching it, I also think it is too rushed. You cannot pack that much TV into 24 minutes. So it's a videogame challenge show. Well, when you have the like of Take That on? That is a show in itself. And then you throw in reviews. And tips. And plugs for *GamesMaster Live* or the *GamesMaster* Fan Club or whatever other money-harvesting enterprise the show was involved in that week. That's a lot to fit in. Add to that great swooping crane shots for my links on set. And all those lovely graphic arms swinging in and out of the place. Those shots and graphics add four or five seconds to the running time whenever you use them. Now that may not sound a lot, but as someone who had to sit and put the show together in an editing suite, you cannot believe how stressful it was editing reviews so tightly they have barely any real review comment and then having to go back to the beginning and start again because you were five seconds over. Obviously it was a huge hit, so people liked what we were doing with it, so maybe I am literally the only person in the world who didn't. Or maybe the fact that this was the only videogames show on the telly meant we could have filmed me taking a big shit on a Nintendo controller and still got three million viewers.

> C.M. *GamesMaster* was so exhilarating to direct because in many ways it didn't feel like we were making a factual TV series, and certainly not a low-budget one. With the sheer fun and ambition of imagining our own high-concept worlds, we were basically creating our very own movie and videogame in one. I mean, how many other production companies would allow a couple of 25-year-olds to create 26 episodes set in a futuristic gaming platform? We just hit the craze at the perfect time.

> A.W. It was very serendipitous. Sega and Nintendo had just released 16-bit consoles and there were a lot of good games. With having that zero sense of failure we were just having fun, playing games in the office and being quite confident about what we were doing.

> S.C. The joke was always that I was the worst games player in the office, because even people like Adam and Cameron who weren't overtly games players were better than me. Dave was a phenomenal games player. Dominik knew his games as well. The game that was flavour of the month for a long time was *Super Tennis* on the SNES, where we had a real lunchtime tennis league going on. I was infamous for being the person easiest to beat on that, and I was meant to be the games expert.

Damn, I was good at *Super Tennis*. It's all in the angles. Seriously. Same with any tennis game. Get to where you think the ball is going to land as early as possible so you can select your direction quickly to get more of an angle. Thereby making the other player have to run more and have less time to set his return angle.

SERIES TWO

A.W.   It was probably quite blokey, looking back. There wasn't a big female presence on the show or behind the scenes, which is something that wouldn't happen now. It wasn't deliberate but it isn't something that I'd be comfortable with happening now in putting a team together. It was basically me, Cameron, Steve and Dominik as a unified team with the same sensibilities. We complemented each other well with slightly different skillsets.

I really enjoyed my time on the show, but after two series I wanted to progress my career. I could have carried on but I felt like I'd done what I wanted to do with it. By this point Jane had secured *Games World* for Sky, so I helped launched that. Once that was up and running, I was offered a job back with Charlie Parsons as his head of development at the production company Planet 24, which was by then making *The Big Breakfast*.

C.M.   I was really excited about the potential for future series to keep reimagining the format with different styles and precincts, but after two series I was itching to move on into drama. I wasn't falling out of love with the show. Quite the opposite. I had loads more ideas for how we could stage future series. During the first Gulf War I was really struck by the vast burning oilfields out in the desert. I always thought that could be an amazing Armageddon-style backdrop for a later series.

My head was in a very strange place at the end of series two. The show was getting over three million viewers, which made it one of the biggest shows on Channel 4.

There were things I was doing in 1992 that I had literally dreamed of as a kid. I would actually sit in my room as a teenager listening to Steve Wright's afternoon show on BBC Radio 1 with *Smash Hits* posters covering the walls. Now I was doing weekly videogame reviews on Steve's breakfast show and writing about them for *Smash Hits*. I was going out and getting drunk with Steve's Posse and the *Smash Hits* writers and best of all I had my *Smash Hits* Annual Readers' Poll nominations in the celebrity pages in between Richey Manic and Dannii Minogue.

I was making insane amounts of money for a 23-year-old guy. I had a cool flat in Camden Town with every games system and every game. If I got bored playing them I would wander down to the Liberties Bar and have pints opposite Shane McGowan then take Myf and David and all my other friends out to the poshest London restaurants and drop a couple of hundred quid at the end of every night for the bill. And it was all thanks to *GamesMaster*.

However, I wanted more. More money, for a start. I felt things like *GamesMaster Live* were 90% my on-screen persona and hard work, but Hewland International was getting all the money. I was on £1,000 per show for series two. Which is a hell of a lot more than I got for series one, but a fraction of what I could make with videogame industry-based deals on the side like appearances or endorsements. My agent was clashing with Hilary about them all the time because Hewland as a company were trying to make as much money as they could as well.

Cool spot
Standard nineties risqué shot with a videogame character pose. We all did it, eh? Didn't we? Hello? Is this thing on ...?

ARCHIVE II

82/83

Dizzy heights
This lets you see just how massive the series two set was. But you couldn't really see anything from the top tiers. I've only just realized that. Bummer.

Roar of the crowd
Getting an audience of this size into a location like this is like a military operation. I didn't do any of that, though. I was just trying to think of funny things to say to Robbie Williams.

ARCHIVE II

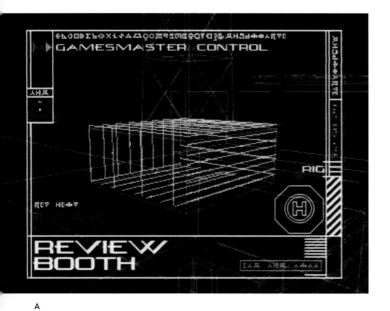

A

B

A, B, D
Quite graphic
'People with money buy sports cars.
We bought Amiga computers with
accelerated processors and more
memory to make complex title
sequences.' Simon Dunstan

C

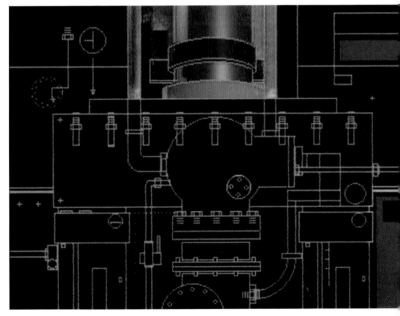

C
Very graphic
'Nobody told me how spaced-out
I looked in filming. But I was told at
school following broadcast. I grew
into a relatively normal-looking
adult.' Dan Tootill

D

ARCHIVE II

Red flag
No, I don't know why I am posing like that
either. I was probably so traumatized by
my outfit I stopped caring. Still.

NEW VIDEO GAME   NEW

92/93

Mega-hero
GamesMaster host Dominik Diamond has more fans than pop stars,' reported the *Sunday Mirror* in February 1992. But Dominic the cameraman was still to be impressed.

pp. 94/95
Seeing double
This photograph was taken in 1992. Before green-screen computer graphics. So I sat beside a life-size animatronic version of me for this photo. It cost MILLIONS!

Widow Wanky
From the series two Christmas panto show. Not gonna lie. I find myself strangely attractive here. Definitely my best-dressed moment of that whole season.

And so was Channel 4. It was a three-way tug-of-war financial clus-terfuck at times.

I didn't actually need more money. It was just a way of getting more control. That's what it was all about, in retrospect. I felt I had no control over this titanic show that in turn was having control over my life and future. Everyone else made the decisions that affected me. Cameron decided how I would look. Hilary decided what other work I could do. Channel 4 decided what kinds of publicity I had to do. I felt I had no say in decisions that actually affected me more than anyone else. I felt series two had humiliated me and damaged my long-term career, I really did. So I decided that moving forward I was going to take less shit, give less fucks and not let anyone tell me what I could and couldn't do. What could possibly go wrong, with that attitude?

SERIES TWO

SERIES THREE

Try as I did to not think too far ahead about series three, it obviously played on my mind. In March I was editing the last few *GamesMaster* shows of series two, and at the same time directing *House of Games* for *Games World* with Neil West and Jane Goldman. This was another example of Jane Hewland giving young people the chance to do all kinds of TV things. I had never planned on directing TV – it just started organically through being the associate producer on *GamesMaster* series two. After doing that Comic Relief *Big Breakfast* feature with Chris Evans, I realized the more I learnt about making TV, the better presenter I would become. And Jane was like, 'OK, then do some more directing.' That continued through to April when I also started opening up a whole chain of Solid Gold Videogame Swap Shop things in Scotland, as well as writing the official *GamesMaster* book. For some bizarre reason I still have my Filofax pages from 1993 and it just looks insanely busy. May has entries like 'Fly to Paris for *Asterix* launch'; 'Virgin sales conference presentation at Richard Branson's house'; 'Disney voiceover for *3 Ninja Kids* movie'; 'Meeting Janet Street-Porter and Alan Yentob at the BBC for new comedy show idea.' Crazy.

So the decision to stay or quit for series three was getting pushed to the back of my mind, but the time for negotiations was getting closer and closer. I was also drinking. A lot. Because I was doing these heavy-stress work days and then there was always some kind of social function at night. With booze. So you would have a couple of drinks to burn off the stress ... then a few more.

One afternoon, I was invited by Manic Street Preachers' management to come and see them rehearse *Gold Against the Soul* in a studio with Richard Easter from the Steve Wright Posse (Richard and I had met them a few times by then; he would plug them on Radio 1, I would plug them in *Smash Hits* and *GamesMaster* magazine). So we go to that, we have a few drinks. Then we went out to dinner with them after. You have a few more drinks. Then we went to see a gig with them after that. Even more drinks. Then you wake up hungover the next morning with a whole day's TV editing to do, so you drink a ton of coffee and by the end of that day you are so wired with caffeine and creative buzz that you need a couple of drinks to chill. The candle was most definitely being burned at both ends. Myf was working back in Bristol, and we weren't getting on well because I was in my 'I don't give a fuck and no one tells me what to do' stage.

To be honest, it would be difficult to not become a bit of a dick after getting that much success that quickly. I felt I had no control over the show, but outside of it? All the extra work? The store openings and whatnot? I was treated like a king, with people getting me everything from lunch to limos. Crowds cheering wherever I went. You get such an inflated sense of your own importance, and that does not make for a good relationship, especially with someone who knew you before all that and can see the change, and points out the change. Myf was my grounding force, you know? She was there to help me keep it real, and I was pushing her away. So I wasn't really in the right frame of mind to make intelligent, measured, mature decisions.

Everything was moving so quickly. Take my June 1993. I fly off to my first CES in Chicago, in First Class thanks to Woody from Virgin Games. Afterwards, I go down to California with her and the likes of Paul 'Ginger' Dowling and Sean Brennan from Virgin, and Alison Beasley and Alison Goddard from Interplay, and we all go surfing. Then I go to Hollywood with Woody and drive around in a limo drinking champagne and taking photos to promote their *Cool Spot* game. All the while being wined and dined at America's poshest restaurants. That was June 1993. Hell of a month! But that was the new normal for me. And I loved it. Who wouldn't? You just think, *Wow!* For a working-class kid who had a tough upbringing, this is what real life is supposed to be like.

Back home, Tony Fox kept lining up deal after deal after deal for me. And Hilary was saying no after no after no. Because they interfered with commercial opportunities that Hewland as a company was setting up with Channel 4. Tony was saying to them, 'OK, if you are going to stop Dominik earning outside of the show, you have to let him earn enough from the show.' And they weren't. The offer for series three wasn't nearly as much as I could make from spin-offs.

And then along came that burger chain. I was told McDonald's were sponsoring the show and it just felt like the ultimate thing I had no control over. Because I hated McDonald's at the time. I had read about their deforestation policies in a great comic called *Crisis* which Simon Pegg and I used to read voraciously at Bristol University. My little brother Michael was a teenage anti-McDonald's campaigner in Milton Keynes. He would draw these leaflets and leave them on the tables in there, pointing out their anti-environmental policies.

So you take the pish offer from Hewland, add the money I could make from the videogames industry without it, plus the fact that I was talking to the BBC about doing non-videogames stuff, and you roll them up into one big hungover bundle with added Big Mac on top. And that is why I quit the biggest new show in British telly.

I'm not doing the next series for a number of reasons. First of all, McDonald's is sponsoring it, and that's, er ... I've got to pick my words very carefully here, for legal reasons ... that's a company which I've refused to have anything to do with, because of my own personal principles. Then there were all these rumours that McDonald's weren't actually going to sponsor the show after all, so I went into negotiations to do the series. But we couldn't agree about contracts, insofar as ... again, I've got to be careful about what I say ... er, they were trying to severely restrict the amount of work that I could do outside the show. For the amount of money they were offering me, I felt it was wrong of them to restrict me so much. I mean, if they want to pay me what Clive Anderson gets, fine – I'll sit on my arse and I won't do any openings or promotions ever, I'll just sit back and cash my cheques. But if they're not going to pay me like that, I have to go out and do other stuff just to make a living.

I'm sad because I bet you any money that if I did the next series they would've put me in really trendy clothes. But I'm glad that I don't have to wear that red jacket again, because that has to be one of the worst TV ideas in history. The person I was on *GamesMaster* is completely different from the person I am in real life, so I don't mind letting go of that – the Dominik Diamond who presented *GamesMaster* was a bit of a dickhead really, know what I mean?
Dominik Diamond, *Megatech*, 1993

MOVING ON UP

Who says no to *GamesMaster*?
Dexter Fletcher, *GamesMaster* magazine, 1993

J.H. Jane Hewland, Executive Producer Dominik left leading up to the new series starting. He had a row with Hilary because we couldn't have him endorsing a particular product and then presenting our show. Everybody in the market wanted to hire him but Channel 4 were saying he can't be paid to endorse any particular market product if he's doing the programme. With the very low budget that Channel 4 gave us, Dominik didn't get very much money from the show. So, obviously, he said, 'Well, I can't live on this', and he was in a very, very hard position. And so were we. At the beginning none of us had any money. I'd left LWT to set up on my own and I had nothing. Hilary had a teeny, tiny salary; in fact, she didn't get a salary until well over a year. We weren't paying Dominik enough to compensate him for not being hired, so in the end he went. Losing Dominik was a terrible blow to the show. It was worse for us than it was for him but I was never pissed off because I understood his position. If you can't pay somebody to stop them taking another option then you can't be surprised when they take that other option. That's the way things are. We suffered for it more than he did. The popularity of the peak was waning, so the immediate craze was finished. There was also competition from Yorkshire Television with *Bad Influence*.

> **We laughed about the competition at the time, actually. The two shows were so different and never pitted against each other in the schedules, so I think they probably complemented each other as much as anything. In fact, when I first met Dominik, I was quite nervous, as I was a big fan of the initial series of *GamesMaster*, which had just gone out. During the last series of *Bad Influence!* though, somebody showed me an article where Dominik had slagged me off in the press. I've no idea why he did that because we'd always been friendly when we met around the place. Maybe these comments are one of the reasons people thought there was competition between our shows. There never was any, as far as I'm concerned.**
> **Violet Berlin, 2003**

I said some utterly despicably horrible things about *Bad Influence!* And Violet. And Andy. Which is utterly unfair because they are both super-lovely people and extremely talented presenters. I met Violet in particular a few times and we got on great. But they were the enemy at the time, you know? They were the big commercial channel's cynical attempt to beat our plucky revolutionary underdog. So they had to die. What a load of bollocks, eh? That was obviously part of my attempt to separate myself from the twee character I was playing on series two and be the bad boy. So sorry about that, to all those responsible for *Bad Influence!* I was a right twat.

V.B. Violet Berlin, Presenter, *Bad Influence!* Luckily I was used to blokes slagging me off because that's what happens when you're a woman in a boys' world. As a TV presenter I was already putting myself out there in a position for people to say horrible things as well as nice, but I was disappointed because Dominik was a snake. He said nice things to my face and then I'd read horrid stuff in print that he'd said to games journalists. It was a shame because I was such a big fan of *GamesMaster* when it first started. Me and my boyfriend made a date to watch it and when I landed the presenting job on *Bad Influence!* I was naively thinking, *Oh great, I'll be friends with the* GamesMaster *production.* I'd have loved to have been on *GamesMaster* and vice versa, inviting Dominik on to the show. It's ridiculous it didn't happen and I never understood why.

SERIES THREE

I was more disappointed that I never got to have a conversation with Jane Hewland because I thought she was so interesting and we were both breaking ground in our own way. Commissioners are very careful about what they put on kids' TV and we had to work so hard to bring something that wasn't considered to be mainstream to a mainstream audience. It's funny, *Bad Influence!* gets painted as the safe option – which it was – but if you look at the context it was still waging its own revolution. We had to get 50% girls watching and we would have been kicked off if we hadn't. In the years that followed I've had emails from women saying that they watched it as kids and now they work as games developers, as well as emails simply describing how they felt like a freak at the time for enjoying games and by seeing me they felt like they weren't one.

M.B. Matthew Bowes, Series Producer (Series 3) I was a producer on *The Word* when the position of series producer came up for the new series of *GamesMaster*. Obviously, I knew of the show as I'd sent Dominik's audition tape to them in the first place. When I went for my interview I did this whole development package on what the show would be like from a prison. By the time they'd offered me the job Dominik had left, so the first major task was to find someone new.

R.W. Richard Wilcox, Researcher (Series 3) Of course, as the new producer it was down to Matthew to sign up the new presenter, but he did ask the team for suggestions and also ran ideas past us. Then he had to get those suggestions past Jane, and many names would get shot down then and there. We seemed to be continually coming up with new names. Some came in to audition, which was done right in the middle of the office with us all watching. Danny John-Jules was good and we all liked him. And I'm pretty sure there was an actor who'd been in *Aliens* who was very much in the running too. We set up a console and they commentated on a challenge.

> We tested loads of different people. What you try and do is never, in television, try and replace what you had before, because it always comes out as a pale imitation. So we tested masses of different people ... You know, ordinary punters, games journalists – all kinds of different people.
> Jane Hewland, *Mega Power*, 1994

D.F. Dexter Fletcher, Presenter Originally I was invited to be a guest on the new series. That's the context of how I was first approached. There were obvious issues with Dominik in the lead-up to filming and it was clear he wasn't coming back, so Matthew called to ask whether I was interested in taking over.

R.H. Rik Henderson, Researcher (Series 3) I was already working at the office on *Games World* and was drafted in to help with the screen-test auditions, co-commentating with those auditioning on a *Mortal Kombat* challenge. That's when I first met Dexter. Funnily enough, the only other person I remember was one of his co-stars from the *Press Gang*. They were both excellent. Dexter on the day, though, there was something about him that just said he would be a brilliant host. He was fun, friendly and came across well.

M.B.   Dexter was a big star by that point. It was very much the case that we had Dexter Fletcher interested so let's have him. He was big news.

D.F.   I wasn't getting much acting work at the time and I was in a bit of a low personal point, not that it reflected my decision to do the show, but it was one I made for the money and a hope I'd get busy again. But you know I did think it would be fun too. I had a passing interest in games, already having had a Commodore 64 and buying my first Atari when I was 11. The games even in their infancy were incredible bits of work.

I think it was Jim Douglas who told me about Dexter. I had just got back from a holiday to Thailand and headed straight to Bournemouth to do the BBC Radio I Roadshow with the Steve Wright Show gang, which was another one of my bucket-list dreams ticked off the list. I remember thinking, *Damn! Dexter is actually quite a clever choice, because he is so unlike me. He is the opposite of Scottish. He is a good-looking guy. Girls fancy him.* I thought he was a really good actor. I mean nobody else could have played Babyface in *Bugsy Malone*, could they? And *The Rachel Papers* is one of my favourite books of all time and I thought he was great in the movie.

I didn't give it much more thought than that because I was trying to stop Mr Blobby from killing me at the Radio I Roadshow. No word of a lie. I was playing this camp character Baron Shaft and I was interviewing Blobby at the top of a massive gantry 100 feet above the crowd. He kept banging into me in that way Blobby did to people, but he hit me so hard he nearly knocked me off. So every few seconds while going out live on air I am covering up the mic and saying to whatever pyscho was in the suit, 'Fucking stop it, right? You're going to fucking kill me, you twat!'

So, yeah. I was too distracted to be that bothered about Dexter taking over. I certainly didn't bear him any ill will. Or Jane. Or anyone. I thought I had just moved on. Tony Fox, God bless him, had sorted out a deal for me hosting this enormous nationwide tour to promote the new *Mortal Kombat* game, which paid me more than I was offered for that whole *GamesMaster* series, so I wasn't missing the money.

Also this was the time when Dave Lee Travis walked out on Radio I. As a result Nicky Campbell moved to his slot, which meant he had to stop doing a show called *Sportscall* on BBC Radio 5 Live. Tony got me an audition for that and I nailed it. So that was me on with a proper weekly BBC radio show. Bam! Another dream fulfilled. And what was great about this particular dream was that it took me out of video-games and into sport, which I also loved. And that just opened up a whole new avenue of work and career.

So I sat down to watch the first show of series three wishing it all the best. I saw the opening titles and thought, *Holy fuck! Cameron has* really outdone himself here. They were like an action movie. Wow. And then Dexter came on and I thought, *Damn, that is a much better outfit than I ever had! He looks cool as fuck.*

And then he held up the sooty remains of the red jacket and broken glasses and said, 'Sadly, this poor chap burnt himself out on level two.'

And time froze. I felt like I had been punched in the stomach. I thought, *What the actual fuck? Why would you say that?* I almost started crying. It felt like such a personal attack. It was so unnecessarily nasty. And the fact that they had reduced me to the red jacket, knowing how much I hated it? That was very deliberate. I still don't know who was behind it. But I thought, *Fuck the show. I hope it dies on its arse.*

P.S.   **Peter Scott, Researcher** It wasn't intended as a dig. It was to explain the transition between the change in presenter. I liked Dominik a lot. Jane liked Dominik a lot. She was upset he left, but put his leaving down to him being young and impetuous.

Dexter and I had written loads of really good, funny scripts together, but Jane ripped them up, saying he needed to be spontaneous – 36 hours before we started filming. Literally months of work had been binned, so we went out feeling more than a little deflated and drank two bottles of whisky. Without a script, we presented Dexter with a running order and notes that he would memorize. Obviously, the introductions were always scripted, as no sane person could think of 26 amusing, off-the-cuff ways to say hello to a prison full of children.

M.B.   It quickly became obvious presenting wasn't a natural fit for Dexter. When we started filming he felt the pressure of the sort of precision I was trying to get from him. I think that ran him down a little bit.

D.F.   I felt like the new kid at school. I didn't really know what was going on a lot of the time. What quickly became apparent to everyone was that I was completely ill-equipped to be the person they needed fronting the show because I didn't have that passion or deep knowledge of games.

F.O.   **Frank O'Connor, Co-Commentator (Series 2–3)** I remember being a little wowed by the celebrity of Dexter. While he was an actor first, he did genuinely seem to enjoy and understand the appeal of games. But it was also obvious to me that he was even more into the craft of making TV, something I guess that really steered his eventual career as director.

P.S.   Dexter loved games but he just wasn't as knowledgeable as Dominik or able to bring that across on screen. Matthew was terrified of Dexter accidentally saying something that might make him seem unknowledgeable to the audience.

D.F.   That's what set Dominik apart. He cared about it in a way I didn't. And all of these kids who were so into games and wanting more of a technical understanding of what was going on, I couldn't provide that. I was just this berk running around and, you know, shouting, 'Whoa, that was a good one' and 'Oh, he's really smashed him there'. [Laughs.] It didn't mean anything.

M.B. Had I been a little less hands-on, I think he might have been able to relax into things. He quite frequently went off-script where I wanted things to be very precise. He would get loose around the edges and I would get frustrated, literally wanting things done in this particular way. It could be a bit of a drain, but he was a very nice guy to work with. Very friendly, and he wasn't at all up himself. He really wanted to do a good job and I think that was one of the reasons why he didn't feel too great about the experience or the aftermath. Unfortunately, circumstances conspired to make it not the job he signed up for.

R.W. Though he was always professional, I think he realized pretty quickly there was no turning back. We all just had to get to the end of it. Along with Peter, we tried to support him as much as we could by briefing him about the games and things to look out for, so at the least he had something to say during commentary. I was definitely in his corner and I hope he knew it. Despite his energy, it was always going to be a losing battle.

> I'd say it's a very nervous Dexter Fletcher, but yeah, it's more or less me up there. It's a very unforgiving atmosphere, quite intimidating, and just getting up, taking a deep breath and going out there and doing it was the toughest part of the challenge. Also, the kids can be pretty ruthless. They come along expecting a show to run smoothly for half an hour but, of course, in TV it doesn't work like that and they start shouting, 'You're crap' and 'Where's Dominik?'
> Dexter Fletcher, *GamesMaster* magazine, 1993

J.H. It was the trouble and the strength of the show that it had such a passionate fan base. They all took ownership of it because it was a live audience show and they were all part of every world we created. It must have been awful for Dexter, and I feel very, very sorry that he went through any cruelty at the hands of the audience.

D.F. It's why I don't talk about the show and feel slightly on the back foot about it all, aside from many other personal issues that were involved in my life at that time. My role as an actor coming in and trying to be a presenter and talking about something that I didn't really have a passion for, it was a disservice to a show that was very loved. It needed someone who really gave a shit about it, and at that point in my life I didn't.

It was so hard refusing to comment on the show when magazines were asking me to, but Tony Fox advised me to rise above it. Tony was a good soul, and he also was very clever about not burning more bridges than you ever have to. Because he was a good soul who was also an agent! I didn't watch any other part of that series, because I was so angry about how they opened it. Obviously, I was pleased that he and the show were getting hammered. At the time I just assumed that if he hadn't actually written the line about me burning out, he had gone along with it. So he was guilty by association, so fuck him too.

SERIES THREE

Looking back now and knowing how out of his depth Dexter felt, I feel sorry for what he went through, because it wasn't his fault. It wasn't just me the show lost – it lost Adam and Cameron, and they are also very hard people to replace. Adam is a brilliant producer, especially in a crisis, and for all my issues with Cameron he is an utterly unflappable hand on a directing tiller. The three of us together could handle anything thrown at us. As a presenter, you need a good producer and a good director. It's like making a cake. As a presenter, you might have some fantastic ingredients, but the producer mixes them together and the director bakes the thing. I was extremely lucky in my TV career because I can't think of a time when I didn't have good people in those roles.

There were stories at the time of Dexter getting into bother, so he was obviously going through some issues. I've subsequently read interviews where he described having drug problems around the same time and – having gone through that myself – I feel desperately sad that the reaction to him on *GamesMaster* may in any way have contributed to them.

I have had that a few times in my career. Any time you take over a breakfast show from someone on the radio there is a flurry of online bile from their old fans, especially if you do that as a foreigner, as I have in Canada. You can get some quite toxic racist abuse. And as an openly Catholic Celtic fan in the media in Glasgow I have had people post online where my kids go to school. I made a documentary, *Crucify Me*, for Channel 5 that even today I get utterly destroyed for on Twitter.

So, every time someone posts some nostalgic thing about *GamesMaster* and tags me? It is only a matter of time before the same two people get slagged. Dexter and Dave Perry. And I know when that happens to me it really hurts. It shouldn't. And we like to pretend it doesn't, but anybody who wants to put themselves in front of a camera or behind a microphone is ridiculously sensitive to criticism because of the nature of the job. It is not like being a bricklayer and building a wall that someone says is a shit wall. That's OK. You can rebuild it. But as a presenter your job is to be you. Your product is you. So all criticism is deeply personal. And you can't redo it. Even if you knew it wasn't going well. I realized during *Crucify Me* that there was no way I was getting out of it unscarred. I know I made wrong decisions. I can't rebuild that wall. Dexter can't redo series three. So to still get burned for it years afterwards is particularly infuriating. Although in Dexter's case, I kinda feel after you have become one of the top movie directors in the world it's easier to handle!

J.H. I feel very guilty. We should have known and we should have protected him better. We did the one series together, everyone moved on and the years passed. He's gone on to greater things and he recovered, we recovered and the show recovered. It was a happy ending for everybody, but it was an unfortunate thing at the time.

Years later, Harry and I went to see *Lock Stock and Two Smoking Barrels* and there was Dexter. I thought, *Wow, he's seriously made it.*

He was brilliant and this film was fantastic. He's a fantastically talented director now, and I'm very happy for him.

D.F.   I'm critical of myself over it all because there was a lot of pressure to be something I wasn't. It was all happening around a very personal period of my life that is so long ago that I've just put it behind me. I made the decision to do it at a particular time when I ordinarily wouldn't have, so that played into it. The show suffered for it and in retrospect I'm not best proud of myself for it. Of course, I did it to the best of my ability, and you know the people were great and I did have fun along the way. It wasn't all doom and gloom and anxiety.

It wasn't me at my finest, but I'm not embarrassed by it. *GamesMaster* is part of who I am and whatever my achievements now it played its part. People still remember and love the show so how can I ignore that?

DREAMS

M.B.   It was a nightmare. A series that swung from being a job of great ego-boosting beauty to a complete nightmare.

> The third series of *GamesMaster* is set in a videogame academy.
> It's for improving your games-playing excellence and your skills.
> And the idea is that it's only the best who get to play there –
> the elite. It's where they train to become better, and part of
> the GamesMaster's elite squad. Erm, as it were. I'm the bad boy
> of the academy. I'm a bit cheeky to the GamesMaster.
> Dexter Fletcher, *Mega*, 1993

C.M.   Cameron McAllister, Titles Director (Series 3) When we came to begin development of series three, I'd decided that I didn't want to series direct this time but I did still want to do the opening titles. I'd come up with this idea of setting it in a prison, but what was really exciting was suddenly the show was successful and established enough to attract money from sponsors, allowing us to do things on a much bigger scale. Suddenly we had to work with proper grown-ups. So when McDonald's were the chosen sponsor we had to work closely with their advertising agency and attend meetings with them where they were like, 'Who the fuck are you, because you all look about 12 and we're about to give you hundreds of thousands of pounds to make a title sequence.'

We couldn't get by making it on the cheap any more, so we went for a meeting with their advertising agency and they said, 'Right, give us your pitch.' So I went into all the detail, that we were going to have this American high school bus with kids pulling up and security helicopters flying above as the kids were transferred by speedboats to this prison fortress out at sea. They said, 'Yeah, great. Right, what's your next pitch?' And we had nothing. That was the pitch. We had nothing else. They were really annoyed with us, complaining that you never come in to a pitch with just one idea, as how would they pick their favourite? And we said, 'Oh, well, that's the one we want to do.' They approved it but I suspect they had never worked with anyone so unprofessional in their lives.

By the time we came to film it, I felt like I was directing a movie. I was so excited and I'd even hired a professional storyboard artist in to design it. We went to Portsmouth to one of those fortresses out at sea to film it, and took some kids with us who had won a competition where the prize was to appear in the title sequence. We put them in a speedboat but it was driven so fast out to sea that the kids arrived at the fortress hysterical with fear. Their parents were so angry we had traumatized them.

R.T. Russell Thomas, Series Director (Series 3) I didn't actually have an aspiration to be a director but the opportunity came along to series direct the show and Jane offered it to me. Honestly, I don't think I'd been a particularly good editor on the first two series so I'm not sure why. I was quite creative but technically speaking I was bloody rubbish. So when an opportunity came along that meant I didn't have to edit any more, I jumped at the opportunity. In retrospect, that was the main reason for me to accept it rather than some kind of amazing drive in my career to become a director.

I was really nervous though, because going from being an editor sitting in a room with one or two people to suddenly being in a position where you're calling all the shots and have to understand things like lighting and how to manage relationships with people, it was very much diving in at the deep end. Quite frankly, I shat myself on numerous occasions. Every time we finished a show I'd be going, *God, I managed to get through that.*

M.B. I liked Russ very much. Very eccentric and a very talented director. However, we did clash a lot in the gallery because I was brought up on *The Word*, where everything was made to fit perfectly and almost scripted beforehand. Quite often things wouldn't go to plan and there were barneys between me and Russell, who was saying we should just go with a take and move on. And I would be saying, 'No, we need to redo it.' He most likely thought I was very pedantic and, do you know what, he was right. [Laughs.]

P.S. I worked on the first block of filming for series three and have nothing but fond memories of Matthew. He was very good to me and the one who told me I would be good at this mythical thing called television producing. I knew nothing much about telly but had picked stuff up quickly and worked hard. Matthew was such a lovely, helpful bloke, even in the dire times of making a show who'd lost its presenter, gained an unpopular broadcast sponsor and had to deal with Jane being in New Zealand for most of the shoot, which meant she didn't get to see it causing trouble down the line and step in.

J.H.   By the time we got to series three we had other shows we were developing. I would go down to set maybe once a week but I really didn't get any sense as to what was going wrong, certainly not at the start.

R.W.   When talking about what Matthew and Russell wanted to do with the show, I seem to remember the word 'cool' being used a lot. Neither was a particularly big gamer. Matthew had a console, but his knowledge of games and in particular the industry was slight. Russell had no interest in them at all. In fact, I'd go further and say he didn't like games or anything that they represented. I found his distaste for games quite difficult to deal with. It certainly didn't encourage you to display any enthusiasm for what you were doing.

R.T.   I was very definitely not a computer games person. I don't think I'd ever played a game in my life prior to that moment and certainly afterwards I never played a game again. I was so nervous about directing that I was too distracted in worrying that I knew fuck all about what it is I was supposed to be doing. There was a lot of trying to cover up my own inadequacies and trying to learn as quickly as possible on the job.

R.W.   I'd been a computer whizzkid in my teens. I'd written a couple of Spectrum games, *Blue Thunder* and *Airwolf*, that were big sellers in 1984 and 1985. And on the back of their success my brother and father built the games publisher Elite, a pioneer of licensed games and quite a big deal in the 8-bit era. They were still going strong when I went for my interview with Hewland. *Striker*, a terrific football game, was topping the SNES charts and would go on to be one of the biggest-selling games of the year.

Jane knew all about *Striker*, and the fact that my family were behind it almost certainly got me the interview to work on the show. In the following six years that I worked for her, I saw her repeatedly give people their first break because they had connections or a background that she thought would be far more useful over traditional TV experience or academic excellence. She was quite intrigued as to why I wasn't involved in the family business, which was obviously making a lot of money. It was complicated, but I don't think she ever really understood why I would want to pursue a career in TV when she argued I could have been making much more money writing games. She maybe had a point.

GamesMaster was my first real job. I was moving down to London from Birmingham for it and I really had no idea what to expect. I imagined that as it was 'media' everyone would be wearing swanky suits. I'd never worn one apart from at a wedding, so I spent a couple of hundred quid on a suitably dazzling lime green number before heading down. I turned up to the office on my first day wearing it and some very shiny black shoes. I probably looked like I'd come to sell them a photocopier. I never wore that suit again.

J.F. Jonny Ffinch, Associate Producer (Series 3) We had a production meeting ahead of filming where Matthew asked, 'Right, who's in charge of getting all the review games? Richard? OK.' Then he moved on to the challenges and asked, 'Richard, you're getting the challenges in, right?' And then it was on to who was gathering tips for the Consoletation Zone and who was prepping the machines to be set up ready for the show. It was all Richard. I was sat there thinking, *Is anybody else doing anything on this show?* It was just ridiculous. He was doing absolutely everything. Obviously that's an insane amount of work for one person, so he'd literally be deciding on challenges the night before filming. And because a lot of those games were generally finished very near upon their release, we'd be getting very early chips on a board with some levels that worked and some that didn't. It was all very, very hairy. Doing that the night before is folly, as it turned out to be. It was just chaos.

R.W. I was responsible for ensuring that everything to do with the games would run smoothly. When one challenge finished, I had to jump in straight away to replace the console and set up the next one with the new game, paused at just the right point so that when the contestants arrive and the presenter gives them the nod, they can just pick up the controllers and start playing. It sounds easy but 99% of the time filming was behind schedule due to lighting issues or guests turning up late. We had a mighty big crew working on the show, so going into overtime meant an awful lot of extra money, even just by a few minutes. The pressure to catch up time was immense. And the more we fell behind, the bigger the pressure. What you really don't want in that situation is to be the person holding up filming, even for a second.

To help things run smoothly all key members of the crew were on talkback, so we could listen and speak to the director and producer in the gallery wherever we were. So when Matthew, quite rightly, was impatient to get filming under way, he'd ask me whether the game was ready. I always wanted to be in a position to be able to say yes. There were times when I wasn't, or we'd start filming the challenge and for some reason filming would stop. At those times, the presenter, commentator, celebrity, camera crew, audience, producer, director, God, every eye in the house was focused on me, as I desperately tried to get things ready to begin again. Quite often there would be cheering and encouragement – and sometimes I really enjoyed those moments – but it was enormously stressful trying to keep a calm head. As I look back on those big shoots, I think, *Forget the contestants. It was the researchers who deserved a Golden Joystick.*

R.T. Richard did an amazing job setting everything up. I don't recall us having major downtime. None of these games or arcade machines were set up to be broadcast on TV this way. To technically manage to get TV feeds out of them for us to film and record with was a great undertaking. It never stuck in my head as, 'Oh God, what's going on? What's the hold-up now?' There was a lot of that elsewhere, but the games always seemed to work.

I LIKE TO MOVE IT

Contestant	Sonya Blade vs. Johnny Cage
Game	Mortal Kombat (Sega Mega Drive)
Challenge	Beat the opponent in a best-of-three fight

J.H. Our big treat was to go to the Electronic Computer Trade Show in Chicago once a year ahead of filming, which is where I saw *Mortal Kombat* on consoles for the first time. I said to Acclaim there and then to give me exclusivity to show the game. So we launched series three with the whole show dedicated to the game.

M.B. My fondest memory is mostly tied up with that particular show. Everything really worked well in terms of that show within its original prison location. The way it looked and the way the studio audience was arranged. The whole look of the show was fantastic. Everyone was just on such a high when we were making it.

R.W. It was an inspired move to dedicate the whole show to one game. *Mortal Kombat* was a phenomenon, and to have the actors playing their characters was a brilliant way to kick off the new series. Of course, they were actors not gamers. I know Acclaim had given them some game training before bringing them down to the set. And when they got there it was my job to remind them how to pull off their special moves before they went on.

D.P. Daniel Persina, Contestant I played Johnny Cage and other ninja characters in *Mortal Kombat* and *Mortal Kombat II*. A group of actors from the game flew over to the UK for the first time to be on the show. Due to our accents it was difficult sometimes to understand the small details of what we needed to say to camera. The producers asked if one of us could perform and recite some lines. We huddled and Liz, as Sonya Blade, said she was very nervous as she was not a martial artist and was nervous about acting on TV. HoSung, as Liu Kang, mentioned that he was having trouble with the accent too, so I said I'd do it. To say the least, it was fatal. I was asked to say 'GamesMaster' on camera and for some reason I had a real problem as I kept saying 'GamesMasters'. The director would cut and tell me to try again, but I kept repeating 'GamesMasters', about 10 times. They didn't use any of the takes in the end. [Laughs.]

EVERYTHING CHANGES

M.B. My main task on the show was finding its location. The beautiful thing about the show and one of the reasons why it was so successful is that it was an incredibly integrated world. So there's this kind of backstory to everything that you're seeing. It's in a prison and that influences the graphics, the script and the programme editorial. It's obviously influencing the presenters' clothing and so on. So I was deeply involved in the set-up and formulating of that.

J.F. A university friend of mine who was working with Jane knew that she wanted a stringer in LA. Basically someone who is based there and sends celebrity guests over to be on the show. I had just come back from living there, so they recommended me. I met Matthew over a curry and prepared by watching a tape of a show. I spoke to my brother, who's a videogame programmer, and was like, 'What the fuck is this?' [Laughs.] He told me to mention the Atari Jaguar. So, while I was having dinner with Matthew he asked me, 'What would be the hot issue now with videogames?' I just went into extraordinary bullshit about the Atari Jaguar. Enough to get the gig and I thought, *Amazing, I'm going back to LA.*

R.W. Matthew and Russell had come up with lots of location ideas for the prison but Jane had shot them all down. They were realizing that being in charge didn't mean you got an easy ride. As the filming deadline loomed, the pressure in the office started to rise. They would pitch idea after idea and invariably come back browbeaten, having failed to persuade her. They'd go outside for a fag to gather themselves, and it fairly quickly became a siege-like atmosphere in the office, with them kind of at war with Jane, while the rest of the team watched as bystanders. I was surprised at how different the experience of making TV was to how I had imagined it. Having grown up being a massive fan of TV and dreaming about how great it must be to be a part of the behind-the-scenes team, I was shocked at how little fun we were having. So when Jane gave the nod for Oxford prison, it wasn't a moment too soon.

P.S. The production locations were always miles away from Hewland's offices. So as a researcher I was sent off in my tiny little Fiat, full of Golden Joysticks and bombing up the motorway to Oxford prison at 5.00 a.m. for filming.

R.W. My main recollection of Oxford prison is that it was intimidating. It was, after all, a prison, so it's not meant to be nice. And this one was built by the Victorians, who were good at scary. We had a little room right at the very back of the prison where we kept all the games and consoles and where I was based for the most part, helping prep the contestants by talking them through the challenge, showing them the controls and giving them tips.

We filmed 13 episodes in the prison over the course of about two weeks. To keep the show topical and ensure the games weren't old hat when episodes were finally broadcast several months later, we had to beg for games months before they were released. That was the biggest challenge as a researcher, to figure out what games would be big over the next four or five months and sweet-talk publishers into supplying us with at least part of the game in time for filming. Thankfully, most of the games we were interested in were on consoles, but even then there were issues. There were NTSC ROMs that had to be run on NTSC consoles. Another game might just be debug code that had to be run on a development console, and some games might be both NTSC and debug so you'd need a different console again. It was a lot of work, and involved hours and hours on the phone talking to publishers and PR companies.

Part of my job too was to wangle the necessary hardware out of Nintendo, Sega or the publishers. And the games TV shows were all fighting over the same few machines. The games room at Hewland, where all these consoles were stored, was a complete mess. Each time you went in there to try and run a game, you'd invariably have to put it all back together to get the machine you needed working again. Only then could you plug your game in. Many times you'd find someone had taken out the cable or machine you needed to use for filming in their show and not put it back.

M.B.   Due to having 26 episodes in the series, filming was done in two blocks. For the first block, we shot an episode a day over a period of two weeks. And then there was a break in the middle before the second block. At the time the Conservatives were in power and there was a whole thing in the news about Britain's prisons overflowing.

J.F.   I turned up for my first day at work thinking I was going to be given a briefing and a ticket and jump on a plane. Instead, Matthew burst out of a meeting room, red in the face, and went, 'We've lost the location.'

M.B.   Curse of God, in the middle break the government said they were going to use Oxford prison again. I'll never forget walking into the production manager's office saying, 'Shit, we've lost the prison. What can we do?' to which they said, 'I don't know. Bad luck.' I was like, 'Great, you're my production manager and that's the support that I get.'

R.W.   I remember the day pretty well. Relations between Matthew and Jane by this point were already bad, but when she learnt about the prison fiasco, she hit the roof. She was mortally embarrassed.

J.H.   Look, Matthew was incredibly talented. These were all incredibly talented, smart people. If you have a company like ours trying to do things with no money then it's going to be chaotic. I like things to be under-managed. It's much better if it's one person's vision and they're trying to do too much than rows and rows of producers. They'll sink or they'll swim. And most of the people who worked for me would swim. They had to learn and they had to do it themselves because there was no support system for them. But it made them stronger. It made them better producers and directors for it.

J.F.   I never did get to go back to LA. Instead, I spent the next few weeks driving around trying to find a new location. We found some stupid place underground and went with it because we were desperate.

> **GamesMaster is switching locations mid-series not through choice but necessity. You see, that disused prison is being used again, by prisoners. Real prisoners. Prisoners that, no matter what they've done, don't deserve to be made to sit through the filming of every single episode of GamesMaster.**
> **GamesMaster magazine, 1993**

M.B.   There was the kind of whole reformatting of the show. I had to come up with an idea to make logical sense of how we would move from the prison to this other location and why it happened. I had to come up with a whole background to that. We did some kind of graphic sequence about an escape but for some reason it was never used.

F.O.   It was a skit I took part in with Brad Burton. I had to do some sort of stunt pratfall as an inmate escaping. It didn't make much sense and we didn't really know why we were doing it, but the background to doing stuff like this was always chaos. [Laughs.] We were both complaining between takes like hackneyed RADA drop-outs or Equity members. And of course it was unpaid. Presumably we were taking a job away from someone, but likely not one they'd want.

> **We are still within the academy but we have moved on a level. In fact, we've moved down a level, down towards the furnaces at the heart of the structure where the GamesMaster is holding his ultimate, final examination of candidates.**
> **Matthew Bowes, GamesMaster magazine, 1993**

R.W.   That's how the team championship came to be born. To disguise the fact that we were moving from the prison to a new location, we radically changed the format of the show. Instead of having each challenge be a standalone show, we would create a 13-episode-long knockout tournament, comprising heats, semis and then a final. The winner of which would take home a pretty big prize.

M.B.   I had to organize that in an incredibly short time. I felt quite sorry for myself. It was horrible. We had to find all the people who would be in the teams, and do it all in about two weeks without any extra budget.

R.W.   The audition to find the teams for the tournament was pretty epic. We took over a school with Sega's double-decker bus and the Nintendo bus, both of which had game stations that we used for gameplay auditions. The best candidates would be sent off to be interviewed by Jonny and Matthew. It was all done on a pretty industrial scale, not unlike how they do the auditions for *The X Factor*. We advertised the auditions on the show, so we had no problem getting people down there. In the course of a weekend I think we saw over 500 potential contestants.

It was strange working in TV before social media. You made a show that was often watched by millions but at that time you never got to see how the audience reacted to it. At the auditions we got a chance to hear from the fans and I was always keen to listen to their feedback. I'd also quiz them about what games they were looking forward to. I remember coming away from auditions with a renewed energy and focus, knowing much more clearly what things we had to secure for the show.

M.B. Everybody had been flying high during the first block, but going into the second half everyone picked up on the atmosphere. We found this disused, underground prison but shooting in it was a nightmare. It was an incredibly small, confined space. Whereas before we had camera cranes and fancy stuff that Russell was in seventh heaven with, this place was a poky little hole that you could just about squeeze a couple of cameramen in and shoot straight. It was really unsexy from the point of view of the directing and for the host. It must have been a real crash-down.

R.W. If Oxford prison was scary, this place was actually terrifying. Often after filming had finished and everyone else had left I was still down there prepping for the next day's filming. I don't think I'm that much of a fraidy cat, but I was genuinely unnerved being there alone. More than once I'd be in there by myself when someone turned the generator off and all the lights would go out. It was also damp. Condensation ran down the walls at the best of times, but when you put more than a hundred people down there breathing out moisture, the place became positively sopping. It wasn't the ideal place to have a load of games consoles and pre-release games, let alone TV cameras. I had organized all the games for the challenges into several cardboard boxes, but when we got there the next day the boxes had melted. It was a tough environment to film in. Each day when you left you had black bogeys because of all the soot and dirt you'd breathed in.

D.P. **Dave Perry, Co-Presenter (Series 3)** I'd done a bit of commentary in the first filming block at Oxford prison. It was a nice setting but I wasn't stoked on it for some reason. Something about it didn't grab me. I've had this kind of snobby opinion of *GamesMaster* that because I was there at the concept that I had a right to have an opinion on every stage of it, even though I probably don't. Ahead of the second filming block, I was asked to meet Matthew and Russell at the new location and they said, 'Jane likes what you do on *Games World* with the challenge commentary. How would you feel about coming in and holding this together as the the co-presenter on the show?' I was like, 'Fuck, yeah.' It's what I wanted and I felt like I could do this. So it was great for me to get out there at the front and partner with Dexter.

J.H. Dave was a great personality with the bandanas and his leather trousers. He was very, very good at presenting and we desperately needed that stability.

SERIES THREE

D.F. He spotted that I was a bit at sea with it all. He wanted the show to be good and he'd share what information he had with me to help me along, so it meant that his role was even more key in a way. I was thinking, *This guy knows his shit.* He was very kind to me and I always appreciated that. To have an ally like that meant a lot.

D.P. There was one day I was stood on that tiny, cramped stage with Dexter, surrounded by kids. There'd been an argument going on in the gallery between Matthew and Russell, which we could both hear through our earpieces. Dexter had enough of it and went off for a cigarette, followed by the cameraman, who had put his camera down on the floor to do the same. So I was just stood there by myself and could hear through my earpiece somebody saying, 'Right, let's go. Action!' I had to say to them through the microphone, 'Can you look through the camera? There's no one here.' The guys had been having such problems in the production area that they just didn't realize everybody had wondered off to have a little break. Matthew and Russell were really nice guys separately. But when they were together they just seemed to clash. It was really funny but it was a strange experience. The things that are hard and a bit broken tend to be the things that bond you best. There was a shared feeling between us all that we were in it together and we had to get the best show out we could. It pulled us all together very, very strongly because we all had to work that bit harder to help each other. To help the producer, the director and the presenter.

EVERYBODY HURTS

R.W. A big tournament needed a big prize, and after the location situation Matthew was determined to try and make amends by securing something special. But even that turned out a nightmare. He'd persuaded Atari to commit to giving us the first off the production line of their new console, the Atari Jaguar. The console ultimately turned out to be a dud with criminally few games to play on it. At the time – and even though there were more elements to the tournament prize – this was the prize that everyone wanted. The problem was that when it came to the final, the machine's release had now slipped. Atari asked us to delay transmission of the final, which we politely declined.

M.B. Somehow we managed to get all the way through to the final, and I remember calling Jane the night before because we hadn't actually decided what the final challenges would be. By this point in production, I'd developed flu with a temperature of 100 so I was not in a good place. When we filmed the show the next day there was some kind of technical hitch on an early challenge – *Rise of the Robots* – and I pulled the game. We had to reshoot it.

J.F.   These things barely fucking worked. They would crash halfway through one of the kids doing really well on a challenge, so they'd have to start again and, inevitably, wouldn't do as well the second time. They'd lose and everyone would get really uptight.

M.B.   This happened in the final and caused one of the families to think I was rigging it. They were very cross. I took them into the production office and spent half an hour calming this family down with my temperature and my flu getting worse. The pressure was hideous. I managed to calm them down and we went back to film. To make it fair I substituted the game for another. However, one of the things with the show that's really important is how the games translate into something that's exciting for a viewer for who it's the first time they've seen it. It has to be understandable so you can feel all the tension and excitement that the player is feeling. It was a brand new game I chose in its place. I can't remember what.

R.W.   It was *Vortex* for the SNES, which was the next big FX chip game at the time. All the challenges on the last show were chosen as being the most anticipated and cutting-edge games.

M.B.   I then made a really bad decision. I stopped the game. It didn't make any sense to my flu brain. Russ was sitting next to me saying, 'Just run with it.' And I snapped, 'It doesn't make any fucking sense! We can't run with it.' So I changed the game again for another. *Sonic*, I think. And this time it wasn't the first family who were now upset. The family of the *other* team were now saying I'd rigged it. And they did not calm down. I could not calm them down. All of this was going on with Mike Miller watching. Oh, it was horrible.

J.F.   Oh, poor Matthew. It was so funny and so painful. The fatal mistake Matthew made was inviting Mike to hand over the prize. I mean, as if the kids cared about him. He's this geeky channel commissioner they've never heard of who showed up in a combat jumpsuit just as everything started to go a bit badly wrong. Matthew was in the control unit with all the monitors and cameras, panicking, and I remember thinking, *Matthew, you could at least try and look like you know what's going on*. But instead he had his head in his hands going, 'Oh no, everything's fucked', and I'm like, 'Matthew, your boss is right there. You need to spin this, mate.'

M.M.   **Mike Miller, Head of Sport, Channel 4** There's always a bit of chaos in any production, especially when you're trying to put together a show like that in front of a live audience. If you look back at the programmes, they were bloody sophisticated for the time. All I care about is that the end product is good and that the viewers enjoy it. As long as the viewers don't see when it goes wrong, it's fine. And even when they do see a little of that it just adds to the whole experience.

D.P.   These kids were livid. Dexter and I were both at the front of stage with the audience watching and we both thought it was wrong. We were both protesting that they had to redo the challenge but everyone was so adamant that we couldn't. By that stage of filming there'd been so many technical issues and so much that had been going wrong with the show that 50% of you wanted to see it sorted out but the other 50% just wanted to get the show done and go home.

D.F. Winning a Golden Joystick was a serious thing to these kids, let alone a team championship. It didn't surprise me when things would go wrong that they would get up in arms about it, especially where they felt they were being short changed.

M.B. I went home that night thinking, *Oh shit, I'm in trouble here* because this family was so upset. A couple of days later Jane called me and said, 'Look, the family are threatening to picket Channel 4 and go to the press about this. You've got to go. I've got to fire you.' So I was fired. The family wanted blood and a public apology. Actually I think what they'd initially asked for was a reshoot, which we obviously wouldn't do. So they threatened to go to the press to say '*GamesMaster*'s rigged and my kids are so disappointed.' So I got the elbow. It was dreadful at the time. It wasn't a particularly pleasant experience.

I was too pedantic. Too stuck on the show following a very rigid rulebook. I think that was partly why it went wrong at the end. If I'd sort of relaxed and said, 'Oh fuck it. You know, who really cares if viewers don't understand the last game' it would have been fine. But I didn't. I really wanted to get it right. I really wanted to make it perfect.

R.W. Jane assuaged the families of the losing team by agreeing to give them the same prize as the winners, although both teams had to wait months before they finally got their Jaguars. By then word was out that the machine was a crock of shit and basically worthless. The issue with the prize and unfortunate events of the final meant that a series that had already lurched between several disasters ended on a monstrous, painful howler of a fuck-up, witnessed in person by the Channel 4 executive who had commissioned *GamesMaster* in the first place.

M.M. Although it was entertainment, it just shows how seriously people took the show. Which is good. It meant that it was important in their lives. Just like when I was a kid at school. If you didn't watch *Monty Python* you didn't have anything to talk about at school the next day. You wanted to be part of it. And I think *GamesMaster* had that. It's really lovely to be involved in something like that, which is serious and not serious at the same time.

M.B. I completely destroyed quite a few of my brain cells through the experience. Do you know what, though, I really enjoyed the first block of shooting. Although it wasn't perfect, it was good and well executed. Working on the first half was an absolute crack. Working on the second half was not. Yes, I had a bad experience at the end of it, but looking back at it all, it's really funny. *GamesMaster* was a really great show. I actually had a little moment recently where I went into a secondhand games shop in search of a game we'd featured on the show, *ClayFighter* for the SNES. These are the little memories that are associated with my time on the show. On the whole, good memories. Shit happens.

R.T.   You very rarely come across stupid people in TV. They always tend to bright people. There was always this feeling that I was slightly out of place there because I felt everybody else was brighter than I was. It was a very exciting kind of environment with lots of young people, but it was probably more fun in the early days of it when I was an editor. Stepping up as director was a very steep learning curve but it was a very happy time of my life. That's not to say it was always easy because it definitely wasn't. It was one of those times of youthful optimism. Well, I say that, but I was 31. I wasn't a young person at all.

J.H.   I'm ashamed to say but if you're running a company – and I only realize it now – there's a lot that people below you protect you from and don't let you see because they think it'll reflect badly on them. Morally and ethically, there's an awful lot on your shoulders because it's your company, but often you've no idea what's going on. I knew there were problems with the series. I mean, the whole idea of the championship was terribly complicated to begin with. We just had to put it down to experience. It was like we hit the wall and when you have a crash like that everybody gets hurt. Dexter got hurt, Matthew got hurt, we got hurt and the brand got hurt. That's series three really.

I was having a great time! The *Sportscall* show on BBC Radio 5 Live was doing great, and I was loving finally being in radio. Especially in Broadcasting House. You would bump into Terry Wogan in the corridor and he'd say hello, and you'd be like, *Fuck! I'm in this gang now!*

Sportscall led to me doing the radio version of *Fantasy Football League*, and that was me in BBC Radio 5 Live for the next 10 years. I managed to write another videogames book, *Dominik Diamond's Guide to Videogames and How To Survive Them*. And I was still getting tons of appearances opening videogames shops. I made more money in the year I quit *GamesMaster* than in any year I actually hosted it!

But then there was *Trash TV*. I was so close to getting my own comedy show on BBC Two. My best mate from uni, David Young, was now working for Hat Trick and we wrote a comedy show for them. We had Richard Easter from the Steve Wright Posse, David Walliams, and what would have been the first time Richard Osman ever did telly. We even interviewed Simon Pegg for it. Janet Street-Porter at the BBC loved it. She championed it and said when she was made head of BBC Two it would be greenlit. And then Janet Street-Porter didn't get the job. Michael Jackson did instead. And he rejected it. Which broke my heart.

Thankfully, Tony Fox managed to get me another TV show. Unfortunately, it was *Swot or Wot*. It was like *University Challenge* but with school kids asking questions, split between school subjects and popular culture. It wasn't a bad show but it wasn't a good one either.

So basically I had started the series three era thinking I would become the biggest new comedy face to the BBC and ending it doing a kids quiz show in Norwich. Them's the breaks, eh? In the aftermath of series three, both *GamesMaster* and I needed each other again.

SERIES FOUR

SEPTEMBER 1994

ven though I wasn't presenting *GamesMaster*, I was still very much part of the games industry. One day I'd be doing a report for Richard and Judy from ECTS, the next I'd be presenting a Virgin Games sales conference in Richard Branson's house, then the next day I'd be on plane to Belfast to open up a new games shop over there. And my lovely friends at Virgin were still taking me on trips to California, more for the banter than anything else.

In January 1994, they also flew me out to the Consumer Electronics Show [CES] in Las Vegas with Paul 'Ginger' Dowling. We were playing this porn game called *Virtual Valerie* where I was literally dragging a cartoon dildo in and out of the cartoon character, giggling away like a loon. And I hear this voice saying, 'What are you playing, Dominik?' And it was Jane fucking Hewland.

It was all a bit surreal because we had got there the day before, after the famous 'flight from hell'. Half the games industry were on that flight to Los Angeles and there were massive storms raging. We hit an air pocket and dropped 5,000 feet in a second or two. We all thought we were going to die. I remember looking across the other side of First Class past Danielle 'Woody' Woodyatt and Sean Brennan and seeing legendary artist David Hockney in one of the seats. I thought, *Oh, that's just champion. If we crash? He'll be the one in the headline, not me!* The weather was so bad we couldn't actually land the plane so had to divert to Vegas, which was luckily where CES was. We were all so relieved we drank until dawn. That was the start of my fear of flying, so I was still a bit shaky the next day. Then up comes my old TV boss while I'm playing a porno game.

It was so embarrassing. I tried to explain that I was writing a feature for a magazine about the boom in adult gaming but I don't think Jane believed me. We ended up having a funny chat about this game and that really helped break the ice between us. There was obviously this elephant in room. An elephant that was obviously losing ratings and credibility, but neither Jane nor I even mentioned the word *GamesMaster*, even though series three was still on air. I'm glad she didn't, because it was taking everything in my power not to say, 'How's my show going? I hear it sucks now.' Which would have ruined this lovely, bizarre moment.

Instead, we stuck to the safe conversation topic of porn games. And I'm not sure whether we would have negotiated my return to the show if that ice-breaking event hadn't happened. So thank you, *Virtual Valerie*, for saving *GamesMaster*.

How ironic.

BACK
FOR GOOD

This autumn we could witness the return of the videogame golden boy and all around nice guy, Dominik Diamond, to Channel 4's cult videogames show *GamesMaster*. This return has yet to be confirmed by the Scot himself, but apparently Diamond is seriously considering moving back into TV. Although not necessarily due to Dominik's leaving the show, audience ratings for *GamesMaster* have dropped rather worryingly. A dwindling interest in videogames has been fingered as the cause to the drop in viewers
Megatech, 1994

J.H.   Jane Hewland, Executive Producer I never wanted Dominik to go in the first place. I could see immediately that Dexter that wasn't going to work. There's nothing you can do about it. You can't fix it. I remember Hilary saying to me at the end of series three, 'We need to get Dominik back.' And I said, 'Thank God you said that.'

My favourite part of any negotiation for any job of my career is for series four. Tony Fox got to the point of agreeing a figure with Hilary Goldman for me to come back, and it was finally an OK amount of money. Tony said, 'OK, I'll get back to Hilary and tell her it's a go.' And I said, 'Yup.' Then just before Tony hung up, I screamed, 'No! Hang on. Wait a minute. Those fuckers said I had burned out at the start of series three. They killed me off. Fucking double it, Tony.' And that is how I got paid twice as much for series four as they originally wanted to pay me.

J.H.   It's weird to think that when the show was most popular we were most cash-strapped. We only got reasonable money once the bubble had burst. That's how it works in television, as it always takes broadcasters years to get on board. That's why Dominik didn't get paid very much at the start. I didn't even take a salary to begin with. We had no production team, no overheads whatsoever and nothing to pay for the offices. It was all coming out of our pockets. Literally, we were cutting costs on camera crew and editing with total faith in the idea. It was a big gamble and if it hadn't worked, I would have been broke.

R.W.   Richard Wilcox, Senior Researcher (Series 4) Though it was big news that Dominik was returning, he had a reputation for being outspoken and someone who didn't suffer fools. I'm sure it was quite a nervy time for him, returning to a series he had left. If it didn't go well his career would have been damaged, possibly irrevocably.

House of pain

'The things that are hard and a bit broken tend to be the things that bond you best. There was a shared feeling between us that we were all in it together and we had to get the best show out we could.' Dave Perry (with Dexter and Richard Baynham as the Caretaker)

A

B

C

A
Day one
'Right then. I'll 'ave a bit of this
GamesMaster malarkey, guvnor!'

B
Day two
'Hmm, no one told me it was going to be a
total shitshow behind the scenes and I'll
have to carry the can for it.'

C
Day three
'Yes! Future Dexter has told me I can
get through all this one day, become
a Hollywood movie director and have
the last laugh! Pukka!'

A

A
Patriot games
So here we have it. The moment
Cool Britannia started. Dave in the
Union Jack bandana.

B
Deeper Underground
'We found some stupid place underground
and went with it because we were
desperate.' Jonny Ffinch

C
Linger
'Condensation ran down the walls [...] It
wasn't the ideal place to have a load of
games consoles ... let alone TV cameras.'
Richard Wilcox

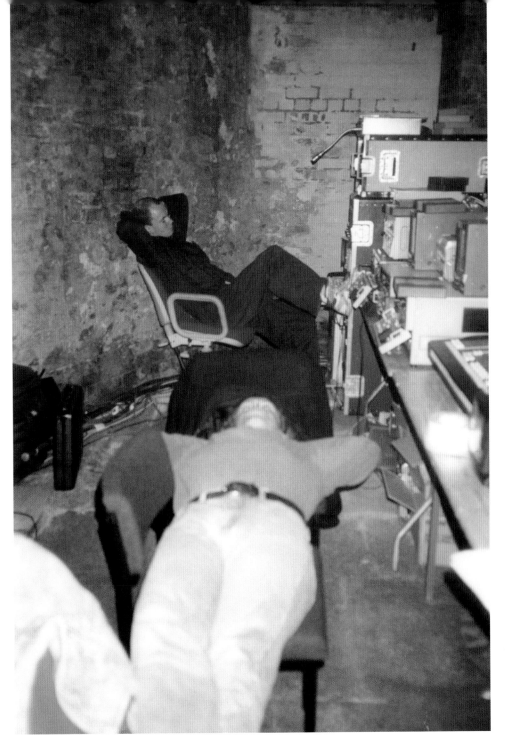

c

Living the dream
The Notting Hill flat. Obviously it didn't *really* look like this. It was a mock-up for a newspaper photo. So I removed all the booze and drugs that were lying on top of the games.

A

A
Life's a beach
The dreadful celebrity impersonators show with Fake That, John Major and Michael Jackson.

B
Breaking balls
Jimmy White and Archer Maclean.
My favourite ever celebrity challenge.

B

Hard knock life
This was in a hotel next to George Lucas's ranch. The lovely *GamesMaster* magazine guys were there as well. A glorious week of bubbles and bedlam.

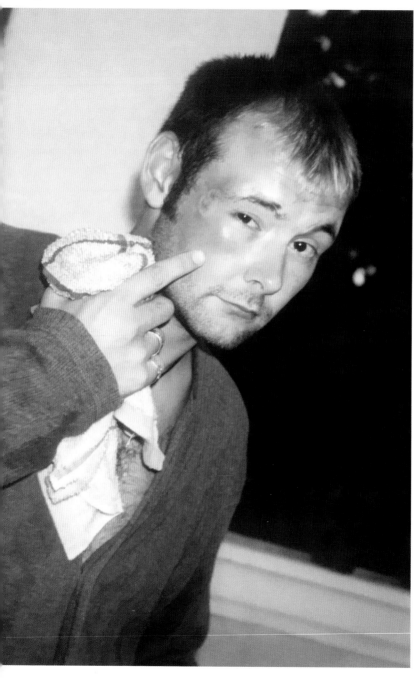

Surf dick
Recovering in Jaz Rignall's California
house after I nearly died surfing.

B

B

Hollywoody
Lovely Woody from Virgin took this pic. Cool Spot was also in the limo as we cruised Sunset Boulevard and nearly missed another flight through sheer fun.

C

Not remotely board
I didn't have a surfing accident this time but I did get the worst case of sunburn in Californian medical history and my skin fell off my face like in that movie *The Fly.*

p. 144

He's back
My favourite ever publicity photo. Praying. In Hell. With clothes I chose for series four.

C

What was great about being asked back is that it was now completely and utterly on my terms. We would never have a setting, a concept, an outfit or a single word coming out of my mouth unless I was 100% on board. I now had control. I was really excited because it was finally going to be my show. But I was also nervous. I mean, the show's reputation was in the toilet. Ratings were down. Was that all just because I wasn't in series three? Or was the audience bored of the show in general? Could we get them back? Because if we didn't, then that basically would be my fault. If it became my show then I would carry the can if it failed. And my career would probably be over.

J.F.   **Jonny Ffinch, Series Producer (Series 4–7)** When I was working on series three, we did a live show at Olympia London where I'd booked Nigel Benn and Barry McGuigan to play *Sonic Blastman*. After the show finished, I was helping offload this big arcade machine into a van. Everyone else had gone off to the pub but Jane was still around, watching me working. She approached and said, 'Please produce the next series.' I responded, 'I've got no idea what I'm doing, I can't!' And she said, 'No, you're doing it.' So I thought, *Fucking hell, all right then.*

R.W. For any production team to work well there has to be a good relationship between the key creatives. The most important of which is between producer and presenter. In simple terms, if they don't trust and respect each other then everything becomes a battle where no one wins and the show suffers.

I met Jonny in the Hewland International offices. It was the first time I had been back in there, so I was really nervous about going back in, nervous about meeting this new team. This tall, thin guy who looked like Jesus skipped across the room with the biggest smile I had ever seen. And he said, 'Hi Dominik, I'm Jonny.' And I fell in love. Seriously. There was something about this guy. His smile, his energy, but most of all his language. Within a few sentences I felt he was the most clever, well-read person I had ever met in my life. And the most unique thing about Jonny is he has this wonderfully gentle manner and speech delivery but he says the most caustic things. It's like a knife sheathed in lambswool. I love that contradiction and contrast. So yeah, I think I genuinely fell in love with the guy. I mean, sure, he'd never actually produced a TV show before, but I didn't care. He had great words and a lovely smile.

J.H.   Jonny's incredibly calm, sensible and mature. He's who you want sitting next to you in a situation of chaos to help bring order. Sometimes Dominik and Steve the director would get very stressed. Jonny could just handle anybody and anything.

J.F.　There wasn't much of a plan around series four beyond it being great
news that Dominik was back. We were a new team finding our way
and our own voice. Speaking of which, we made some quite serious
mistakes with Dominik's voice. He wanted to come back as a more
sophisticated personality as he regarded the old, nice presenter
style as embarrassing. So his first link to camera was, 'I'm Dominik
Diamond. I'm back and I'm grumpy.' It was all very antagonistic
and sarcastic, but that doesn't work. People sitting at home are like,
'Oh, fuck off.' [Laughs.]

I had a deliberate scorched-earth policy with my presenting style on
series four. I wanted to be the complete opposite of this character
I had been crammed into for series one and two. Right from the start.
So that first line was really important to me. No presenter starts a TV
show saying they are grumpy. That's immediately different from the
start. And I was thinking, *OK, you thought you could burn that character at the start of series three by torching a red jacket? Amateurs.
I will burn that character far more effectively using just words.*

J.F.　It was the beginning of a voice that we perfected in the subsequent
series. Dominik and I shared the same sense of humour, so between us
I'd write all the scripts and he'd add to them.

It is a measure of Jonny's brilliance with words, and how much I instantly
trusted him, that he is one of only two people I have ever let write stuff
that I say on telly. And the other one is Frankie Boyle. That is the lofty
company he is in.

R.W.　Apart from the occasional change in presenter and location,
GamesMaster had remained largely unchanged for three series. Jane
felt it needed freshening up, saying she was sick of the challenges
and giving us just one word to work with: events. She wanted events
rather than challenges. Frankly, we were mystified.

J.F.　It's hilarious we found it so difficult to grasp. These were the absolute
basics of making entertaining TV. God, we were shit. We got hold of
a load of big, exciting, arcade machines which were all shipped off
a massive truck on forklifts and handed over to our vision engineer.
They were all spitting out weird, Japanese NTSC signals and after

about two hours he said, 'Look, I can't get any kind of signal out of these things.' So they all had to be shipped back on to the truck and we instead played *Mickey Mouse* on the SNES. That served as a good lesson for me, so before we filmed each new series I'd take him to the arcades with all his kit, where he'd open up the back of the machines and he'd make notes about how it was all going to work.

That is one of the problems with series four. People really knew what they wanted to do, and the direction the show should be going in: bigger challenges with arcade games and events. But we didn't collectively have the experience or the technology to make it happen yet.

THINGS CAN ONLY GET BETTER

R.W.   Series four looks nothing like your typical TV entertainment show.

The first conversation I had with Jane after agreeing to come back, I mentioned setting it in Hell. The last series was so bad the show deserved to be in eternal damnation. I said to her, 'Well, you fuckers killed me at the beginning of series three. There's only two places I can be, and Hell is much naughtier.'
    I don't know if I was being serious or just making a flippant point-scoring gag. But it works perfectly. Series four is a savage reboot of the show. A show that had become this big commercial behemoth that basically destroyed itself because of money.
    There are many parallels between series one and four. Both are set in churches, both feature production teams that haven't done this kind of thing before. And it has a 'new' presenter as well. Because I am a totally different character. The show has to go back to the bottom and start again. And the ultimate bottom of everything? Is Hell. No TV show like this had ever been set in such a place. It was a big, bold, controversial statement. And we needed that. It was the job of me and the new team to raise the show up from this to the heights of TV Heaven again.

R.W.   The features in the previous series had been the responsibility of Steve Wright. He came from the pop promo world, where he'd directed music videos for songs like Jona Lewie's 'Stop the Cavalry'. Like most young pop directors he had aspirations to make the move into film directing, so unsurprisingly he was always looking to make things as cinematic as possible. He particularly loved Terry Gilliam and *Brazil*, and he never missed an opportunity to go a bit Gilliam. Steve was unquestionably cool and talented, full of ideas that were often leftfield. He also subscribed very strongly to the notion that creatives shouldn't be judged by the same standards as mere

mortals, especially when it came to boring things like organizational skills and punctuality.

Steve came up with idea of having goblins played by dwarfs, though. I would hate to take that away from the man. Because that was an utter stroke of genius. Just another thing in there that makes it a bit controversial because I don't remember *Bad Influence!* having dwarfs. Ever.

R.W.   He went all out to make the shoot as cinematic as possible, securing the services of an old mate and talented production designer he knew from his pop promo days.

D.M.   **Drogo Michie, Production Designer (Series 4–7)** I'd just fallen out of art school and this was my first and only ever television job. When we found the church, I started thinking about how we would dress it as Hell, so my starting point was mixing in Edgar Allan Poe with references to ancient themes and Greek mythology. The church lent itself to lighting which could fade into pockets of black and was very suggestive of hidden depths but were actually just areas we couldn't afford to dress. On camera it was the right size, but it was a pain in the arse filming and getting cranes in to shoot.

H.W.   One of my jobs was location finder so I found the church in Silvertown, East London. Although it was a disused church it was still owned by the diocese. When they asked, 'What do you want to film?' and we told them 'Hell', suddenly they became a little uncomfortable. Not enough to block it, but enough to double the price. [Laughs.]

D.M.   It was a lot of fun dressing the church but there was also a lot of background politics. When you're new to this stuff you don't understand the departmental boundaries of responsibility. The enforcer at Hewland International was this woman called Dina who I had a sketchy relationship with from the off over the river that would serve as the celebrities' entrance. I wanted it to be like this vision of Charon, the boatman on the River Styx. We tanked what would normally be the aisle leading up to the dais of the church and flooded it so we could have a rowboat with Charon bringing on the guests. But someone pointed out that the church might not have the load bearing capacity to put a river in. There was a crypt underneath and the tonnage that we were going to suzzle the floor with instantly became my problem. Suddenly, it was the art department's responsibility to structurally sign off and reinforce an entire location.

J.F.   Steve also brought in this maniac director of photography who insisted on having a fucking great dolly and crane for smooth camera shots. It must have weighed well over a ton. As it travelled up and down the aisle on the first day of filming we began to get the feeling that the 200-year-old wooden floor wasn't much enjoying it. After shooting, I went down into the crypt with Dina and instructed the grips above to roll the dolly up and down. We both looked up at the ceiling in absolute horror at what was a swollen, wooden wave rolling backwards and forwards, groaning and creaking as it bulged. It looked like it was seconds away from collapsing, so we had to hastily bring a team of scaffolders in overnight.

R.W.   The efforts to transform the church into Hell took longer than planned, so we were behind filming from the get-go and spent the entire shoot trying to catch up. We had that classic tension between producer and director that you get on film sets where the director wants to spend more time doing something so it's perfect, and the producer is pushing to move on, stay on track and on budget.

Series one, two and three used real locations. Which means there wasn't any set construction at all really before series four. So that was a quantum leap. You could not have had a better person to do it than Drogo. He was just utterly, utterly cool as fuck. They were like this trio of male models – Steve, Drogo and director of photography Nic Sadler, who came from the world of music videos, which obviously and immediately made me love them. They were creatively top-notch and fascinating guys to hang out with. Drogo in particular was incredibly eloquent, well spoken and super smart. I love people like that. And he used to wear this really cool flat cap. Between them, the set they created was incredible. I mean, they built the River fucking Styx! Drogo built an actual waterway! And then filled it with fire! That was mind-blowing. And they were all big, confident characters, which was also good because so was I. I needed them to match that, because I was so pumped up to make the show brilliant.

D.M.   Dominik had a sort of schizophrenic relationship between being pretty fucking self-important and a man who knew he was in the right place at the right hour and that it belonged to him. With that there was a sense of him being a bit impertinent and that everything's a bit crap. His unbridled ego was kept in check by his own sense of silliness. It was a wrestling match, which made for quite an interesting watch. [Laughs.] He was a bright guy interested in a cultural zeitgeist, which back then didn't have any of the credit that it has now. It's so expansive and immersive with scriptwriting and a sophistication that's on par with film. In a way, his intelligence was bottlenecked by his niche interest in videogames, because videogames couldn't mirror his intelligence. They didn't have the breadth and the depth, whereas now you can take the best film critic and give them a good videogame and you'll get an equally interesting and thoughtful response.

The one thing I do remember about him is that if you quaked in his shadow, or if you bent the knee, then you were fucked because you were pandering to an ego. The people who came back at him with a wry smile and an amount of wit he was fine with. Enfant terrible. But some people get tongue-tied and some don't have a rapier wit. And if you're not gentle and kind to them then you get a reputation as a bit of a wanker. It's a fairly primal victory, scoring points over someone who's designed by Darwin to not to survive your wit.

This was the first time I ever felt like I was the leader on a set. So what I did – and interestingly this became the template for every show I worked on afterwards – is make it all about what, I hope, is gently mocking humour.

My boss at Q107 Toronto, Blair Bartrem, who is the only producer figure to have become as good friends with me as Jonny, he calls it The Fire Hall. Like in that TV series *Rescue Me* with Denis Leary. You rip the piss out of each other. All day. What I think that does is create an environment where anybody can say anything, so it's a really fertile creative space. It also tells me very quickly whether people are on my level comedically and intellectually.

That may sound arrogant, but it's actually the opposite. I am utterly, passionately committed to visions of whatever I work on. And because of that you cannot tell me your idea is better than mine, unless I feel you are as clever and funny as me. If I do think that? In the case of Jonny, Steve, Drogo, Nic, The Dickster? Then I listen to you tell me when my stuff is shit. And that's important.

It's important with people further down the pecking order. Runners who are getting people coffee and whatnot. People who are easy to just ignore on set. I don't like that. I want everyone to feel part of the gang and part of the family. So I will turn everyone into characters, by picking something about them that becomes a running joke and that builds them up. For example, if a runner is wearing an Arsenal baseball cap then every day I will make a comment about Arsenal. If a lighting grip has a beard, I'll ask him funny stuff about facial hair management. Just little things to lift people from the background and give them a bit of identity, make them feel noticed and important. And part of my gang!

Sometimes, though, it goes wrong. If I don't feel you are as smart as me, or creative, or funny? Or most importantly, if I feel you don't work as hard or care as much as me? Then I can get a bit cutting. But if you don't tick at least one of those boxes then we shouldn't be working together. And you probably shouldn't be in the creative industries. It gets harder to run shows in that way these days. You can't make jokes about their little hats. Or anything really.

So the whole on-set atmosphere of *GamesMaster* from series four onwards I led more like a light comedy roast. And that is the key to the continued success of the show. It isn't really a show about videogames. It's a show about hanging out with your mates taking the piss out of each other. Mates who just happen to be playing videogames.

LET'S GET READY TO RHUMBLE

R.W. The opening titles to each series were always a big deal, and between series three and four, when most other people were on a break between contracts, I stayed on staff and spent quite a bit of time researching features. I came across a motion simulator ride in America that featured cutting-edge 3D films rather than the usual racing or helicopter simulator rides at the time. Like a good researcher, I got these companies to send us tapes, and when I played them in the office everyone was blown away. One of the films was a minecart rollercoaster ride through a deep underground cavern, filled with death-defying jumps across broken sections of track. We got them to tweak it a little and we added a short black and white film at the beginning. Everyone loved it apart from Steve, who had hoped to direct his own title sequence.

D.M. **Dominic Murphy, Titles Director (Series 4)** We shot the black and white sequence in an old steam train railway station in Sussex. We wanted it to be like a horror film and had some ideas to make it more dark, but we were told they didn't want us to have anything too satanic. In the end – and without telling anyone – we made the destination of the ticket read as 'Reef Hill', which was an anagram of 'Hell Fire'. I don't think anyone ever twigged.

J.F. As a new team, we wanted to put our own stamp on the show and move away from the videogame graphics and the iconography of the earlier series. Steve, quite rightly, said, 'I think we've seen enough of that.' It was the right time to freshen things up.

S.D. **Simon Dunstan, Graphic Designer (Series 1–3)** I can't remember what the budget was for the first three series we worked on. It was never that big but it was reasonable enough that we'd look at it and think, 'Oh that'll keep us going for six months or so.' Ahead of series four, some financial type turned up to our studio, arriving in a brand new TVR sports car. They said they wanted us for another series but the only glitch was that unfortunately the graphics budget was very tight this year and that they could only offer us £300. So we thought about it long and hard and I said, 'Well, I'll tell you what. How about you fuck off?' [Laughs.]

There was no big falling out. They'd obviously just decided they had enough material in the can and with editing technology having moved on so much they could carry it on in another way. I was very busy at the time, personally, so it didn't upset me too much, but I did think, *Who invented this bloody show?* In terms of that whole look and design and the logo, that was all us. As far as we were concerned the meat of the show was that it was a visual concept, which we were responsible for. We felt they had a duty of care. We were a team.

J.F. Steve just wanted to do something different. We replaced all the animation around Patrick with a head prop for him to wear. However, the first hat we had built looked absolutely ridiculous. I was so inexperienced and passive that when the prop guys handed it over, I just said thank you and took it. I walked back to the office thinking, *This looks really shit*, without the experience or the sense to just tell them it wasn't going to work and to please build us another one. Luckily, when Jane saw it she said, 'That's crap, get a better one.' I planned to use it because I'd already spent the money but Jane was like, 'No, just get another one. Black mark in your book. Off you go.' So we ended up with this plated metal thing that looked kind of shit as well, but not nearly as ridiculous as the first hat.

I don't know why I hadn't met Patrick in person by this stage. It wasn't something I consciously avoided. Though to be honest we were probably hanging out in completely different places at the time. I am not sure we would have been happy bedfellows. I knew anecdotally that we were at opposite extremes, politically. I can't think of any other double act to have that level of success without meeting. Ebony and Ivory by Paul McCartney and Stevie Wonder? Where they recorded the song and the video without meeting? We were the TV equivalent.

J.F. This series also marked the last time I had a live audience in filming, because it just made shooting so much more difficult. It was such a technically demanding show and to have a bunch of kids and their parents standing around when everything is going wrong and trying to keep them happy, it was just a nightmare. We kept them all in a cage to fit with the vision of Hell and then shoved 5,000 watts of lights underneath them. They'd be standing in this cage literally being roasted alive. Every now and then we'd be halfway through a take and one of the kids would complain, 'I'm going to faint if you don't let me out.' I'd be like, 'Shut up', and keep filming. [Laughs.] Those poor kids.

A live audience works both ways. As a performer you get more energy to feed off, but you also have to behave more. Anybody who has met me for more than five minutes off-air knows that I really do like a jolly good swear. And you can't do that in front of kids, even if most of that audience were kids from the Diamond Theatre School run by my mother. Actually, that makes it even more imperative to keep 'fucks' and 'shits' off the menu.

What was glorious about filming without an audience was that we were all such great friends by then. So filming this show was just like hanging out with your favourite people and saying what you want all day without having to censor yourself in any way. Total creative freedom. And getting paid to do it.

R.W.   Due to being behind schedule, some essential shots and elements for various challenges and episodes weren't recorded and this created quite a few problems in the edit. It all made for a very pressured set, but it was still fun because there was no animosity and no recriminations. We were all friends trying to make it the best it could be.

J.F.   When I look back at series four now, it looks like it was made by a complete halfwit. Some of the edits are just terrible and I can't believe Channel 4 broadcast anything so amateur. I'd never produced a TV show before and nobody tells you how to do it.

The first few shows of series four are a clusterfuck. There are so many bad edits. In one show, poor Simon Byron from *The One* magazine doesn't even get a proper introduction. They just throw his name up in a caption.

S.B.   **Simon Byron, Co-Commentator (Series 4)** I can only assume everyone else they asked was busy. There was absolutely no need for a slightly stammering games journalist like me to have ever have found his way on to the show. As editor of an Amiga magazine I was asked to explain what was happening on three games I'd never played nor had any actual knowledge of. Mainly because none of them were Amiga games.

   The production team did what they could to brief me. But in the chaos of filming I managed to forget almost everything they told me and provided literally nothing of worth. I caught one of my broadcast appearances to find an entirely different voice commentating on a challenge. I was so shit they actually dubbed another voice on to me. [Laughs.] I've spent all these years certain that none of my contributions were of broadcast quality, so I'm delighted to hear that actually the series was a technical shambles.

H.W.   **Hugh Williams, Production Assistant (Series 4)** It was partly because I was doing those edits, even though I wasn't really allowed to be. Steve just left me in the edit suite and went out for the day. [Laughs.] But he came back to check how I was getting on. He was my hero and became my mentor. He only told Jane at the end of the series that I'd done most of it.

Now, as much as I would go on to love that team, in series four I was the only one on set who had actually made a decent version of this show before. I was the only one who knew what they were doing. Jonny and Richard had been involved in series three, but series three doesn't count.

   Actually, no, there was one other person on set who had been there before. And that was Dave Perry, of course. I didn't like Dave any more because he had kept banging on about how great series three and Dexter had been, which I – delicate flower that I am – took very personally. You add that to the burgeoning ego of the Games Animal malarkey – his self-proclaimed 'I am the greatest games player' schtick that he'd relentlessly promote – and I felt I had to take him down a peg or two. Puncture the pomposity, so to speak. I should have done it face to face over a beer, really. Sorted it out like men. But no. I decided instead to make funny faces behind his back like a child.

D.P.   I knew something was wrong. Immediately on set there was just this problem between us and it was never clear to me why it was happening, but I was made really uncomfortable by it. He just never spoke to me off the camera. All I could put it down to was that I'd shown support for Dexter in the press and maybe Dominik felt that I was on the other team.

D.F.   It was really kind of Dave, but I didn't take any of it personally. If jokes were ever made at my expense by Dominik or in the press I was a big boy. I could handle it. [Laughs.] When I presented it I didn't have Dominik's swagger. I wasn't like that. I was more timid.

D.P.   Dexter was a nice guy and he was still taking a lot of flack. Having shared that experience with him just a year earlier, I was coming out in his corner when literally no one else did. I'd have done the same for Dominik. We'd been, I'd like to think, pretty solid pals in the early days.

J.F.   The awful thing was that the growing rivalry between them both was quite entertaining. Dominik was always persuading us every series that we shouldn't get him back, but the fact is Dave was good and that's why we kept booking him. I know Dominik's very contrite about the whole thing now but I could see why they didn't get on. Dave's ridiculous Games Animal persona was there for the taking. And to be fair to Dominik, I think Dave always felt he should have been presenting the show.

D.P.   I was perfectly within my rights, ego-wise, to believe I should have been in line after series three, because why not? Dominik had left. I had a presenter contract with *Games World* and Jane liked me enough to make me a co-presenter with Dexter, who was clearly not coming back. It seemed like a natural succession. But then, of course, Dominik returned, which made more sense. Of course it did. Nowhere along the road though did I say I wanted or expected to be the presenter. I just sat hoping. There was certainly no animosity from my side or any underhand move that I was vying for Dominik's job. Magazines were my day job.

When I came back for the new series, I was happy to keep plodding on. What mattered to me at the time was the show. And even when Dominik started making faces behind my back as I introduced the challenges, I actually thought it was quite funny in a childish sort of way. That was his sense of humour and these are the kind of things people look out for. But I was perfectly happy to be game for a laugh. I took the jokes and even presented a show with no shirt on, so I wasn't taking myself too seriously. However, when it carried on beyond what I thought was a reasonable joke I decided to put an end to it, as anyone would.

So. I have a horrible confession to make. Yes, I do think it was a terribly mean thing to do to Dave. The faces behind the back. It really was. I mean I humiliated the guy on TV without him knowing. That is shitty. And he was right to complain about it. And Jonny was right to stop me doing it. But I'll be honest. It is still fucking funny to watch. Embarrassing. Guilt-inducing. But still funny.

DON'T STOP [WIGGLE WIGGLE]

Contestant	Opponent vs. opponent vs. opponent
Game	Earthworm Jim (Sega Mega Drive)
Challenge	Collect the most neutron capsules within 1 minute

J.F.   One challenge we lined up early on in the series was *Earthworm Jim*, which was a huge title for Virgin. They gave us an EPROM – a board with a chip on with the level on it – and I think they'd even written '*GamesMaster* level' on the background as a copy protection thing. But it got leaked and ended up online. And Virgin went absolutely ape shit about it.

D.W.   **Danielle Woodyatt, Head of Global Communications, Virgin Games** David and the team at Shiny were so upset because this was their first big game release for which they developed a level especially for the show, so it was a big exclusive. Dominik had been out there discussing it with them and getting everything in place. When it leaked, Dominik was so pissed off and initially firing off at everybody because this was his big comeback show.

I was furious about the *Earthworm Jim* leak. Because by that stage the people at Virgin were my best mates. Woody, Ginger, Sean – I was hanging out with them every week. That is how we got exclusives like *Earthworm Jim*. That is how we ended up getting features from Skywalker Ranch. And because I was the only person on the team who was actually hanging out with games industry people on a day-to-day basis, I was more aware of the commercial implications and how seriously they viewed things like piracy. Tim Chaney was the president of Virgin Games, one of the most powerful men in the industry at the time, and I was fucking terrified of him because he never really hung out with us socially. And he hit the roof. I was the one who had to go in there and grovel and apologize. But I didn't mind doing that because they must have spent a million pounds on dinners for me over the years.

D.P.   **David Perry, Shiny Entertainment** Interestingly, I don't actually remember the leak. I'm not going to say I wasn't told, but I don't remember it. In reality, leaks were just a part of the industry. At that point every game ended up in a market in Thailand. I think it upset Virgin more than it did us.

R.W.   I was the one responsible for looking after all the ROMs and disks we were sent by games companies. So, yes, it happened on my watch. I was pretty organized and did what I could in an open-plan office to keep the games safe and under wraps. But after the big challenge filming shoot we all moved on to editing and getting the other parts of the show together. That would probably have been when it was taken. It's not something I've ever really talked or thought about. It just happened, and we had to move on, but it was fucking embarrassing, that's for sure. I don't know who did it but I have my suspicions.

J.F.   I couldn't get that uptight about it myself. I mean, it was bad that one of our researchers had done that, but on the other hand my feeling was, *It's an early version of one level of a game. I mean, knock yourself out and play it, kids. It's not the end of the world.* But Virgin were like, 'This is it. This is the end of our relationship.' They were going nuts. Luckily, we knew them and they calmed down about it. But yes, it was considered very bad and I had to pretend to think it was a terrible, awful situation. I didn't really care. [Laughs.] People were still going to buy it.

D.W.   What made the situation even worse was that David also sent over a one-of-a-kind maquette and limited-edition film cel for the winner of the challenge. There was only ever one maquette produced, and whoever ended up with that is incredibly lucky.

D.P.   It was handmade by Sandy Collora and initially used when we were pitching *Earthworm Jim* as a cartoon, which was then commissioned by Universal Cartoon Studios and aired in the USA on the Warner Kids Network. However, in sending it across to England someone clearly sat on it before Dominik handed it over, as it's supposed to be standing upright. Just look at it, for goodness sake. [Laughs.] I wonder if the winner ever realized and fixed it.

I'LL STAND BY YOU

Contestant	Baraka vs. opponent vs. opponent vs. opponent
Game	Mortal Kombat II (Super Nintendo Entertainment System)
Challenge	Beat Baraka in a best-of-three fight

A.H.   Andy Hutchinson, Co-Commentator (Series 4) I was commentating on the latest *Mortal Kombat* game with Dominik, and as it was an exclusive and such a controversial game, Jonny asked us to really play up commentary around the violence. So, of course, that's exactly what we did, salivating over the now frankly hilarious and tame end moves. We had a real laugh doing it. The only problem was that *GamesMaster* went out before the watershed, after which all the good boys and girls would brush their teeth and go to bed. So the show aired and it caused something of an immediate shitstorm with outraged parents jamming the Channel 4 switchboard complaining about the distressing violence their children had just witnessed.

It caused such a stink that we ended up being the lead item on *Right to Reply*, which included a cross-section of the correspondence they'd received from the mums and dads of suburbia and how their kiddies were now suffering from PTSD. I think that Hewland International were reported to the Broadcasting Complaints Commission as well, but apart from a slap on the wrist I don't believe anything further came of it.

J.F.   Jane went on *Right to Reply* in my place as I remember saying to her, 'There's no way I'm going on, you'll have to go on.' I'm so glad she did. In the cold light of day you've got Roger Bolton quoting lines from the show and asking, 'So, Jane Hewland – will you "nex that boy, mince him up and cut him to pieces"? Do you think that's suitable teatime viewing?' This was an 18 certificate game. She just had nothing. And she was up against the person who had written in to complain: a dinner lady. Jane said, 'You're dead against a dinner lady. The dinner lady has all the moral authority.' So Jane just came out with this line of saying, 'We are just reflecting the games culture as it is', but obviously showing games that aren't meant to be seen by under-18s is a bit dodgy at 6.30 p.m. or whenever it was.

A.H.   Now that I look back on it, I reckon they knew exactly what they were doing by glorifying this violent videogame on a TV show pre-watershed. It was actually a pretty transparent effort to be controversial and generate a bit of much-needed press about the show and prop up its flagging ratings. I am, however, still very proud of the fact that I appeared on *Right to Reply*.

CONFIDE IN ME

Contestant	Kylie Minogue vs. John Major
Game	Windjammers (SNK Neo Geo)
Challenge	Beat the opponent by scoring the most points

L.H.   **Louise Hynd, Contestant** I became Kylie Minogue by accident. I would get stopped in the street or when I was being served in the shops and told that I looked like her. It happened on my way to college so I told my friends about it, who fell about laughing while trying to persuade me there was a resemblance. I sent photos to lookalike agencies just so that I could get a rejection letter, which would have been the end of it. Instead I got these letters back inviting me to go on their books. That's how I became a lookalike Kylie Minogue model.

There is no excuse for the Christmas beach fake celebrity special, by some stretch the worst idea in the history of the show. It is one of only two times I have ever fallen out with Jonny in any way.

> J.F.   And he never lets me forget it.

When it was suggested, I just assumed the fake celebs would look and sound like their counterparts. But then John Major turns up and he is fucking Scottish! At least Macaulay Culkin and Kylie Minogue try and put on something vaguely approaching the accent of their real-life counterpart.

> L.H.   I realized I was a bit rubbish at my Australian accent. The only thing that saved me was that I felt John Major's was worse. [Laughs.] It was all a bit of a shambles and Dominik did take the piss. Now when you think of a lookalike you expect an impersonator, but back then it was different. The agency knew I couldn't act or sing, but I was typically booked for fashion shows and nightclubs, not videogame television programmes.
>   When I arrived for filming, I saw Ant and Dec hanging around the trailers outside the church signing autographs. I went inside and was met by Roger Black and David Coulthard, so I was slightly overawed thinking what I'd gotten myself into it. Stage fright doesn't cover it. I'd just graduated as a theatre designer so I was normally in a boilersuit painting scenery and making props.

It was excruciating to record. Every second I am speaking to them I know how terrible this is going to be. Robocop was also originally supposed to be on that show, but we held it over on to the Gore Special. That outtake of me looking pissed off when he enters? Is basically how I looked between takes of every single bit of filming that Christmas show.

> L.H.   I was terrible at the videogame from the brief practice I had, but the thing that powered me through filming was thinking, *I can't lose to John Major.* Even if it is someone pretending to be John Major, I could not lose to him. Somehow I managed to win, and I still have the trophy.

It's great when you are such close friends with someone that you still have something that is an argument ender. Even 30 years on, Jonny can disagree with something I say and I just reply, 'Yeah, but you were the guy who thought fake John Major was a good idea.' And that is game, set and match to me.

LET ME BE
YOUR FANTASY

Contestant	Frank Skinner vs. opponent
Game	Super Sidekicks 2: The World Championship (SNK Neo Geo)
Challenge	Beat the opponent by scoring the most goals

J.F. Dominik loved that Frank Skinner was booked. He'd make jokes to me about how I was shitting myself that I wasn't going to be able to be as funny as him. For the comedians who appeared on the show it was a faintly intimidating arena. They'd arrive and step into a weird, very elaborate set being run by young people all tapped into a culture they didn't really understand. They never felt so comfortable that they would attempt to start deconstructing it.

Getting Frank on for the first show in the series was such a big deal to me for two reasons. After *Fantasy Football League* he was the hottest property in telly. He was everywhere. So he would be the biggest guest we'd had since Take That. With my return and the reboot of the show, it was a great statement for us to make. Also, Frank had seen me back in the day working my first professional clubs as a 21-year-old standup comedian. I wasn't very good and he gave me some great tips. I wanted the chance to show him that I'd done OK in the end.

H.W. David Baddiel was meant to accompany Frank given that they were presenting *Fantasy Football*, but at the very, very last minute he pulled out due to illness. I was working on the show as a runner and as they knew I could play the game well Jonny was like, 'Right, you're going on. But there's two things you've got to do: lose, because Frank Skinner is more important. Secondly, we're massively behind schedule, so get the game over as quickly as possible.'
    I ended up taking the game to penalty shootout and beating Frank. I was desperately trying to let him win. At a couple of points I'm running towards my own goal with the ball. When it ended up going to penalty shootout, I was discreetly telling him which way to dive but he still cocked it up. He was the worst player. When Dominik's talking to me at the end of the challenge my head is kept down because I think I'm literally going to be sacked the minute I walk off set.

GIRLS AND BOYS

Contestant	Natalie Imbruglia vs. opponent
Game	Kid Klown in Crazy Chase (SNES)
Challenge	Beat the opponent by collecting as many coins as possible within 1 minute

S.B. **Scott Bradley, Contestant** I'd joined the Diamond School of Performing Arts. I was a fan of *GamesMaster* anyway, but after finding out the son of its founder, Paula, was Dominik Diamond I was starstruck. After the first year, Paula asked me if I would go on the show. I can't remember if I'd pestered her to be on it. Probably. [Laughs.]

Without her drama school I wouldn't have dreamed of going into entertainment, and I've been working ever since because of everything she taught me. We would get experience on film sets and appear as extras. Between her, Dominik and Michael, their comedy and direction are kind of ingrained in my psyche. When I'm presenting on stage in a holiday park, I'm very much in the style of Dominik.

It made sense to use the kids at my mum's drama school in challenges and features and whatnot. They were being trained as performers so they would actually bring something to the chat and not just stand there with rigor mortis. So I would say to Mum – keep an eye open and let me know if there are any kids that you think have a bit of star quality. Scott was one of them, so he appeared on the show a few times in various features.

S.B. My mum took me over on the train. It wasn't until I arrived I found out I'd be playing a celebrity. When I was then told it was going to be Natalie Imbruglia who had just left *Neighbours*; well, being a 14-year-old boy, that was obviously quite exciting. I met her ahead of filming and we practised the game in a Portakabin around the back of the church. Natalie and my mum got on really well, chatting about her new haircut, which had just been cut short. Before the challenge she said to me, 'Don't worry if you lose, I'll give you the Golden Joystick anyway.' It was good of her, but I still wanted to win. I was a bit of a gamer anyway so I really wanted the game to be something like *Street Fighter II* or *Mortal Kombat*, which I'd practised religiously once I found out I was on the show. And then it ended up being some stupid clown game.

There was obviously a feeling of elation at having won, but it was a strange experience at school when it was broadcast. To be honest, there was a lot of jealousy and I ended up getting quite a bit of stick for it. It's only now I'm older people recognize how cool I am. [Laughs.] I work as an entertainer and singer now, and in the holiday parks we always do gameshows for the guests. I actually put on a *GamesMaster* challenge where I go into the story of being on the show. Then I throw it open to the audience to challenge me on *Mario Kart* on the SNES. I still want to beat them given it's my professional reputation on the line, though I do occasionally let the younger kids win.

THE REAL THING

Contestant	Jimmy White vs. computer opponent
Game	Jimmy White's 'Whirlwind' Snooker (Sega Mega Drive)
Challenge	Clear the snooker table before the computer opponent

J.F. Jimmy White was a great challenge. We brought him on to clear a real snooker table while he competed against a computer opponent of his own game.

The Jimmy White challenge is the one more than anything else in series four where we got it right. Jimmy playing on a real snooker table versus his computer opponent. I mean, that takes ages to set up, and is beset with problems. But that is one time our result matched our ambition on series four.

A.M. **Archer Maclean, Developer** I came back to the show again with Jimmy to find they were filming inside yet another deconsecrated church. Jimmy turned up to play on a full-size snooker table where they struggled to fit it on this raised platform area in front of all these flames and caged kids. But the table was too sodding big. Jimmy had to teeter on the edge of the stage without falling off, then appear to be relaxed taking a shot down the table while cueing up a ball. In one shot he was bending over the table when his bum went too far back and was scorched up by one of these flames. He reacted pretty quick, dumped the cue and was seen exiting stage left pretty sharpish, clutching his smoking arse. Luckily he saw the funny side of it, although I remember Woody doing her nut thinking he would never help out again.

Jimmy White and Natalie Imbruglia to me represent the polar opposites of guest reactions from that series. For example, years later I was opening a videogames arcade in a caravan park in Tenby, South Wales. I walk into the hotel afterwards and I hear this cockney voice, 'Dominik!' And it is Jimmy White, who had been playing an exhibition match in the area with John Virgo. And he was like, 'Come and have a drink, mate!' I spent that night getting shitfaced with him and Virgo. And it was lovely that people of his calibre remembered the show so fondly that years down the line they would still want to have a pint with me. Natalie Imbruglia on the other hand? I actually found it hard to breathe in her

presence. Seriously. I was smitten. I saw her about two weeks later at some showbiz party in London. And I was like, *Oh my God, this is a sign! We are destined to be together.* And I went up to her and said, 'Hey Natalie, how are you doing?' And she had no idea who I was. I said, 'It's Dominik?' Still no recognition. 'From *GamesMaster*?' Nothing. 'The videogames show?' And finally she said, 'Oh yeah.'

In the show there'll be more emphasis on the features, which will improve it no end. We always tried really hard on *GamesMaster* to make humour the most important thing. We did that for the first two series. But in the last series, for some bizarre reason, the humour was missing, whereas this series is going to be hysterical. Dominik Diamond, *GamesMaster* magazine, 1994

J.F. I wanted to broaden the show out, subject-wise. Certainly in terms of the features, I wanted to cover entertainment technology in the broadest sense of the word, which is why we started covering things like rollercoasters being designed by computers. Basically, I wanted to do anything that would be vaguely fun to cover.

I don't know how we did it, but we managed to sweet-talk publicists in the States to let us come over and film on their big-budget movie sets. So over we went and it was the most incredible fun. The films we covered were terrible in retrospect, but it was the right direction to take the show. We actually wanted to do a bit of that in series three, which was partly why I was being sent over to LA.

There are two brilliant aspects of the series four features. First of all, the content itself. *Lawnmower Man 2* and *Mortal Kombat* are two of the best features any show did at that time. We were on Hollywood film sets, for fuck's sake. That was as big as it could get for me. And also it wasn't about videogames. It was beyond videogames.

The other great thing about filming that batch of features was it was where I really bonded with Jonny. Travelling makes or breaks a new friendship, doesn't it? Because you spend so much time stuck in little spaces with each other just talking. And it was simply brilliant. This is why the second half of my career has been devoted to doing breakfast shows on the radio. Because that is all about being stuck in small spaces talking to (hopefully) the most interesting and funny people you know.

This wasn't any ordinary piece of travelling, either. We were in America! In California! And every time I have been there for work, whether it was back then for *GamesMaster* or even a few years ago covering Rush's induction into the Rock and Roll Hall of Fame for Q107

Toronto, there is such an unbelievable energy to the place. So many times on that trip Jonny and I would just look at each other and giggle. And I think because we quickly realized our relationship was one built on mutual love of each others' intelligence, there was that sense of feeling intellectually superior to Americans in particular. That is why all those features involve me taking the piss out of them in some way. And that was very much what life was like on those trips even off-camera: Go to America. Hire a convertible car. Eat in nice restaurants, Get drunk. Laugh at Americans. Of course, years later they got their revenge by electing Donald Trump, the cunts.

> D.W. Virgin was the first games publisher to start to do international press trips, so Dominik was on one of the first trips. We took him to LucasArts for a feature on *Full Throttle* and stayed at this lodge just outside of Lucas Valley. There was a coach to take us all from the lodge to Skywalker Ranch, and Dominik didn't like the music. So he put on his music tape and well, for God's sake, it was all 'Fuck, fuck, fuck.' He put this rap music on and all the other journalists on the bus were complaining. And he would not stop. Honestly, he was a law unto himself.

No matter what feature we did, whether it was on the set of *Mortal Kombat* or on some shitty Loch Ness Monster motion ride? It was always about three things: How fit were the 'birds' and could I pull them; how hard were the blokes and could I take them in a fight; and what could I say about people's hair? Now, from the lofty heights of Woke Mountain, today some of those things may seem a bit iffy. But that was the nineties. For everyone. It was birds and blokes and beer whether you were a bird or a bloke. Or a beer. Even in America. So when I ask out Talisa Soto on the set of the *Mortal Kombat* movie, it's an extension of the laughing and joking and pissing about on set with her I was doing off camera. Ditto with Bridget Wilson.

This is why pre-chat with guests is crucial. That's where you get a sense of where to go with them. Whether it's in a feature or doing a challenge. You suss out whether they get the show and its humour. So you don't end up saying anything that makes them feel uncomfortable.

So when we did a feature on *Phantasmagoria*? And I interviewed the legendary game maker, Roberta Williams? Chatting to her beforehand I felt she didn't quite share the same sense of humour, so I didn't think that was an appropriate time to roll out the 'do you fancy me?' stuff on camera. Even though she most probably did.

HERE COMES THE HOTSTEPPER

J.F. We developed a Gore Special that was intended to be the last show and part of the normal run of the series. It was far tamer, but nonetheless it was still quite graphic, and when our immediate bosses at Channel 4 saw the rushes they hit the roof. They said, 'We can't possibly broadcast this. You're insane.' I had an emergency meeting with the head of department, Dawn Airey, in which we viewed the original cut. It had seemed such a good idea when we were shooting but seeing it in the cold light of day, in a bland Channel 4 office, it suddenly seemed rather difficult to defend as acceptable teatime viewing. To Dawn's credit, she didn't seem too pissed off and suggested a late-night slot instead.

Now, the Gore Special might have been out of order at 6.00 p.m., but we had the opposite problem with it going out at midnight. It looked terribly tame and we thought we'd have to up the controversy content as much as we could. So we started shoving as much gore and as much porn into it as we could. We just cobbled it together. When you sit down and watch it now it's just a horrible mess. And then bizarrely it was even released on VHS and Video CD. I mean, they must have sold about four copies.

R.W. The Gore Special was pretty much built in the edit suite by scouring rushes from the challenge shoot mixed with new features and Dominik's expletive-laden asides between takes. We had such little time to put it together in time, we were working from three edit suites simultaneously, through the night. Factor in how expensive an edit suite was to hire and it was a very pressurised environment if you weren't prepped. Jonny was an absolute master in that regard, working ad-hoc and dealing with hundreds of tapes while I was up in the attic capturing scenes from dodgy games at the same time. Even just to get the gameplay onto tape was quite the achievement.

H.W. To up the gore content we created some sting transitions to edit one sequence into another. There wasn't really any existing material to use, so at the request of Steve I was sent to a meat market to buy a sheep's head and then a fishing tackle shop to buy maggots. Travelling on the underground with a carrier bag of body parts and a huge meat cleaver was bad enough, but I had to then sneak them all into the post-production facility house in the West End without being spotted. I managed to sneak past, lock the door of the edit suite and put all this stuff under a rostrum camera, which is a fixed camera looking down on a desk. So I gently placed the sheep's head down and poured maggots all over it. I assumed it was a perfectly normal, natural thing to ask of a runner. It isn't. [Laughs.] We were still finding maggots in the edit suite days later.

I actually really enjoy the Gore Special to this day. Sure, it is a little over-stuffed with adult content just for the sake of it. 'Oh, here's a sprite with its head splitting open. Fuck it, let's shove it in there. Oh look, here's a game with tits. That's in too.'

But I think as an episode it is better than 90% of series four. And I love the outtakes of me swearing and – best of all – smoking a cigarette on set. After all those years of hating playing a character on TV that wasn't really me? This is absolutely, unfiltered, unfettered, unchained Dominik Diamond. In real life? Back then? I was a sweary, chain smoking Scotsman who got angry if he messed up doing a bit for the show. Lo and behold, the fans finally get to see him!

Also, including footage of Robocop from the Christmas beach fake celebs special allowed me to cut away from that challenge in a voiceover, saying 'the only crime being committed is arse actor in crap costume. Let's forget this ever happened and go to the Consoletation Zone'. I hated it that much we cut away to the fucking Consoletation Zone. I think including the footage at all was Jonny's way of saying, 'OK, Dominik. You can now say how shit you thought that idea was.'

> J.F. For later series we used to push Channel 4 for a later slot because we just felt it would get it away from being a kids' TV slot. We'd sit and imagine, *Wouldn't it be great if we could swear?* I wonder if Dominik would agree with me now with the benefit of age and hindsight that, no, the time slot was actually perfect as it was because it felt like you were doing something naughty and getting away with it.

After all that fun? After the great return of Dominik Diamond? Series four isn't actually very good. It really doesn't stand the test of time at all. My performance is decent. And I think the scripts are great. Ending each show by telling viewers I'm off to do something horrible like tell kids at boarding school their parents don't love them? That stuff is good. True story, the original version of that line was, 'I'm off to tell kids at boarding school that their parents have died.' I am so glad we shot a safer version.

I also like the way I am quite cutting and rude with the contestants. And obviously I love what I was wearing. Finally. But I don't think I really checked on much of the show after we filmed it. I wasn't an associate producer on this series, so I wasn't sitting in an editing room putting it together. And I didn't actually watch many shows go out. When I watch that series now I barely remember half of it. I mean, booking C.J. Lewis? Whoever made that decision?

> R.W. Looking back, series four is pretty grim and downbeat. Just in terms of visuals, it's unremittingly dark. At times it's a bit choppy and staccato. There were signs that the series was evolving, but it was embryonic and we were a new team finding its feet.
>
> J.F. Steve's direction of the visuals – of how ambitious, rich and amazing it could all look – was something we very much got right. We hadn't

thought about that stuff before. I'd say the show looked good, but it was quite pedestrian really in terms of content. I remember after one of our creative sessions in the pub going up to Jane saying we'd decided we wanted to do a black and white mute show like the old films. We were deadly serious. We were convinced it was the best idea anyone had ever had.

In many ways series four is our *Spinal Tap*. It's a series of excess. Setting it in Hell and having the actual River Styx in there. Flames everywhere. Dwarfs. Snooker tables. Hollywood movie features. Gore specials. We really did turn it up to II. And it got away from us a bit. My own life was about to lurch into its own rock excesses. Not too long after filming series four I was at a games industry party in London and was introduced to both cocaine and speed on the same night. And that was love at first sight, sadly.

I was never comfortable with the level of recognition that comes with fame. I would go to all these videogame events and whatnot and have to talk to everyone. Everyone. It is exhausting. And to be blunt, most of those conversations are the same and they can get quite boring. So I used to drink a lot to make it easier to deal with. And then you get too drunk too quickly so you go home. But when you find a drug like cocaine, whose most potent superpower is the ability to help you drink more without feeling woozy, and makes boring people tolerable, giving you boundless energy? It really is a match made in Hellish Heaven.

I never directly mixed cocaine with work. Or alcohol. At no point was I hoovering up a line of marching powder and downing a shot of tequila before throwing across to the GamesMaster in the Consoletation Zone.

Jonny and Steve were learning on the job. And it is ironic that, having worked so hard to be a leader on set during the main filming, I kind of failed them and the show as a leader when they were putting it together afterwards. That is one of the reasons series four isn't as good as it should have been. I was very lucky – and the show was very lucky – that by series five Jonny, Steve and Richard knew what they were doing. Because my personal life was chaos by then. My life of incessant partying in London meant I wasn't really heading back up to Milton Keynes to see my family as much as before, and when Myf wasn't working in Bristol we were rowing all the time. I was growing further apart from the only people who could tell me to calm down a bit.

The only bit of series four, apart from the foreign features, that I think stands the test of time? And this is strange because it wasn't a part of the show that I was ever really that bothered about before, even though I had to film it and edit it, is the reviews section. Those three guys: Tim Tucker, Adrian Price and the utterly glorious Frank O'Connor are the dream team, basically. Three distinct personalities, each of them with something really interesting and unique and entertaining to say about the games. I feel the reviews are much better edited than in previous series as well, because they are given a bit more time to make salient points.

So it is ironic, that after me coming back to save the show, on reflection, the best bits of series four are actually the bits I don't appear in or have anything to do with.

That said, this series is the first time I remember us having a wrap party after filming. It's a measure of how well this new team bonded that we had an insane drinkathon in east London, which ended up with me wearing nothing but my pants, egged on by the whole team, launching myself on my boogieboard from a hotel patio into the water in Docklands. That kinda sums up the experience of series four. Messy but fun.

SERIES FIVE

SEPTEMBER 1995

ineteen ninety-five. When the show finally came together as my life finally fell apart.

The team were so good by series five. Which was just as well. I had undergone a total life change before we started filming. Thanks to my new best pal cocaine, by this stage I was partying hard while Myf was working down in Bristol. I was out of control.

Actually, it was hard *not* to do cocaine in London in 1995. It was everywhere. The Atlantic Bar, Quaglinos, every single pub in Notting Hill. It was flying. Literally great big clouds of it in the air. You would go into any pub or club toilet and every cubicle was full. I remember one time with my mate David at the Camden Underworld and the bouncer knocked on the door as we were doing a line. 'Sucking or snorting?' he shouted. We looked at each other, and both simultaneously said, 'Sucking!' And then put on assorted sex noises while giggling. So he left us alone.

There was a very famous person who I was good pals with who was about to leave Tony Fox's agency. I was sent out with him and some of Tony's people to give him a great night out and persuade him to stay. This involved bags and bags of powder, which he gleefully hoovered up with us. And still left the agency.

Don't get me wrong. Cocaine is a horrible, vile drug. It destroys lives and it certainly fucked up mine – I still feel its effects today. But back then? In London, in 1995? Doing cocaine was like putting salt on your food. You just did it without thinking.

It made all those people wanting autographs and a chat a lot easier to handle. And it does give you confidence. A horrible, cruel, selfish confidence, but a confidence I lacked in real life.

And then one night I met Kirsty Young. She was beautiful, intelligent, this glamorous figure in Scotland and, most important, she was Kirk's wife's sister. The four of us went out together one night in London and there was the most insane spark between us. So it didn't matter that I lived with someone or that she was engaged to be married. Boom. It happened. And I dumped Myf. And Kirsty broke off her engagement and it was all front-page news in the Scottish tabloids and her fiancée was obviously not happy. At all. It was a scary situation, but it was also incredibly exciting and thrilling. It felt like being alive in a more multicoloured way. Your life is like watching a movie on a brand new telly. Because of cocaine. Cocaine makes you addicted to adrenalin.

Kirsty and I only lasted a couple of months and I tried to get Myf back afterwards but she rightly was like, 'No fucking way, you've changed.' I had no one to rein me in or ground me. So the stuff I joke about on the show? Booze and birds? That was my life, for the next two years. Sex and drugs and rock and roll and videogames! But I think in a weird way, it helps my presenting on this series of *GamesMaster* and the next. Because I finally felt 'cool'. And what you see on the next couple of series of the show is a presenter who is willing to try anything, because my confidence was at Mount Everest-like heights. So I would go, 'Fuck it, let's ask Whigfield to marry me!'

SERIES FIVE

ROCK 'N' ROLL STAR

I think you'll find *GamesMaster* still is about videogames. We've had more exclusives on this series so far than any other games show in Britain. We're the only show that features the latest arcade games for a start. But for every *Chart Show* you've got to have a *Tube*. Ten or twenty years from now, people will be sitting in the pub, saying, 'Fucking Hell – wasn't that an unbelievable show?' They certainly won't be sitting there talking about *Bad Influence!*
Dominik Diamond, *PC Gamer*, 1995

J.H.   **Jane Hewland, Executive Producer** Successful TV shows reinvent themselves at some point. Look at *The X Factor* and how they keep modifying it with small tweaks. Formats get boring after a while and you have to keep the audience on their toes. Once you appoint the Jonnys and the Steves, you have to trust that they know better. All the way along they were far closer to the audience than I was, and also it was an audience growing up with us too. The kids that started watching us at 10 were now teenagers coming to the end of secondary school. We were never a kids' programme, but we had to keep being more grown-up than the audience.

M.M.   **Mike Miller, Head of Sport, Channel 4** I wasn't nervous. I had faith in Jane and in the team around her. People are always a bit nervous where there's change, but things reach a natural peak and then need refreshing. I thought it was handled well. I was also the commissioning editor for *The Big Breakfast* for four years, which went through the same sort of issues over a change in presenter when Gaby Roslin and Chris Evans left. We went through a period where we tried lots of different people before settling on Johnny and Denise. I ended up being involved in that because they thought being only the commissioning editor for sport I had loads of time on my hands. [Laughs.]

With a show like *GamesMaster* you have a decision to make. Do you grow with your audience, or do you move back and try and catch the next generation? Or can you do both – and probably not – so do you do a spin-off? Those were the sorts of questions Jane would have been thinking about, and it probably made sense to grow with the audience and to create a completely different show for the next generation.

R.H.   **Rik Henderson, Co-Commentator (Series 5–7)** Series five feels like the first of the new era. It just seemed like it finally all clicked in as to what the show was about. The setting for Hell was kind of too dark in many ways. Series five was just this totally different thing. Something a lot more structured and a lot more fun to watch.

After the steep learning curve on series four, Jonny, Steve and Richard knew what they were doing. And it was the start of our amazing pre-production sessions. We did them for series five, six and seven and each series followed the same pattern.

The four of us would meet in a pub in Notting Hill. We would get absolutely off our tits. We would come up with ideas for the next series, including settings and assistants and guests and other crazy shit. We would meet the next night and do some more, probably with Drogo there as well. Sometimes we would spend three or four nights in the pub coming up with stuff over a week. it's all a bit hazy, but I do remember most times I would try and steal something from the pub at the end of those nights. And at the end of the week we would have this massive book of initial ideas, along with a giant pepper grinder from the pub in my kitchen. The ideas would get sent to Jane who would go, 'Love it ... Love it ... What the fuck? What are you guys on?' And throw out the more mental ideas we had come up with at 3.00 a.m. In particular, every year we wanted to set the show on a pirate ship but that never happened. So Jane is still very much there as the arbiter of all this stuff, and it is important to have that editorial boundary there. Especially because Jane does not drink alcohol.

It really was a glorious way to work. We had all become such great friends, immensely respectful of each other's work and ability. So it was this group of four of us – and Drogo – who shaped the final three series. And that is basically how I work with breakfast shows on the radio, except you go to the pub at 11.00 a.m. rather than wait til the evening.

I am a great believer in certain substances aiding creativity. And I think series five shows a quantum leap in terms of fun and ambition that was a result of a wonderfully loose creative process for all of us, shall we say ...

> J.F. Jonny Ffinch, Series Producer (Series 5–7) It was very simple, really. After setting the previous series in Hell, we thought, 'What are we going to do now?' We do the opposite and set it in Heaven. One of the developments we came up with that Channel 4 didn't particularly love us for – and that I can't really defend now – was bringing in professional models dressed as angels to be on-screen assistants. Our audience was predominantly 15-year-old boys. It made the shoot so much easier because we had all these hairy camera and sound men who are usually such grumpy bastards, but you stick these two gorgeous women in the middle of it all and suddenly they're on their best behaviour.

We knew we didn't want them just standing there. But then you see them on screen, Helena and Tanya, and they have such an enormous charisma and presence that they just dominate the screen. It was a superb bit of casting that involved legions of the most beautiful women in the UK coming into the office to meet us, and I was honoured to be a part of it.

SERIES FIVE

H.T. **Helena Tepper, Angel (Series 5)** I was with a good London agency where it was normal to be working on shoots during the day and get a phone call to audition elsewhere in the evening. I always had my passport with me so sometimes you would literally get a call saying, 'Right, you need to fly to Germany', and you'd just fly across, do the shoot and fly back. One of those phone calls was a request casting from Hewland International down in the Docklands. They wanted someone who had blue eyes and dark hair to be teamed up with someone with blonde hair and it was for a TV show called *GamesMaster*. And I was like, 'I've heard of that because Dexter used to present it.'

That is brilliant. That there was someone out there who thought of *GamesMaster* as being Dexter's show. I love that. Especially considering it was someone who became such an integral part of the show. I only hope she wasn't disappointed that it was me she ended up working with.

H.T. I was a bit uncertain about doing it, as I just thought, *This is a kids' programme.* But I was in London so I went along to it. It was pretty standard with the usual introductions and them looking at my portfolio. Then I got a phone call by the end of the week to say they wanted me for the series. They hadn't yet hired the other angel but narrowed it down to about three blondes, so I had to go back and audition again. I was a bit pissed off to be honest because I was saying, 'They already want me so why have I got to go back for a recall?' My agent was like, 'Please, it's not going to take long.' Anyway, I met Tanya who they hired as the other angel and it was the start to us becoming lifelong friends.

T.K. **Tanya Kecskes, Angel (Series 5)** The dynamics of power within the set was all balanced. There wasn't any hierarchy or sexism. It all just seemed really nice where Helena and I were in our own little bubble enjoying everything going on around us. It was always a pleasure, but it was hard work because filming was intense and they were long days. There was a very chilled-out atmosphere so it was really friendly. Professional but friendly.

H.T. We had to be fitted with these white togas and, of course, look very heavenly. So we went along for the fitting and were given tall heels in which they stapled on angel wings. They were really uncomfortable and I had to put Blu Tack on the inside of the shoe to try and pad this little staple out. A nice little toga and high heels. What more could a girl want? [Laughs.]

T.K. Dominik used to wear the most amazing shirts. Being a proper celeb, he used to get his Issey Miyake white shirts laundered and delivered and ironed on set. He was quite a snappy dresser.

My outfit for series five is not that different from series one. It's still black trousers and a white shirt. Take away the waistcoat and cravat from

series one and replace it with a black jacket. But it looks totally different because it's a great Paul Smith suit with a lovely Issey Miyake shirt, and the result is an outfit I wear with confidence. And a show I present with confidence. That's why it looks so different without actually being that different. And with the angels on each side wearing white? That's a fantastic composite image of colour contrasts. We almost look like a band. So the outfit, the angels, all of that gave me the level of confidence which resulted in me finally hitting my groove as a TV presenter.

> H.T.   I was told I received the most fan mail. It was ridiculous. I never thought that would happen. I didn't realize people held the show so dear and that it affected people, hopefully in a positive way. Some of the people who wrote in really opened up about their lives. There was one chap who was in the army. He was stationed somewhere overseas. He said that he'd seen one of the episodes on the plane and he just really wanted to have a signed photograph because he was going to be stationed somewhere for quite a few years. His letter was handwritten and was very much about his life and surroundings. I felt as if he was trying to have a conversation in a very nice, respectful way.
>
> Obviously, people remember the show, and if you think of the gaming industry how it was then, it was an exciting time but it was more than that. We became part of this incredible journey of new technology and innovation. Looking back, we've all realized we were there at the beginning of a lot of things. I think that's why people are still so fond of it.
>
> J.F.   We had a very passionate audience but we use to suffer from the terrible inverse ratio between social skills and videogames, so the better you were at games, usually the worse you were at talking. Dominik would also get people who'd follow him around and try and attach themselves to him. And I did try to always be friendly and respectful of fans because they were our audience and, above that, they are people.

I don't remember getting so much as one piece of fan mail. I remember not being able to go anywhere without being hassled by gamers, so I can only assume that my particular sect of the cult follower were not literary types. Or, which is more likely, in the midst of a beer and cocaine hangover that I'd get a call from the office about what to do with correspondence and I probably said, 'Bin it.' So, sorry if you wrote to me back then. You can put your question to me on Twitter now if you want.

> T.K.   We had a wrap party where Dominik put drinks on at his place and we'd all go over and watch the opening show. What stands out for me in working for them was just how welcoming an experience it was.

We all hung out a lot, outside of filming. And I remember having everyone round mine for the first show. Everyone. From every level of the show. And thinking, *This is a real team, here. Everyone is just part of this great big lovely thing.* As much as I loved Adam and Cameron – and I did, in spite of my creative differences with him, always enjoy Cameron's company – but now the show felt like my big family, especially when I got my big hairy Scottish brother involved.

> K.E. Kirk Ewing, Co-Commentator (Series 5–7) Dominik asked me if I'd be interested in joining as a co-commentator. I thought, *Yeah, that sounds like a lot of fun.* It wasn't much money and it was a case of coming down for the first show and hanging on set for a few days. It was like being invited into a really brilliant little club. I loved the guys instantly and everyone made me feel incredibly welcome.

For series five we wanted to take the role of commentator to the next level. It's not about being a credible games journalist any more, necessarily. It's about personality. And being different. And being genuine. Mates having a laugh. Kirk had the largest personality of anyone on the planet. Physically, he is striking. Nobody looks like Kirk apart from Kirk. And Gerard Butler, once Kirk got his hair cut. He was the funniest guy I knew and he loved videogames. It was a no-brainer. So that new trio with Kirk, Rik and Derrick was what made series five, six and seven for me in terms of challenges. We had a good split of commentators for particular game genres. Rik would do sport games because we hung out and watched sport together, Derrick did the arcade stuff cos he was Mr Namco, Kirk did anything that was a bit random and Dave hoovered up the rest.

Rik and I had been mates for a few years and he knew what he was doing. He was good on camera from the start and we had a fine banter level in real life. Kirk and Derrick were filming virgins. Not media people. So there were teething problems while they learnt their craft. And I worked really hard at that with both of them. They were both very different puzzles I had to unlock to get that massive talent inside to come out on screen.

> K.E. Honestly, I thought I was terrible throughout. Dominik would be really pedantic, like, 'Fucking say this. I'll say this and then you fucking say that', and I just never said what I was meant to. And I can see his face like, *What the fuck are you doing?* and I'm like, 'It's fine, right.' [Laughs.] Just a big, lumbering stone oaf. That was my role.
>
> Like most people, I blank out when I go on camera. I'm just like, 'Argh. This is insane.' I might not have looked nervous, but I was. To help, Dominik encouraged me to get ripped. So he'd say, 'Why don't you go out and have a little joint before you do the show?' and I'd be like, 'What?' and he'd say, 'Yeah, you should definitely do that.' It was an approach that culminated in our TV show for Paramount, *Dom & Kirk's Night O'Plenty,* where we both just drank and got stoned before every show.

A

B

A
Dream team
My guys. And Lisa MacNugget. Steve Wright
and Jonny Ffinch standing left, the Dickster
on the right. Beyond love for them all. We
made TV magic.

B
A bit fuzzy
The two funniest guys I knew in the nineties.
Kirk and the legendary Ginger from Virgin.
Kirk starts fights. Ginger finishes them. I was
always somewhere in the middle.

A

B

B
Doubling up
Hugh Williams, yet another member of our production team who was slipped in as a contestant. He played against Frank Skinner in the series four opener.

C
Angelic
'Tanya and I had absolutely no idea what it was going to be like. We arrived into this surreal Heaven setting and walked up this marble staircase in our angel high heels, dazzled by the brightness of the lighting and feeling like we literally had stepped foot into Heaven. This wasn't our usual experience of television.' Helena Tepper

C

A
Heaven sent
'The fundamental point about trying to communicate Heaven is that in everyone's minds Heaven is something of absolute unending grandeur and enormity. [...] It was an absolute bastard to represent as a set on a limited budget.' Drogo Michie

ARCHIVE IV

Moore, Moore, Moore
'I used to dread filming days with Patrick, but he was quite an old, kind man in his own way in life. I remember him once asking me during recording, "What is an N64? Does it have wheels?"'
Jonny Ffinch, Series Producer

A

B

C

SO POWERFUL
NEVER GIVE IN

D.I.V.O.R.C.E.
Oh boy. You really can tell that by this stage Dave and I did not enjoy sharing the podium. Rarely has a photo summed up a mood so well.

Game for a laugh
Ravi never took himself seriously for a second, and was always willing to get the piss ripped out of him for the show.

A

A
American graffiti
Proof if proof be needed that I did write that Anglo Saxon word on Bill Gates's car on a freezing Seattle night.

B
White knuckles
That time I pretended to be terrified of a little rollercoaster. De Niro levels of method acting. Especially from my pants.

B

C

D

C
Cruising
A love-filled threesome in the Californian sun. I made Jonny drive us around the most dangerous gang areas of LA in this ludicrously expensive convertible rental car just so I could get a picture of me throwing up gang signs.

D
Landmark
In 2013 I went back to LA for Q107 Toronto to cover Rush's induction into the Rock and Roll Hall of Fame, and I made a pilgrimage to this shop. It is still there. And still smells of bad decisions.

Birthday boy
Celebrating my 25th in the flat. Behind
me, L–R: Chris Knight. Rik Henderson and
Doug Johns.

Kirk does not realize how good he was on that first series, which is strange, because he is the world's most confident man in real life. And those leftfield challenges like 'Baby Rom', 'PC Impossible' and 'Blokes Who Sweat Rock and Roll' simply do not work without Kirk. They need someone who doesn't take himself or anything else in life too seriously. Someone who realizes that all this is a bit silly. He is in effect the polar opposite of Dave, who knows the games inside out but treats them and himself as if they are Holy Grail. And there is room for that, and you need a bit of that if you are doing a legacy game like a Sonic or Mario or whatever. But we were trying to move beyond that kind of thing now. In fact, the biggest mistake you could make on *GamesMaster* from series five onwards was taking yourself too seriously. It's supposed to be daycare for adults.

> R.H. I was the editor of a videogames magazine at 19 and my first big interview was speaking to Dominik ahead of the first series of *GamesMaster*. I phoned him on Christmas Eve in 1991 and we just got on really, really well. He ended the call saying, 'I hope to catch up with you again soon.' Which he did when he returned to the show in series four and I was working on *Games World*. So we'd meet in the office and became friends. Like Kirk, he invited me to co-commentate on the series and said he wanted to surround himself with friends rather than just a parade of games journalists coming in and out.

Because of *Games World*, the Hewland office was a conveyor belt of researcher talent who were keen to step up on screen. Rik did a feature on football management games alongside Marcus Beer on series four, so I knew he could do a turn. Not sure why we didn't get Marcus as well. Possibly because he was Welsh and we didn't want any singing.

> R.H. My first show started with an absolute nightmare, though, as I got beaten up the night before filming. On my first appearance, I only ever show one half of my face because my other half, my eye, had been punched by a Dutch squaddie. I was with the police until 5.00 a.m. But it wasn't my fault, I was literally just beaten up. When I went to the set, the make-up woman said, 'Oh my God, what have you done?' She spent over an hour working on me and I could just about get away with it. My first commentary was a game Stephen Hendry was playing. He just pissed himself laughing when he saw me.

Weird random stuff happens to Rik that you never really quite know whether to believe or not. We used to call him Rikanory, after *Jackanory*. For example, we played football a lot together. Rik would tell me he had trials for Liverpool or AC Milan or something. If you ever played football with him, it was obvious that never happened. So when he calls up the night before filming and says, 'I've been battered by a Dutch squaddie', you go, 'Yeah, right Rik. Jimmy Hill!' And then he turns up and he looks like he's been lamped by Mike Tyson. I was like, 'Wow. This may be the first episode of Rikanory that is true. Although it's possible he just fell over.'

K.E.   I knew that Rik and Dave were the expert commentators. Rik had that measure with Dominik and perfected all that double-entendre. So I didn't feel like my job was to try and replicate him. Sometimes I think Dominik would have been happier had I been more in that camp. My role was like a bumbling yeti. A big, hairy virtually unintelligible guy. And then there was Derrick. I fucking loved that sweetheart.

> I used to organize international video game tournaments at the Namco Wonderpark arcade. *GamesMaster* got to hear about it and approached me to help them do an audition for players to be featured on the show. I organized an event where the players could show off their skills and the *GamesMaster* crew could take notes. After the event they asked me if I would like to come on the show. They invited me to an audition with Dominik. He gave the nod and I was in. It was great fun. I never got over the novelty of being on TV and working with all those very talented people. I wasn't very professional because I was too busy laughing at Dominik. He was very clever with the innuendos and jokes on and off camera.
> **Derrick Lynch, Co-Commentator (Series 5–7), 2003**

T.K.   Oh, we loved Derrick. Helena and I used to look at each other and laugh, saying, 'That's right' as he said that phrase over and over.

Derrick Lynch. Even just saying his name makes me smile. Loved every single moment of working with the guy. I didn't know him before but it was obvious to me that he was totally different than anyone we had in the booth with me. Gigantic personality. That was what we were looking for. Raw as fuck, obviously. But genuine unbridled enthusiasm. A real person who loved games with no ego at all. The way he would just run names of special moves together. With a word punctuating it at the end? 'Helicopter kick. Blade swish. Helicopter kick. Back break. Splash!' They were like little videogame haikus! So, unlike Kirk, who I tried to feed lines to, I just let Derrick be Derrick and it was up to me to react to that and build his character and confidence by being very generous with my laughter and by hanging out with him a lot on set and basically fast-tracking a friendship. That was a process, and we don't really see Derrick go full Derrick until series six, but when he does? It produces some of my favourite moments of the whole show.

K.E.   The first week Dominik and I filmed our *Fair Game* documentary a few years earlier was how we became firm friends. And we realized that I was making him laugh and he was making me laugh. So we had that banter straight away. He's a good producer because he under-stands what works. Between BBC 5 Live and all these other shows he did outside of *GamesMaster*, I just thought what an amazing broadcaster he is in many ways. So he must have been able to see that we would work well on screen, even though I'd always feel that I could have done more or that I'd let the team down because I hadn't been as quick as Rik or as knowledgeable as Dave. There wasn't pressure to make sure I knew how every game worked but there was pressure in that I didn't care enough. That's why I got the more leftfield challenges to work on.

Even though he plays a stoner really well, Kirk is actually very intelligent and eloquent. And you see that in the 'PC Impossible' challenge with Patsy Palmer and Dean Gaffney, where he says some salient things about boot disks and how Windows 95 is going to make setting up PC stuff easier. In among the giggling and strange-smelling cigarettes.

WHERE I FIND MY HEAVEN

H.W. **Hugh Williams, Researcher (Series 5)** Working with Steve, we developed and edited the title sequence where Dominik gets hit by the bus and transported to Heaven. We filmed it in Walthamstow in London and spent ages on the initial scene of Dominik walking out of a kebab shop, getting hit by the bus and then seeing this kebab splattering on the ground. We did this as a close-up, but Steve wasn't happy with the take so we had to keep doing it over and over with me throwing kebab after kebab on the ground. After the eighth take or so the manager of the kebab shop took it as a personal slight and became very angry that we were disrespecting his craft.

J.F. Once we had Heaven as the setting we thought we'd do it in a studio because it would be easier to control and to key in the clouds. One fatal error, which Steve and Drogo didn't see coming, was the gates of Heaven. When you're doing one of those old nineties chromakey effects of replacing the background of something with other footage, which in this case was white clouds, you need everything to be as solid as a rock. But we ended up with extremely fine reflective metal gates. They keyed like a dog's dinner. They were terrible. We also didn't realize that as you move the camera you need the background to move too. You need parallax, otherwise everything just looks terribly weird and shit. It was only when we were building the set and practising in the edit late at night that I went over to the editor, Lorenzo, telling him we've got to try and fix this. But Lorenzo said there was nothing we could do. You'll see within the show the camera doesn't ever really move. If it does the background looks terrible. It was unfortunate, because it was quite a nice set.

K.E.   I was really blown away by the set. I was like, *This is fucking amazing.* I'd watched the evolution of *GamesMaster* and I guess when I was appearing on it I felt like that era was when they hit their absolute stride.

D.M.   **Drogo Michie, Art Director (Series 5)** I consider the studio set as one of my greatest professional disasters and embarrassments. The budget didn't increase in line with our ambitions. Steve was a really lovely guy and, in many ways, much more talented than the programme in terms of his directorial talents, and was most invested in the title sequences. This was his unique opportunity to make a 90-second film with total creative control and without having to be tied to the mast of all the other factors of a format of a TV programme. Having me being a willing sidekick massively bit us on the arse when it came to designing Heaven in a studio.

Heaven was a conceptual conceit based from him wanting to do a really interesting visual narrative of Dominik and his journey to Heaven as a title sequence. But that great, manageable, 90-second idea turned out to be an absolute bastard to represent as a set on a limited budget for a television programme. For me, it was a disaster. It looked like a Greco-Roman set for a porn movie, which may or may not have starred Joan Collins.

It's a wonderful opening title sequence because it's the first one that actually tells a story. Cameron's titles from series two and three are brilliantly cinematic, but they are like a single action scene from a bigger movie. Steve's titles actually tell stories with a beginning, middle and an end. Which takes amazing talent. I remember a moment when I was lying on the hospital gurney filming the bit where I flatline. And I am realizing, *Oh my God. This is the first death scene I have ever filmed. Wow. And it's just for an opening titles? This show is really rocking and rolling now!* Little did I know then that when we filmed the opening titles for series six a year later I would genuinely nearly die and see Heaven for real.

D.M.   The concept was just too big. The fundamental point about trying to communicate Heaven is that in everyone's minds Heaven is something of absolute unending grandeur and enormity. You're dealing with scale and you're dealing with grandeur. And both are the fucking enemy of a small budget. You can't do Heaven on a shoestring.

When the brief was given to me my bowels turned to ice but Steve was so wedded to this title sequence and the narrative that I think the whole thing had already been sold to Jane and signed off. I was a young pup and didn't have the certainty or the miles on the clock to go, 'Look, this will be an absolute disappointment at best. TV apocalypse at worst.' Nowadays, I'd say that to a director, but back then I went 'OK', and pursued the tail of something uncatchable. It was disastrous.

With an amount of humour I still flinch to think back at it. Just a classic case of ambition getting completely dislocated from means across the board. Everyone should have taken a breath and said, 'Hold on, let's remember who we are and what our assets are', and worked to absolutely wring the neck of those rather than try and build a Rolls-Royce out of a cardboard box and 50 pence.

I don't think the keying looks that bad. I know Drogo and Jonny hate it but I feel that Heaven is by its nature not a geographically exact place. It's very conceptual. So if there are images bleeding into others, you just think, *Oh, well, Heaven has different rules.* Also, if any of our viewers are sitting there concentrating on blue-screen mistakes rather than the rest of the show, we're in trouble. I think the set was great then and great now.

The music helps disguise the set problem. Genius composer George Taylor had taken over, and he started using multi-track choir vocals and crazy reverbs. So you have that audio cleverness over this slightly wonky blue screen of what looks like hundreds of kids with trumpets or whatnot. And the music just makes it all feel a bit otherworldly. So if we have 'coloured over the lines' with the blue screen and the gates, so to speak? It's just part of the crazy feel. George also added little rock guitar motifs to the music – a great contrast to the Heaven setting. The theme of series five is us bringing a bit of rock and roll roughness to Heaven. Which, of course, climaxes with Iron Maiden's Janick Gers in the final show.

Patrick is another thing that is at its peak in series five. He looks brilliant as God. Sure, he doesn't have the Consoletation Zone. In fact, his role is probably diminished slightly from series five onwards, but he still dominates proceedings, literally and figuratively.

Thinking back on it, I wish I had met Patrick at this time. Because this series was when it became a bunch of mates larking around. A bunch of mates who were all extremely good at their job. But a bunch of mates nonetheless. It would have been fun to have had Patrick around for one of those crazy nights. With me and Kirk and Jonny and Steve and Richard. Holy fuck, that could have been mental. How mental? Put it this way. We had a wrap party after filming series five. Nobody remembers it. Nobody.

COMMON PEOPLE

R.W.   **Richard Wilcox, Associate Producer (Series 5)** Series five is where we really started to get going with events. We were moving further and further away from the show being a procession of random kids trying to complete random challenges on a new videogame that they invariably hadn't played. Games had evolved to a point where they had deep gameplay that required skills that had to be earned through hours of practice and dedication. This meant you were beginning to get specialist players who concentrated on mastering different genres.

In retrospect, games were moving towards becoming esports, though no one really realized that at the time. Not even us who were making the show and watching it happen. Nowhere was this shift more true than in the arcades, and it was led by Sega, Namco and Capcom.

We wanted to showcase the very best of this new breed of players. So we staged live events in the studio where the players would attempt feats of gameplay that really demonstrated just how deep, sophisticated and engaging the new games and gamers were. I used to watch a lot of TV for inspiration, particularly sports. I'd watch how they recapped long matches, or how they did analysis post and pre-match. I'd then push for us to do similar things. In retrospect, it's all part of that move to treating games as a sport. I have no doubt we were years ahead of everyone in that, and there's still things we did that nobody else has thought about doing.

If you look at the online world of videogames now, it is dominated by two things. Competitive online gaming on Twitch, and complete game walkthroughs on YouTube. We pioneered competitive games playing as entertainment. Three decades after, things haven't evolved at all. Today it's done online with no wit or humour, because the death of entertainment is taking yourself too seriously. All that stuff today takes itself way too seriously. We just had fun with it.

K.E.   We were after anarchy. That was the real fun we were after with the events. Just these preposterous challenges from which we could be funny. Dominik was very much focused on this transition into a comedy show where games are the format around which we hang everything, but basically we could do whatever we want around it. Along with Jonny they cultured that change and realized the audience would like that we would play with the format and talk about things tangental to videogames.

M.M.   **Martin Mathers, Researcher (Series 5)** I had no experience when I joined as a researcher and I'm not entirely sure what I did for the time that I worked there, but I enjoyed it. One day the phone rang, and as I was the only one in the office, I answered and it was Patrick Moore. I was like, *Wow*. I had a bizarre conversation with him for 10 minutes, asking how his day was going and what he was doing. It was just so bizarre. I walked around the building all afternoon telling people I had Patrick Moore's phone number.

T.K.   They really had a super guest line-up. It seemed to be anybody who was really hot at the time was booked. Johnny Herbert had just won the Grand Prix and yet he came on. That says a lot about what people thought about that show. Janik from Iron Maiden was so down to earth. I was just looking at him thinking, *God, you're famous across the world.*

The hardest thing about having the guests on for series five was that the set had no audience and no background. Yes, it looked amazing by the time it got on your telly, but there was just great swathes of

blue screen in the background. And when I say, 'With that final punch Donna Air is the winner!', I am saying it in front of zero crowd. All that noise gets added afterwards. It's just the crew clapping. So I have to give it even more energy on set. I don't think you notice. That's also because we had celebs on series five that 'got it' and brought a great deal of energy – even those that perhaps were not 'cool'. Mr Motivator, Cobra and Panther from *Gladiators*, EYC – they really played along. Sometimes it falls a bit flat with the likes of Stephen Hendry or certain footballers. Sportspeople need the energy of a live crowd to perform, you know what I mean?

In this series we finally let the interviews with the celebs breathe a bit. So we have extended banter with Donna Air and Vicky Taylor from *Byker Grove* about Ant and Dec slagging me off after their appearance. We have me asking Johnny Herbert whether the better-looking racing drivers should drive without helmets. We have that wonderful extended session of Janick Gers rocking out an Aerosmith song while Kirk plays air guitar and I play air flute. And most importantly of all, I have time to marry Whigfield.

BABY BABY

Contestant	Opponent vs. opponent vs. opponent
Game	Baby Rom (PC)
Challenge	Collect three clapping babies

J.F. This was the first challenge of the series. We brought three babies on, including Dominik's nephew, purely so we could do some funny commentary with Kirk. The next challenge on the show was *WipEout* on the PlayStation, which had just come out. Mike Miller viewed the edit of the first show and said, 'This is just fundamentally wrong. People are excited about *GamesMaster* and they're excited about videogames. And the first thing you put on the launch show is you lot fucking around and making stupid jokes with babies.' [Laughs.] At the risk of some horrific edits we swapped the whole show around so *WipEout* was the first game and *Baby Rom* the second. Mike argued that a lot of the audience didn't want to see us pissing about with gaming and to abandon them at our peril. We tried to balance it and keep everyone with us.

D.P. **Dave Perry, Co-Commentator (Series 1-6)** Everything that they were doing like this, they were all patting each other on the back. Everybody's having a goof and that's great but that's not what people want, or not what it should be. It was *GamesMaster* for God's sake. People at home wanted to see fucking games experts and as the show went on that got diluted. This was the point it stopped being as fun. But I realised the importance of being on the show. It was something very special, it meant a lot to me and I still wanted to be there. And from a selfish, honest point of view, I was getting a lot of perks from it. It was raising my profile, which was the whole end game for me.

'Baby Rom' was a big deal to me because it was such a different direction with regard to a challenge. It was a statement that we weren't taking ourselves too seriously – and you know I love making statements with the first show of each series. The youngest baby was my nephew, Callum. And as a result of that I think you get a much softer, friendlier Dominik than in series four, where perhaps I was a bit too grumpy. Like I said before, that personality suited Hell. But now we are in Heaven, with angels, so it is nice to see the gentler side of me rolling on the floor with my wee nephew. At the same time we have to realize we have things like *Bad Influence!* as competition. So we have to stop the hardcore gamers with a less-than-stellar sense of humour from switching off. It's a fine balancing act throughout the series, which Richard helped address with the addition of the news section.

> **R.W.** In researching events and features, I'd been turning up lots of interesting stuff that didn't really fit anywhere in the show as it stood. Things like crazy tech, and particularly new types of tech-based entertainment. Jane loved all this, and it was her decision to add a news section into the show. We were the first on British TV to show the trailer and clips from the world's first 100% computer-animated movie. That movie turned out to be *Toy Story*. We also did a story on this crazy little event in a San Francisco warehouse where robots fought each other. Jane pounced and attempted to sign up the rights to develop this as a TV show. But she was beaten to it by Tom Gutteridge at Mentorn, and that's how *Robot Wars* came to be.

The news section is the most important development in series five for me. Richard was getting all these exclusives from the world of videogame culture that satisfied the hardcore gamers and allowed us the freedom to be more wacky with the rest of the show. I must also give thanks to *Bad Influence!* here, because they made us up our game. The game being: 'OK, can we show the first clips of the Ultra 64 before they do?' So Richard, Martin Mathers and Ravi Chopra did a hell of job there.

What allowed us to do this? Getting rid of the Consoletation Zone. The least entertaining part of the show. The least funny part of the show. And the least credible part of the show for real gamers. They were now much better served by the news section. Also credit to Jonny, because my voiceovers in those bits are brilliant, and those were mostly written by him. I would turn up hungover to the edit suite, Jonny would hand me the page and say, 'Here's what I've written as a guide, but you make it, Dominik.' And more and more as time went on I would look at his words and realize that he was writing Dominik. I didn't have to change anything. We were in total sync.

TWO CAN PLAY THAT GAME

Contestant	Stewart Lee vs. Richard Herring
Game	Director's Lab (PC)
Challenge	Beat the opponent by directing the best movie masterpiece

Lee and Herring was my Vic Reeves moment of this series because, for me, they were all operating on a higher comedic level. I was a huge fan of Fist of Fun *and I fucked it, basically. I was so intimidated by their level of intelligence that I crumbled, and I didn't have the clubs in my golf bag to make that challenge as good as it could have been.*

> R.H. **Richard Herring, Contestant** It was a strange day filming that show. Me and Stewart didn't do too many things like that and I expect we were both embarrassed and thrilled to be on the show. My main memory is that the studio had loads of props from Blur's *Country House* video stored in it. Also there were some pretty women dressed as angels, who I was too nervous to talk to. And Dominik Diamond was there too. Or was he the bloke from *Saved By The Bell?* We didn't meet Patrick Moore and I don't know if he was there or not, though I do recall Stew questioning how Moore was fit to judge our contest, as it was based on us editing a short film with primitive software and not on who was best at shooting things. Stew had a point, but as Patrick Moore chose me to win I didn't make too much of a fuss.

Stew's bit at the end where he rails against the contradiction of the GamesMaster *making an aesthetic value judgement in what is essentially a point-scoring medium. That is genius. It's gold.*

> S.L. **Stewart Lee, Contestant** I remember absolutely nothing about it, except that Patrick Moore was in a hat on a screen and Dominik had good trousers, but I think these are memories of seeing a film of it on YouTube, rather than of being there myself. I had never played a computer game before appearing on it and I haven't played one since.
>
> To be honest I don't remember much from about 1995 to about 2000, so I don't think it's just *GamesMaster* I have blocked out. I don't think I liked being a half-famous, light entertainment, 20-something celebrity. Without wishing to come across as ungrateful, I found myself expected by others to go on things like *GamesMaster* and taking up space that someone really into computer games could have had. I hope I wasn't rude to Dominik, and please apologize to him if I was. Years later somebody showed me a clip of another television show where I smashed up and stamped on a Golden Joystick

which I had literally never seen and don't remember doing. I hope that I wasn't rude to the children who wanted a Golden Joystick, and please apologize to them if I was.

I watched Stewart smash that Golden Joystick live on telly on *Good Morning With Richard Not Judy* and I was so upset. Honestly. I know the point of the gag was that Stew smashed something that was precious to Richard, and I know true genius comedy needs to destroy something. But it was the most harrowing act of evil committed on television until the Red Wedding. And I think that is an apt comparison, because it was like Stewart killed one of my children. The one I like. Not either of the other two.

R.H. It wasn't the real Golden Joystick he smashed up because I'd already thrown it away. I always say in a skip, but I can't remember if that is true or not. I have no idea why I threw it away. I have been a hoarder of stuff my whole life and hung on to all sorts of rubbish in the hope it would be of some value in the future, if only sentimental. But there we go. It was just a painted joystick in a perspex case. I think. Shit, maybe it was made of real gold. I hope I get invited back on *GamesMaster* soon.

I LOVE YOU ALWAYS AND FOREVER

Contestant	Whigfield
Game	Super Mario Land 2: Yoshi's Island (SNES)
Challenge	Collect 32 coins from two levels within 2 minutes

K.E. Probably my favourite challenge is the one where Whigfield was there, because I reckon Dominik in his mind kind of thought he was going to get with her that night. He was pretty certain that that was going to happen. Man, he's got a pretty big hit for himself for such an ugly fucker. So when he came to me and suggested this thing that he was going to get married to Whigfield, he was like, 'This will almost certainly seal the deal.' I was like, 'What.' He went, 'No, trust me. When girls think they're getting married they just crumble.'

Marrying Whigfield was possibly the single greatest on-screen moment in the history of *GamesMaster* for me. 'How's Whigfield?' Is the second most popular thing people say to me when they meet me in real life or online. The most popular is 'Do you have a Golden Joystick?' It was a totally unique TV moment. It was perfectly pitched, wonderfully subversive, utterly surreal. Whigfield totally got it. *Saturday Night* was this mainstream behemoth of a song, which means it wasn't terribly cool. So she gets a chance to do something a bit different and everyone is a winner. And my mate Kirk gets to marry us. There aren't many shows in the history of TV that have the same sense that anything can happen. *Tiswas* did when I was a kid. *Soccer AM* had it too. *The Big Breakfast* as well, obviously, but not even they would have the presenter marrying Whigfield.

K.E. I've always been very comfortable in the dog collar. Still have a priest's shirt I occasionally take out, and not just for Halloween. I just sometimes put it on, go out and get people to confess to me to buy me drinks. It's a very disarming thing, walking around as a priest. My slight obsession with the priesthood started as the officiator for Dominik and Whigfield.

BOOMBASTIC

Contestant	Martin Mathers
Game	Virtua Cop (Arcade)
Challenge	Complete the game and achieve a perfect score

M.M. Despite already working on the show, I'm not entirely sure who came up with the idea for the challenge. All through college I spent so much of my time in a shopping centre that had a Sega World on the top floor. I'd play *Killer Instinct* and *X-Men: Children of the Atom*, but *Virtua Cop* was my game. So it must have come up in a conversation at some point that I was good at it, because it wasn't something that I needed to practise for the show. It wasn't presented as, 'Can you do this?'

The machine that featured on the set wasn't even plugged in half the time. It was just there where they filmed four or five sections with me pretending to shoot. The actual footage had already been filmed behind the set and was rigged up to a recording device. I would just turn it on and play the game and if I died I'd stop recording and try it again. The actual perfect score was 100% genuine and I did do what was shown on camera, just not in the real time of the show being filmed. It was quite weird, because I remember playing it and getting to a point where I was thinking, *This is being recorded. I'm actually going to do this and win a joystick. This isn't going to go wrong now.* And to get that heart-pounding excitement of getting so close is just a feeling like no other. I'm not in any way, shape or form interested in the idea of a legacy, but it means so much that people still watch that and think it's cool.

Martin's *Virtua Cop* challenge is the perfect example of how we nailed it for the hardcore gamers that series too, in addition to the news section. The events allowed us do silly stuff and things that were genuinely technically impressive. And here we had an arcade game for a start, as those cabinets always looked wonderfully ambitious on set. Then you have the game itself, which was graphically mind-blowing at the time, and you had Martin's games-playing ability, which is almost otherworldly. It tells the audience that yes, the show can make you laugh, but it is also where you will see the best videogames players on the planet.

M.M.   I have done so many cool things with my life and I remember all of them. My life is basically a series of anecdotes of shit I've done. So to appear on the show while working for the show and in this dreamlike position of teaching Panther and Cobra from *Gladiators* how to play videogames, it's so weird to think that was an actual job.

STAYING OUT FOR THE SUMMER

J.F.   The games industry was still quite young at this point. Jane always described it as like the early days of Hollywood. It started off as great fun but then as more and more money came in it just became much more a corporate business, because serious money was now at stake. In those days though, it was the absolute, glorious chaos of Virgin flying Dominik and a few of us around the world First Class to go and shoot two minutes of TV in which we'd more or less insult them. Why anyone would do that, I don't know, but they did.

R.W.   We really upped our game when it came to features. I remember setting up an American shoot to film five or six features that Dominik came out for. It was the first of many such shoots that would become a real highlight for both those who went on them, and for the stories they generated.

I have done many things I have loved in my career. Interviewed Dave Grohl on a red carpet in Hollywood. Climbed mountains with Jack Osbourne. Had a 10-minute slot with Roger Waters turn into an hour chat because he doesn't want to stop talking. Played concerts with Glasvegas. But nothing in my career has been as much pure fun as those two filming trips for *GamesMaster* series five.

K.E.   The America road trip was just perfect. If I could do that over again I would. It was hilarious. We went on the set of *Wing Commander*, which had this whole *Star Wars*-esque look. The Mark Hamill interview is great because Dominik is very good at making people relax and have fun with it. But meeting Biff from *Back to the Future* while we were there was what we were really excited by. We really clicked with him and had a picture taken where I'm pointing at his crotch. It's just ludicrous for an interview to start with the interviewee saying, 'Sure, I'll stuff a toy down my trousers and you can point at my crotch for a picture, yeah.' That gives you an indication of how well we'd got on in that process.

This was really, I suppose, where Dominik and I took our friendship to the next level given he'd asked me to come along in the first place and really wanted me to be a part of the trip. It allowed me to relax even further knowing that. So when we came back we were firm friends.

What is amazing is that Kirk wasn't even supposed to be on that trip. I was going over with Jonny, and I had bought an extra ticket as I was planning on going with Kirsty Young. So I would do the filming then Kirsty and I would have this lovely romantic few days in the Californian sun. And then we split up like a week before. So I asked Kirk if he wanted to come instead. It became an even more love-filled threesome with the big guy, me and Jonny instead. And it was just awash with stories. On the flight over, Jonny, Kirk and I are sitting at an actual bar in the Upper Class section of the plane, and this wonderfully camp steward takes a fancy to us. He kept us plied with drinks, which was great because after that Virgin flight from Hell into LA the year before I was terrified of flying and could only do it if I drank until I passed out. Anyway, about five cocktails in, Kirk has swapped clothes with him. Kirk has on the Virgin steward's badge and tie, and Kirk is now serving drinks to a bunch of businessmen who've paid £5,000 for the pleasure.

First thing I did when we arrived was make Jonny drive us to the most dangerous gang areas of LA. I was obsessed with movies like *Boyz n the Hood* at the time, so poor Jonny had to drive us in this ludicrously expensive convertible rental car down to Compton or Watts or wherever just so I could get a picture of me throwing up gang signs there.

Then there was some random night where Jonny met some girl in a bar who took a shine to him and she invited us to some party in the middle of the Hollywood Hills. Kirk and I left Jonny there, fully expecting he would end up murdered in some kind of Manson family thing while we went to a diner and got stoned so badly I remember clinging to the bed in our room screaming to Kirk that the hotel was tipping on its side and I was about to slide out the balcony.

So, yeah, when I interviewed Mark Hamill I wasn't in a good space with regard to substances. There are parts of that interview we sensibly left on the cutting room floor where we are talking crazy shit about whether either of us would do porn movies and whatnot. But then again I don't think we would have had the fun we did with Tom Wilson, or the funny gags I did in that feature, if I wasn't coming down off ridiculously strong Californian hash and tequila. I mean, when Jonny and I had gone out before to do features for series four we had a laugh and drank a lot. But with Kirk's terrible influence it goes to a different level.

SERIES FIVE

If you watch back the 'Wing Commander' feature, I arrive on the lot at great speed, the car screeches to a halt and I nearly get thrown out of it. That's Kirk driving that car at around 80 mph. Stoned.

> **K.E.** Dominik's such a nervy person. He's always just been this ball of anxieties, upsets and a real presenter prima-donna. I found it endlessly amusing to wind him up about things, like 'Is that a pimple?' It was as easy as that.
>
> One day we decided we'd go out in the evening to the Viper Room. Before that we went to the big shopping centre in LA. Dominik had a bit of money to throw around while I had next to nothing, and he was like, 'Let's buy a shirt each before we go out.' He bought a $500 shirt and was all, 'Oh, look at this. I look great.' Out to the Viper Room we went, where it was not at all what we expected. Dominik was like, 'This is a fucking nightclub? It's a joke.' He ordered a drink and then literally out of the blue someone just vomited all down his shoulder and on his new shirt. He was absolutely raging. [Laughs.] And this is the problem with Dominik. When he's decided, 'Right, that's it. We're fucking leaving', then that's what we're all doing. We walked outside the entrance, which is where River Phoenix had died. Dominik got down and lay on the ground in front of the doormen and was like, 'Kirk, take my picture.' He turned around to the doormen and asked them, 'This is the place where River Phoenix died, right?' And the doormen go, 'Yeah.' To which Dominik responds, 'Yeah, fucking died of boredom.'

That was the most expensive shirt I ever bought in my life. Ironically, given the subject matter of the show at the time, it was a stunningly beautiful lady that ruined it. It actually happened in the toilets. I was in the queue and this stunning Californian girl pushed in front of me so she could use the gents because it had a shorter queue than the ladies. She said to me, 'Oh, I hope you don't mind.' I was like, 'No please, go ahead.' She smiled, leaned in and I thought, *Yes! I have pulled a genuine California Girl!* And she threw up. All over the world's most expensive shirt. Which Kirk found hilarious.

I got the shirt dry-cleaned and in fact you can see me wearing it in the *Waterworld* ride at Universal Studios feature. But it was never the same shirt after that.

After filming, Kirk and I hung out at the beach and surfed for a few days. Which is not a sight that many Californians will forget. They were wonderful times, when the most wonderful random things happened to us. We were driving around after lunch near Sunset Boulevard and we saw these two ladies advertising a bikini car wash. Kirk and I parked up and asked if we could work for them for the afternoon. For free. And we did. Me and Kirk, and two ladies in bikinis. Washing cars and getting stoned. Best job I ever had.

The trip with Steve and Richard later that year was even more outrageous. Similar thing happened on the flight over, except I was completely out of control by this stage and I invented the first ever case of air rage. Once again, I was so terrified of flying I had to get blind drunk. Luckily the barman in Upper Class made us this cocktail he said was so strong that Keith Richards passed out after five of them. So I made a point of having six. Unfortunately, instead of passing out the Scottish gene took over and I got loud and obnoxious. Fellow passengers complained, and I apparently pulled one out of his seat and asked if he wanted to step outside. At 30,000 feet. Then the captain came out and told me he had radioed ahead and I was going to be arrested at LAX if I didn't calm down. At which point supposedly I passed out, and they were so relieved that I was allowed to land with my seat fully reclined and my feet up on the seat in front. I don't know how I got through customs. I just remember waking up on a bench in a rental car park with puke on my face. And I remember Woody calling me up on my cell phone asking what the fuck had happened because she had a call from Virgin Airways and they wanted me banned from Upper Class cabins from that point onwards.

> D.W. Danielle Woodyatt, Virgin Games He did get banned. Honestly, it was like managing a school trip.
> J.F. When I heard about that I was very annoyed. That would never have happened if I'd been on that plane. I was annoyed with all three of them. Dominik shouldn't have done it but Richard and Steve should have stopped him from doing it. They were thinking it was all quite funny and a good anecdote, but I just thought that it was fucking obnoxious. Absolutely pitiful behaviour. I've had my crazy moments but I was never quite as crazy as anyone on those trips because I was a bit older.
> D.W. It did put a lot of pressure on us because we wanted him to be able to do trips and they wouldn't allow him on the planes. We just gave it a few months and it all settled down and all was forgiven. We spent an awful lot of money on flights across the world, and if I remember correctly we wrote to Virgin Atlantic saying, 'If you don't let Dominik back on we're not going to fly with Virgin any more.' It got sorted out, but at the time I could have killed him for getting banned.
> R.W. Steve is quite the hedonist, and Dominik too. Putting them together was always going to go one way, and it did. The US trip was an absolute hoot, though. We had a brilliant time. Every city we went to we partied hard. In San Francisco we all got dressed up in drag for their giant annual fetish ball.

Oh, man! The Exotic Erotic Halloween Ball in San Francisco! Now there was an eye-opener of a night. Partying with porn stars and people dressed up in bondage costumes and whatnot. I still have a photo of that night, with me standing next to a guy with a wonderful glittery penis head mask thing. Talking of which, at one point we were trying to find a space where we could just have a pint, because it was rammed. I spied a gap in the crowd so we headed towards it. When we got there we realized the reason there was a gap in the crowd was because there was a guy in a gimp mask masturbating openly. I felt at first horrified, then gutted we didn't have the film crew with us.

> R.W.   Steve came back from the toilets saying he'd just seen someone being fisted in the bog. Everywhere you looked there were people masturbating. Outside I decided to try and make friends with a Latino street gang while pissed. It was just a crazy trip. We went to a Supergrass gig and went backstage. We hired bigger and bigger cars every night. Finally, in Seattle, we called a stretch limo as a taxi. And we did it while sticking to a demanding schedule, shooting lots of great material for the show.

We went up to film the launch of Windows 95 in Seattle. In retrospect, this was probably the seminal moment in the revolution of PCs. But all I was interested in was writing the word 'CUNT' on the frozen windscreen of Bill Gates's car.

There was just no one to tell me this behaviour was bad. It was all such a laugh. We were all cut from the same party cloth at that point. We were all at it. All having the time of our lives. It was hilarious.

CAUGHT BY THE FUZZ

The reception to this series was just great. So I was in a very strange position. The show was finally what I wanted it to be. But I was still aware that I was going to pigeonhole myself the longer I stayed in it. I was still at BBC Radio 5 Live. My shows there were getting bigger and bigger. I was even doing a series on philosophy for Radio 4, for fuck's sake. So there was a move I could make in that direction if I wanted to. But at the same time, *GamesMaster* was so much fun. I just want to say again: Imagine you could hang out with your best, funniest mates every day? Fucking around, making each other laugh from London to Los Angeles. And you get paid. Tons and tons of money. What would *you* do?

There is one great story that brings together series five of *GamesMaster*, series two of *GamesMaster*, the peak of the nineties as a whole, and an illustration of the crazy life of Dominik Diamond at that time.

So, I meet a girl one night at the Cream nightclub in Liverpool, who is the funniest, sassiest girl I have ever met in my life. The next morning she tells me she has to go because she can't be late for work. We completely fall for each other and a few weeks later she comes down to London to see me. On the day, I am late meeting her at King's Cross station. The last thing she had said on the phone was not to be late. And I was literally, like, 30 minutes late. I walked across King's Cross concourse and she looked at me with a face that could kill a wasp, as we say in Scotland. She starts screaming at me about what an arsehole I was and how she was getting right back on the train to Liverpool and we were over. At that point I literally feel a tap on my shoulder and I turn around to see this figure in a hoodie. I thought I was getting mugged. But then the figure pulled the hoodie up a bit and it was ... Robbie Williams.

'All right, Dominik, how you doing?' he said.

'Oh, hey Rob,' I said. 'Not great, to be honest. This is my girlfriend Paula, and she's pissed at me for being late picking her up.'

Without missing a beat, Robbie replies, 'Oh yeah, traffic is a nightmare out there. Were you on the Euston Road, yeah?'

And I realized he was backing me up. 'Yeah. Euston Road. Nose to tail going right back to Ladbroke Grove.'

Then Robbie, once again turning on that incredible charm, took Paula's hand in his, kissed it, looked deep into her eyes and said, 'Give Dominik a break, eh? He's a lovely chap. I was on his *GamesMaster* show, did you know that? I beat Jason Orange to the Golden Joystick!'

He was just brilliant. I would love to say that Robbie saved that relationship and Paula and I are now happily married but, alas, when we got back to my flat that night a local drug dealer had left a message on my answerphone about a delivery. And that is how you piss off a girlfriend. Who is also a police sergeant.

That really was peak nineties for me. I still feel very fond of Paula. But not as fond as I am of Robbie Williams.

SERIES FIVE

SERIES
SIX

etween series five and six I had this lovely little TV experience called *Dom and Kirk's Night O' Plenty*. Although Myf and I had split up, we ended up still being friends, which was a good thing because she became head of production at the Paramount Comedy Channel. She asked me to come in and meet the bosses because they were looking for people to pitch shows. I loved them instantly, as they basically said, 'Come up with whatever you want to do and see what we think.' Thankfully they liked what I came up with: a live, late-night chat show set in a studio recreation of my flat where Kirk and I would interview beautiful women and play phone-in games.

It was like playing in a wonderful comedy sandbox, which became a playground for a lot of funny people to do a lot of funny stuff. Simon Pegg did *Dan Doyle Space Person* directed by *GamesMaster* director Steve Wright. Simon also made a wonderfully dark and ambitious comedy called *Asylum* with Edgar Wright directing and also starring Jessica Stevenson. That was basically where the seeds of *Spaced* were sown. Dom Joly was there doing some of his pranks on celebs that later turned into *Trigger Happy TV*.

And there was Kirk and me. Getting drunk and hoovering up lines of cocaine then going on live TV in between sitcoms to talk utter, utter stoner shite. It was a total riot from start to finish.

K.E. **Kirk Ewing, Co-Commentator (Series 5–7)** It was a real buddy experience. Dominik worked really hard on that show and I could have done a better job if I'd just had two pints less. He worked so hard on building these little games like 'Play Your Cocks Right'. It was on once a week, every Thursday. I'd fly down from Scotland, do the show, stay overnight and catch the flight at 6.00 a.m. the morning after and go back to work. So invariably I didn't sleep any of those days. I would just turn up at work stinking of drink. It was a hoot but my wife hated it. We made six episodes and then we got an extension of about another four. I hoped that it might go on, but I guess all shit things come to an end.

Each week we had a cock-based version of a famous UK gameshow. So for example we would have 'Play Your Cocks Right' which had a series of panels, behind which were cartoon chickens with their necks at different angles of erectness. Listeners phoned up live on air had to guess whether the next cock was going to be stiffer or limper than the one before.

We had this designer on the team who would draw these fetid innuendo dreams of mine every week. To perfection. He also fancied himself as a comedy sketch performer. He had one character he came up with called Bobby Stark, this council-house lounge lizard who was obsessed with lovely ladies, Irn-Bru and Scotch eggs. It was hilarious. His name was Leigh Francis, now better known as Keith Lemon.

It was really just an extension of *GamesMaster* in many ways. Birds and booze, basically. And it fed back into series six because people like Tracy Shaw and Bear van Beer were on *Night O' Plenty* as guests first.

K.E. When people meet me now, regardless of whether they know *GamesMaster*, at some point somebody will google me and see this clip of Geordie Gunter appearing on the show. Thankfully, I find that a pretty brilliant clip. Honestly, the contributors were better than us on that show. The Matt Lucas and David Walliams appearance was the one night I didn't turn up, and that was a disaster because Dominik is really easy to wind up. They hit a nerve with him and had I been there I think it might have been better, because I knew how to calm things down more than Dominik.

There were only two times we didn't have a beautiful woman on as a guest. One was this guy Geordie Gunter German Porn Star who basically came on and humped the furniture. And then we had my so-called mate David Walliams who came on with Matt Lucas and fucked the whole show. I still don't know why. I suspect Matt was behind it because he always felt a little bit outside of our Bristol University group. They just behaved like twats live on air and I got angrier and angrier and at the end of the night had to be dragged off Matt by a security guard as I tried to put his face through a wall. Good times!

K.E.   I was the worst influence during this period. Dominik is fairly conserv-
       ative in a lot of his outlooks. He's family oriented and he aspires to
       that sort of normality. Whereas I was just sort of poking him saying,
       'Let's be bad.' I liked that he would get you into these kind of silly situ-
       ations and I was the solid big guy beside him prodding him.
       I also sort of helped defuse any trouble. [Laughs.]

That really was The Summer of Dom and Kirk. We were at the centre of
everything: Euro 96? Dom and Kirk were at Wembley in tears watching
England beat Scotland. Movie premieres? Dom and Kirk were there. We
were out in London what felt like every second or third night. Tons of
bad behaviour. Tons of stories. There was a party that involves me, Kirk,
Alex from Blur, Dave Stewart from the Eurythmics and Kylie Minogue. An
arse was touched, cocaine was requested and there was some aggressive pushing and shoving. I cannot give any more details of that story
because we now live in very different times, thankfully.

    What is interesting though is that if you take what I was doing with
Kirk on Night O' Plenty, add in the fact that I was playing in a Sunday
League football team with Rik, lived round the corner from Jonny in
Notting Hill and was going out to the pub with him, Steve and Richard
most weeks ... series six is me and my mates getting even closer on
screen and off. With one exception. And boy what an exception that
turned out to be.

READY TO GO

I've quit. This is totally, definitely, incontrovertibly my last series,
so I dunno what's going to happen next year, but it's an amicable
enough agreement. I am sick of knowing that I am potentially the
best presenter in Britain. I've got to convince 50 million people of
that, and I'm not going to do it at six o' clock on Channel 4. There's
no other presenter alive who could do a videogames show like I've
done it, and if you can do that and be funny at the same time, you
can do anything. I look at Chris Evans on TFI Friday – that's not hard,
to be funny about stuff like that. Try being funny about Sega Rally.
I've got to move on, I've been lazy, I need to break free from the
financial safety of GamesMaster and get on.
Dominik Diamond, GamesMaster magazine, 1996

It was the features from series five that did it for me, basically. I had so
much fun shooting stuff like Wing Commander and Lawnmower Man
and Mortal Kombat. You know? Hanging out on movie sets and interviewing celebs and doing funny stuff. It spoiled me. It was all I wanted
to do. Don't get me wrong, GamesMaster was still so much fun on set.
But from a professional point of view, I felt I had to get away from

videogame challenges. Been there, done that, can do so much more. I was now four years into live weekly sports shows for BBC Radio 5 Live, so I felt I had already proved that I could do into an area outside of videogames and be a success. But it was difficult to convince TV producers of this. Coming back and successfully saving *GamesMaster* from series three made me even more synonymous with it, making it even harder to be associated with anything else.

My agent, Tony Fox, was in two minds. He agreed that for career longevity I had to branch out, but he also was very aware that lightning never strikes twice and it was unlikely I would do anything that would have the same money-spinning potential as videogames. But I wasn't concerned about financial security, or any form of security. My personal life was anything but secure. I was literally shagging, drinking and snorting my way across London. I hardly saw my mum or my family. It really was utterly debauched. Whether it was a bar or a girlfriend or a TV show, I felt I didn't want to be tied down to anything. I couldn't stop. I had to keep moving on to new things. I guess I felt that if I did stop any one single aspect of my life that everything else would stop. If I kept going? If I kept absolutely kicking the arse out of life on every level then life would keep getting bigger and better. It was all quite mad.

So I decided series six was going to the last one for me. And I think we all agreed that, after the Dexter fiasco, that they couldn't do the show with anyone else presenting. So we were like, 'OK – balls to the wall, let's make this one the most fantastic TV series about anything ever.' And you know what? I kinda think it was.

> [It's] Funnier than ever, I think. The show generally is a lot funnier this series. I don't say 'pants' any more. Dropped 'pants'. Say a few 'trousers', though. And I still say 'quite literally' too many times. Less 'pants' this year, anyway.
> Dominik Diamond, *GamesMaster* magazine, 1996

R.W.   Richard Wilcox, Associate Producer (Series 6) For me, series six is the pinnacle of *GamesMaster*. It looks the best, it's consistently the funniest, filled with great news stories, features, and hosts unique, well-staged events, some of which still haven't been equalled anywhere else. All that work largely fell to me and the other researchers. We'd spend weeks on the phone, trawling magazines and newspapers, basically doing the spade work.

I sat directly opposite from Jonny and we'd be talking all the time, throwing in ideas and acting as an immediate sounding board along the way. Jonny was getting a stronger idea of the things that worked and he would push us that way, and he began to start setting things up himself too. Very soon it became apparent that each event was unique and required its own development time for us to to really flesh it out and work out how we might stage it.

What became really crucial in the development of each series were the nights Jonny and I would head to the pub to do event development. I'd have a load of ideas, some half-baked, others fully formed. And over the course of the evening we'd take those ideas and try and get excited about them. It takes courage to not just play it safe and to try and do something new, and as each night would go on and we basically got a little more drunk, we'd get more confident and adventurous. Jane knew what we were doing and in the morning she'd come over to us and with arms folded she'd say with just a hint of challenge and sarcasm, 'Got it all sorted then?'

Richard 'The Dickster' Wilcox was a machine. Pure and simple. I have never known anyone on any production I have been a part of who has worked harder. He was locked into pre-production 24/7. Especially when we neared filming, there were times when I would see him and I'd say, 'Dickster, you're a wee bit less than fragrant, pal, when was the last time you had a shower?' And he would reply, 'I haven't left the office for three days, for fuck's sake, give me a break!'

He and Jonny were a great team as well. And it's strange because you take me, Jonny, Steve and The Dickster and put us in a pub – which was pretty much our natural habitat at that time – and Jonny, Steve and I will be chatting ten to the dozen. And The Dickster says nothing. For great long stretches of time. He's a really quiet guy. And then he would come out with a zinger. He's a thinker. And we needed that on the team. He was the anchor in many ways. The foundation. I like to think we brought him out of his shell a bit over the years. Well, us and the dazzling array of liquids and powders we were indulging in.

D.T. David Tibballs, Director (Series 6) I was a freelance director finding my way and at the time working on another Hewland International production for the BBC, *The Technophobe's Guide to the Future*, which was a sort of updated version of *Tomorrow's World*. I was working on that show with Dominik and Jonny and remember being around the *GamesMaster* team before they went into pre-production. They asked me to do some directing work to support Steve so I felt like I was really lucky to get to go along for the ride. I only did the one series, so I was aware of arriving quite late on into a very established show. I did a lot of the short-form features like filming in Japan and I also worked on a lot of the edit of the show.

R.D. Robin Delbourgo, Runner (Series 6) I left university in the summer and went back to live with my mum and dad in south London. I was quite enjoying doing absolutely fuck all, just lying in bed all day watching children's TV. But my mum and dad were less on board with this as a lifestyle choice and they gave me a weird sort of ultimatum. I don't know if they'd been watching some American teen movies because it was like an intervention. They told me I had four weeks to get a job or they were going to throw me out. A friend of mine from university was temping and had a job as a receptionist at Hewland. And she said there was an opportunity to be a runner on *GamesMaster*. So it was pure coincidence. I was so directionless and unmotivated that I fell into television.

D.T. It felt like I'd joined a cult having been invited into this special world, because it felt like everyone cared so much about games and the show. It wasn't really like making television. In fact, Jonny felt like the only one who had more of an interest in television beyond the show.

R.D. I didn't really know what a runner was or what I was supposed to be doing. I turned up and was placed next to a researcher, Kyle, who was on a work phone with his feet up on the table, idly flicking through the *Sun*, and chatting to a girl going, 'Oh yeah, I really like it when you wear that cardigan with just one button done up.' I sat there thinking, *This is different.* He was obsessed by the fact that I lived with my mum and dad, so throughout the two years I worked with him he would riff about me wanting to call Mummy General. And that I slept in a racing car bed and stuff. It was low-key bullying but it really made me laugh so I didn't care.

K.P. **Kyle Prince, Researcher (Series 6)** I loved being part of that team. We'd go out for drinks every evening. Steve would turn up in his leathers and tell me my work that day was shit. [Laughs.] But you took it because it made you feel included. I liked Jonny too. He could lose his temper but he was an honourable guy and he loved that show. He could take on Dominik too, who was a big personality. Afterwords I worked on *The Big Breakfast* and that production team had the same kind of attitude.

J.F. **Jonny Ffinch, Series Producer (Series 5–7)** Dominik and I were great friends by this point. He really helped me learn how to be who I really was. Growing up in television I had lots of attitudes and opinions I thought I ought to have because they were respectful and nice ones. Dominik taught me to be comfortable with expressing more offensive and unpopular opinions. Similarly, he liked me because he knew that I was quite well read and Dominik respects things like that. We both just really, really got on. He's still one of my absolute best friends. In fact, he's probably the best friend I've made since university.

I tried to get everyone loosen up a bit. I mean, I didn't give a fuck about anything at that time, why should anyone else? Say what you want, do what you want. Everything will be OK because it's the nineties and we are all indestructible! It was very *Wolf of Wall Street*. So if you were one of my pals? If you were in my gang? Then I would be the most enthusiastic encourager of your talents and abilities and try and get you to join in my 'fuck it' sensibility and take chances. Professionally and personally. And in return I will take a bullet for you.

What I love about Jonny is that he really was this super-polite posh bohemian Notting Hill intellectual, steeped in classical literature. Utterly charming to everyone when I met him. But that brain of his is so honed, his literacy so profound, that when you get him to turn that to wicked ways it is dazzling to behold. I have seen Jonny destroy idiots with one single sentence in the same manner Luke Skywalker takes down the Death Star with that one single rocket down the hole.

R.D. Jonny always struck me as really cultured and aristocratic. He spelt Ffinch with two fs, for fuck's sake. He cultivated quite an eccentric, bohemian existence, like he would be in The Clash. But the show really felt like it was more than a job to him. He was all in on making it as hilarious as it could be. It's rare to work with people like that in TV who want to make something excellent but not treat it like life or death. Quite a lot of people take it so seriously. Jonny wanted to make it great but he also knew that what we were doing was really silly. Everyone worked really hard and the hours were appalling and it was filmed in the middle of nowhere but I can genuinely say, without being a rose-tinted bullshitter, it was always fun. Even when I was desperately trying to find whatever B-list celebrity had vanished from the location that we'd left them or nervously knocking on the door of the Portakabin to see if Michael Fish was ready.

One thing I remember really clearly about Jonny is he used to carry a little bit of fabric around, like a ribbon, just constantly twiddling. Occasionally, someone would steal the ribbon just to fuck with him. And he'd come in the next day with a new one, like he had a bobbin of this special twiddle ribbon.

The ribbon really sums up why Jonny is my favourite person in the world. Because here is a guy who is smarter than anyone else in the world. Who has read every single book ever. Who can organize anything. Who can destroy mere mortals with a withering word. Yet he needs a little ribbon wrapped around his fingers or he literally fucking loses it. That is the kind of character flaw, the tenuous hold on reality that appeals to me. And it was me who stole the ribbon, Jonny. Every single time.

R.D. My friend Tom and I were both runners but there was a difference in that he could drive and I couldn't. So he got to drive the glamorous mermaid assistants around which he was very pleased about and pick up celebrities from the nearest station. I basically got sweeping and tea-making. My most important job was ironing Dominik's shirts every night, ready for filming the next day. Obviously as a 22-year-old boy I had no fucking idea about ironing shirts. As a 46-year-old man I still don't know how to do it. So I would take them back home with me every night and my mum would iron his shirts. I'd carry them back on the train, sneak them back on set and go, 'Here you are.' I didn't give my mum a cut from my £30 a day. So I got all those jobs but, you know, I had my run of a tea urn and I put all those tea-making skills down to working on *GamesMaster*. The trick with styrofoam cups is you put the milk in first or the cups will melt when you put hot water in.

R.H. **Rik Henderson, Co-Commentator (Series 5–7)** Series six was my favourite by a long way. There was such a confidence in who we were at this point and the kind of show we were making.

Rik is brilliant on series six. He hits this really nice groove of sending himself up which makes him very likeable. He is also part of the two best celebrity challenges of that series, perhaps *ever*. The Zoe Ball challenge on *Manx TT Super Bike* and the challenge on *Athlete Kings* with John Regis and Tony Jarrett. He also has this thing he does where he accentuates totally random words like 'garbage' and 'throttle' for no apparent reason. We didn't use Dave as a reviewer after his Christmas show meltdown so Rik became my number two in terms of screen time. In fact, I wish I had thought about that when were making the series, because I would like to have called him My Big Number Two.

R.D. I liked Rik a lot. It felt like more than a job for him. The thing about him is he had amazing stories but he used to embellish them as a storyteller. So we often used to guess whether he was talking fact or 'Riktion'. He was really enthusiastic and sort of like a mentor figure. I don't think he would ever consciously describe himself as such but he'd always try and bring you into other shows he was involved in or producing.

R.H. Throughout my career I've become known as the person who will always mention *GamesMaster* to you. I go on a lot of press trips and every single time I meet someone new and get drunk, talk of *GamesMaster* will emerge. I learnt a hell of a lot but I also learnt it from people I hold very dear to me. Looking back, the show stands up as well as anything else from that time period, bar the videogames themselves. The subject matter isn't timeless but the challenges are. We set the trend on that. We set the format. It hadn't been done before.

R.D. I learnt a life lesson on *GamesMaster* because up until then I'd just been a normal young person who had never interacted with the real world. Essentially being a runner is not that much fun because you're there before everyone else. You leave after everyone else. You get paid £30 a day. You get your mum to iron Dominik's shirts. And you make 400 cups of tea a day. But I noticed that if you're basically nice to people, don't moan and you're vaguely upbeat about it, like, 'Yeah, I'm sweeping the floor of Atlantis in a church in Woolwich' that people would just offer you loads of work. If only I'd had that can-do attitude at other points in my life.

K.E. I was more prepared for the series and my role this time around. I think I was more relaxed and the whole thing just felt like it had really hit its groove. When I walked on to the set, I was just like, 'Right, OK, let's do it'.

You cannot underestimate Kirk's influence on the show at this time. Not just the work he did on camera. But his actual presence on the set. *GamesMaster* was an antidote to this terribly serious mega-million-pound gaming industry. Kirk is the embodiment of someone who doesn't take anything seriously, just wandering around the set stoned as fuck and being big and loveably funny.

R.D.   I've worked in TV since *GamesMaster* but nothing has ever replicated that same feeling of magic and the Wild West about it. Everything is all built around health and safety now and, you know, all focused on target demographics and everything. *GamesMaster* really felt like the product of the people who were making it. Who were all utterly eccentric.

Series six was perfection. Everyone knew what they were doing. Everyone was at the top of their game. It just felt like one big love-in. Except for, you know, *that* bit later in the series.

BORN SLIPPY

> Because we were in Heaven last time, we tried to think where it'd be possible to go after that, and we just imagined Dominik falling from the skies above and where he might land. And of course he'd land in the sea. It's all set in this ruined underwater splendour, with a giant, magnificent vista out onto the open seas. And a glorious golden beach, and an old shipwrecked galleon.
> Jonny Ffinch, *GamesMaster* magazine, 1996

R.W.   When it came to the sets and the concept of each series, Jonny and Steve worked that up with input from Dominik. Steve always had a stream of outrageous ideas that were practically impossible to stage and Jonny would have to talk him back down. Then as we approached the shoot Dominik would get involved. There were some ideas he would hate and push for us to drop and others he would love and add something to. By the time we got to the shoot most of the stuff I had to do was already set in stone, so it was a case of delivering it. But scripts would evolve, as would staging, and that would really be down to Dominik, Steve and Jonny working it out as filming progressed. Dominik had a very strong naff sensor which would lead him to rewrite parts of the script and eject potential naff moments. He was invariably right and Jonny was rarely, if ever, precious about changing things. As time went by we really all began to develop a strong sense of what worked and what didn't, so during shoots it became much less a case of Dominik wanting to change something because he didn't think it would work and more that he was excited and wanted to run with it. We were a very good team. Of course, there were moments when not everyone agreed, but all in all Jonny steered a very happy, hard-working ship.

Things were slightly different in terms of my input this series. I let Jonny and The Dickster sketch out a lot more ideas for scripted parts because a) I was tied up with BBC Radio 5 Live stuff and *Night O' Plenty* and

b) because I utterly trusted them and their brilliance. They knew the show and they knew my voice. So it was more a case of them writing a lot of scripts around the challenges and me coming in at the last minute and saying, 'That is brilliant. That is shit.' And rewriting the bits I thought were naff. In some ways I was taking on Jane's role she had in series one and two.

> H.W. Hugh Williams, Production Assistant (Series 6) Initially we were considering filming the series in a disused water park I found, which would have been the most amazing filming location but unfortunately it didn't have a roof on it. We ended up reusing the church which had been the location for Hell.
>
> D.M. We made it into Atlantis and carved a giant shell, which was a play on the famous *Birth of Venus* renaissance painting. We built the carcass of a wrecked ship, which was on the right-hand side of the church.

I think it's the best set for a British TV show ever. When I think of the most memorable sets from telly that try to create a different world? I think about *Noel's House Party* and his Crinkley Bottom. That was brilliant, but you never forget you are in a studio. *The Crystal Maze* is obviously incredible. But the sets are an integral part of the games. Atlantis was a completely separate world that – brilliantly – had absolutely nothing to do with the world of videogames.

What was great about Steve is that, like me, he loved the show and he loved playing games. But he felt he should be doing something else. And that is why he comes up with these big fuck-off set ideas each year. Those are the things that set the show apart. Those are the reasons there has never been a successful videogames show on telly since. Because TV bosses don't play or understand gaming culture so you need that level of ambition and thinking totally outside the world of videogames to get their attention. You need people trying to do more.

> D.T. David Tibbals, Director (Series 6) Steve was very much the lead director. It was pretty clear that it was his show and his vision so I was there to support how I could and was involved more in the edit which was ludicrously laborious. I was doing the offline edit which involved assembling all the recorded footage into a first pass that's cut down to time. He helped train me up in the online edit, showing me how things were done and adding in all the graphics so we had a final version of the show ready to broadcast. I remember those sessions really fondly. He was a really talented, very creative maverick.
>
> D.M. Steve is just a giant, lovely guy who clearly wanted to be doing more than the show but did it as well as he could, which was a lot better than other people. There was a lot of friction between his working practice and the jobbing television studio camera departments and the electrical department who had all been used to shooting variations of gameshows for 40 years. He and I came from sort of pop-promo backgrounds, so we had a very different working language to

a lot of the old-school TV guys. Quite a lot of bullets were fired and quite a lot of us and them scorning and going, 'This isn't how it's done.' I'd like to suggest we were revolutionary anarchists but we weren't at all. We were just young prats doing things the way we needed.

These are unbridled cliches but Steve was definitely a filmmaker rather than a gameshow director. His love affair was with always the title sequence. That was the reward to the schlep of the programme.

H.T. Helena Tepper, Angel (Series 5) I was asked to go back on this series as a mermaid assistant but the title sequence required diving into this deep pool of water. I'm actually quite a strong swimmer, but I can't dive and this pool was really, really deep. They took me to a swimming pool somewhere in the Docklands to practise because they really wanted me to continue doing the show. I turned up in my *Baywatch* red swimming costume, just trying to style it out, but I simply couldn't style out the fact that I couldn't dive in and do what they needed me to. I had to be able to hold my breath and dive deep down into a tank, as this was where they were filming all these mermaid scenes. I was absolutely petrified. So they had to get somebody else and I was gutted. In fact, I heard it was quite a scary shoot actually. There were quite a lot of things that went wrong.

Series six doesn't just have the best set of any TV show ever. It also has the best opening titles. Can you think of a TV show that has an entire movie as its opening titles? A movie about a man falling from Heaven, nearly drowning and being rescued by mermaids, waking up in Atlantis? No. And again it has nothing to do with the subject matter of the show, which is brilliant. Would they try something like that for *Bake Off*?

It was a crazy shoot. The closest I will get to making an action movie. I was flying around in harnesses in a studio, then hanging off a ladder 50 feet above a pool. Then dropped into that pool and then filming underwater, drowning then dying.

Which I nearly did. For real. I was underwater and they were filming me thrashing around then lying still, basically dead. But I started running out of breath. The safety guy swims up, taps me on the shoulder and gives me the thumbs up to say it's a good take. He gives me the oxygen mask which is on a long tube. I take a scoosh and give him the thumbs up. He swims off. I go to push up from the bottom to swim back to the top forgetting to remove the weights from my pockets first and my calf muscle just pops on my left leg. So I am trying to swim up to the top with one leg, the weights are still on me, and I am stuck there, flailing and panicking for what feels like ten minutes. I have dropped the oxygen line, I am getting dizzy, I think I am about to die for real, wishing that I had gone on that second date with Jadine from *Don't Forget Your Toothbrush*.

Then at the last minute I feel the hands of the safety guy. I have never felt more happy to have a strong man's arms around me in my life. And that includes all those nights with Kirk. He got me up to the surface, at which point I announced there was no way I was doing any more fucking underwater shots and that is why we brought in a stuntman.

D.T. I was the one who volunteered to take over the underwater shots. When the show was broadcast, I told everyone there's one or two shots of me as Dominik floating face down in the water. That was my starring role. I was not in any way trained for this or had any real ability to hold my breath for long periods of time, so we had to retake that shot over and over again. It was actually quite scary and a little bit terrifying but such a fun thing to do. Those sequences were stunning productions. I mean, nobody could afford title sequences like that anymore.

T.T. Theresa Tilley, Mermaid I'd never swam in a full wig and a long, heavy dress so that was quite something. We did all those underwater scenes in a hired house which had a massive outdoor pool. It was really cold that day so in-between takes I was just sitting upstairs in this room being soaking wet.

S.D. Sammy Differ, Costume Designer (Series 6) I'd not been out of college very long and I was doing lots of different shows like *Zig and Zag's Dirty Deeds* and then *GamesMaster*. I had to dress these two models as sexy mermaids that could swim underwater. But the costumes had to work both under and out of the water. I made them myself and at that time I was a little nobody starting out in costume. It was only me. I spent a whole week virtually not sleeping to make these bizarre stretchy things, thinking they would be amazing. I just wanted them to be textural and beautiful but sexy because that's what Dominik wanted. I remember thinking, *Is this for kids or is this for adults?* [Laughs.]

T.T. They were quite tight and obviously when you're filming all day, it's not just something that you take on and off. You just have to keep it on all day for 10 or 11 hours. It had a bit of a slit in the middle so me and Leigh Ann always used to laugh, because in filming they just feed you 24/7. It's one of the bad things about filming. You arrive and they give you a bacon butty. Then they give you morning snacks and a big meal for lunch. And quite a lot of the time you're just waiting and hanging around waiting for scenes to be filmed. So you're normally eating more than you should and honestly we were like, 'Oh my God, if we keep on eating we'll just look like the biggest mermaids ever'. It was a kind of material that didn't stretch with your chip butty.

S.D. I also took Dominik to a tailor I used to work with in Brixton and had his suit made.

Mark Powell Bespoke Tailoring made the green suit for me from scratch. That was great. First and only time I have had someone do that. Utterly gorgeous thing with lovely gold lining. And great to see how far things had moved on from series two, where I was made to wear something I hated, to series six where I am now asking one of the UK's best tailors to make something for me. Sadly I threw it out recently because it had sat in boxes in Canada for about five house moves and was full of mould. Now there's an analogy for you!

T.T. There was a big difference as an assistant to standing there looking pretty and not saying anything to speaking and delivering funny
lines. It made us feel that we could connect with the audience rather
than just be smiley and giggly. We could pretty much say that we
were co-presenters – although we didn't actually say that – and not
just dolly birds on the side. I mean, we didn't say too much to be fair
but it was really nice and I'm glad that they did that because it would
be horrible to put forward that we were there to only look pretty.

Theresa and Leigh Ann were terrific. Great professionals. There was
just something about the contrast in their looks and charisma they
threw off. Leigh Ann looked so pure and innocent but Theresa had this
real vividly wonderful Kate O'Mara/Joan Collins naughty, fun, evil look
– and I mean that in the nicest possible way – so that we thought, 'OK,
let's come up with this schtick where Leigh Ann says nice things and
Theresa says nasty things.' And I think that really works. Theresa was so
good in particular that we got her to do that funny remote challenge
with the wee cocky kid driving the full-size car in an arcade.

BEAUTIFUL ONES

This was the first series we had a proper celebrity booker, like the chat
shows have. And you can tell. It's not necessarily the calibre of guest,
because we'd had people from *Eastenders* before, we'd had top bands
and we'd had famous sportsmen. It's more about the mix. A chat show
has to have an eclectic mix of guests otherwise it gets boring. It can't
all be actors, or all sports stars. So on this series we have soap actors,
comedy actors, hypnotists, spoon-benders, footballers, athletes, pop
stars and TV hosts who just happened to be the most beautiful women
alive. And Michael Fish. It's a giant variety big-top circus with me as
the ringmaster.

J.F. To be honest, I was never that plugged into popular culture. So a
boy band would be booked and I'd be like, 'Great, whatever.' The
celebrity booker for that series was a lovely woman and a very high-
profile celebrity booker that I knew from London Weekend Television.
She used to do all the bookings for the big chat shows at the time and
had really good contacts. So I phoned her up and said, 'How would
you feel about doing *GamesMaster*? It's a bit of a crazy show.' And
she said, 'I'll do it.'
    Traditionally, you credit celebrity bookers as assistant producers.
I don't know why but I suppose on a chat show it's a key role. But when
it came to doing the credits, I thought of Richard Wilcox who just did
so much. And I just thought I can't give her, who's maybe done a day
a week's work, the same credit as Richard, who was fundamental to
every aspect; it was just so unfair. So I did the edit and without asking

Focused

This makes director Steve Wright, producer Jonny Ffinch and me look like we are in a cool band. Which I guess we were. Still with the ciggies as well.

QUALITY CONTROL
Blurred out of focus prints
•Camera shake - hold camera steady
•Focusing error - applies to variable focus cameras
•Subject too close - allow 2 metre distance for fixed focus cameras
•Dirt or condensation on lens
ADVICE LABEL
LIFT & PEEL HERE

A

B

A
Rolling rocks
Jonny, Steve, me and Tanya in some
trendy Notting Hill bar. Could have
literally been any night in 1995, because
it WAS every night in 1995.

B
Le football
Great example of the friends I made in
the games industry. Bernard from
Infogrames. Best player in my Sunday
league team. This is us in Paris after PSG
pumped Celtic.

C
Comfort blanket
Jonny looked after me so wonderfully as
a producer. But he himself was lost
without that lucky yellow ribbon you can
see round his wrist. We would hide it for
shits and giggles.

C

The comic strip

Storyboard for series six titles. What I want to know is, why did we IGNORE the bottom-left panel? I think we're all naked.

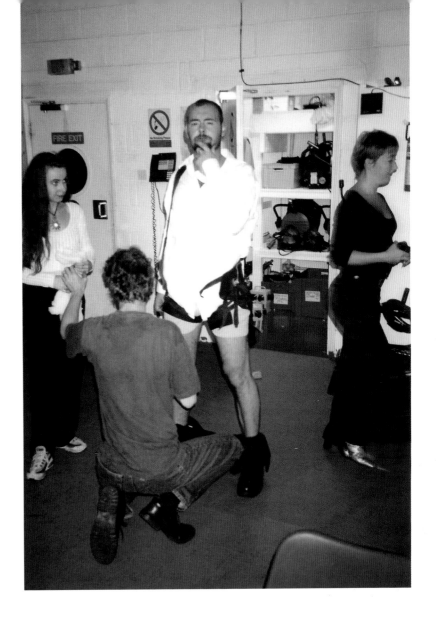

Superman
I thought it would be the best fun ever to fly around in a superhero harness. It was actually really uncomfortable and chafing. But didn't stop me smoking fags.

The drowning
Almost the last ever photo of me, after a combination of weights in my pockets, a torn calf muscle and the wrong sign to a safety diver nearly consigned me to a watery grave.

ARCHIVE V

Splash
'The costumes had to work both under and out of the water. I made them myself and at that time I was a little nobody starting out in costume. I spent a whole week virtually not sleeping to make these bizarre stretchy things.'
Sammy Differ

Sailor mouth
Atlantis. Me and Tracy Shaw. On the right
is floor manager Kate Thompstone, who
was the most wonderfully funny,
potty-mouthed floor manager we
worked with. I still can't believe making
TV in deconsecrated churches was my
place of work.

A

A

Hypnotized
Getting Paul McKenna, the UK's most famous hypnotist, to play a game where you blow up buildings to allow a nuclear missile truck to pass through unhindered made perfect sense to us in the nineties.

B

C

B
Fake news
The strongest mind on the planet. People ask if his challenge was genuine. I am too scared of Uri's power to ever comment. He could tweak my hamstring with a mere thought.

C
Lynchpin
Dear old Derrick Lynch laughing his way through another episode.

International incident
Ah, Japan. Here I am on stage carefully judging an Otaku cosplay party in Tokyo. In retrospect, the guy we filmed wearing pants on his head was the real winner.

anyone gave her the credit of researcher. We had the screening in a pub for the first show, which she came along to and was really sweet and lovely about the show. But then the credits came up and she saw herself credited as a researcher. She went fucking ape shit. [Laughs.] It still makes me break out in a cold sweat to this day because I had no defence. She said, 'I haven't had a researcher credit for 15 years.' And I just felt awful. Stood there like a wet blanket saying sorry.

R.D. I met the Cat from *Red Dwarf* who I made some tea for and brought some biscuits to. And he was lovely, Danny John-Jules. He seemed to be embarrassed that anyone would bring him anything. It's funny, generally when you're a runner or a researcher, unless the celebrity is a total arsehole, people are nice to you because essentially people are quite nice. I would go home and tell my mum and dad who I'd met. I also remember making tea for two or three members of The Brotherhood. I used to read the *NME* when I was younger and they were always in there as this ultra-radical, political hip-hop group. And I met them and they were sweethearts.

J.F. For me, it was always the combination of the game and the celeb that made a winning challenge – things like Tracy Shaw on the skiing, arcade game *Alpine Surfer*, or that old fraud – and that's personal opinion – Uri Geller playing a mind-control game. I seem to remember Michael Fish being rather smelly but he was sweating because we kept him there for hours and he thought he was going to miss his evening weather bulletin. For some reason, at the time I couldn't see that this was important. You get tunnel vision on a big shoot like *GamesMaster*. The only thing that counts is the success of the shoot. Everything else seems insignificant.

Footballers were the classic good news/bad news guests on the show. They cost an absolute fortune. I mean literally they would be paid four or five times as much as any other guest. And I desperately wanted them on the show because I was a huge football fan, and with my BBC Radio 5 Live stuff and all these columns I was writing about football for *FHM* and *90 Minutes* I was hanging around with them in my outside life.

But they are the most awful interview subjects when the camera rolls. They never really give you good chat. That's not their fault. They have great banter off-screen but they are deliberately schooled by clubs not to say anything remotely controversial on camera, which doesn't work with a show like *GamesMaster*.

J.F. We used to lure footballers on with statements like, 'It'll be all done in two hours' and then keep them waiting around most of the day while we desperately fiddled with a broken arcade machine. Vinnie Jones came on a couple of series, and the rules with him were very simple – any delay would instantly be met with demands for more money. I think he left with three times his agreed fee once.

R.H. I was working in the office and got a call during filming that Stan Collymore wasn't going to turn up. So they asked me to step in and play the game against Chris Armstrong, who at the time was a £3.5-million player. He turned up and they introduced me saying, 'Oh, this is Rik. He'll be playing you at the game', and Chris just went, 'But you're the Violet Blade!' He'd been watching *Games World*. I told him not to worry about it. [Laughs.] Now, obviously Jonny didn't want me in the final as well. To knock out an actual professional footballer. So I spent that entire game trying to let him score. And he didn't. I think it was right at the end I purposely threw my ball towards him and he kicked it in the net so he could win.

GOING OUT OF MY HEAD

Contestant	Uri Geller
Game	Mind Drive (PC)
Challenge	Use will power alone to steer the skier through 15 gates

U.G.   **Uri Geller, Contestant** Our mind power is like an iceberg, with 90% lying hidden beneath the surface, but still there and awesomely massive and accessible. Today there are certain technologies that allow one to tap into that mind power and control a game with thought power alone. The future will be riddled with possibilities to connect to our subconscious. Our subconscious is like the subcontinent of Alexander's days – a vast treasure house waiting to be explored, connected and utilized. In the future, technology will be able to develop artificial instincts, intuitions and psychic energies to comply with new mind games.

I was a total cynic about Uri Geller beforehand. And I was pissed off with him because he claimed he had made the ball move during the England vs. Scotland Euro 96 game, which made Gary McAllister miss the penalty. So I had it in for him. And I was thinking, *I can't wait to expose him as a fraud on air.*

T.T.   I remember Uri because he came into our trailer during lunch and literally guessed my birthday, which I really don't know how he managed to do. God knows how he knew that. And then he took my spoon and bent it before my eyes. He was really sweet and very friendly.

When we do the old 'draw something and then Uri guesses what you drew' on the show I had seen this done before and I knew that people mostly draw houses. So I thought I'd not only draw something random – a pair of scissors – but I would turn the handle round the wrong way on one of the bits. Just to fuck him up.

And he still guessed it. He drew it perfectly. Correct dimensions and everything. So, yeah, I was a convert. I know Jonny thinks it's all rubbish but for me Uri Geller's shit is real. He was a superb guest.

U.G. **Uri Geller, Contestant** *GamesMaster* was a fantastic TV production. I've been on thousands of TV shows over the years but it is still vivid in my mind. There was nothing else like it then and nothing similar in today's TV world.

Contestant	Martin Mathers
Game	Virtua Cop 2 (Arcade)
Challenge	Complete Virtua Cop 2 on two machines simultaneously

M.M. **Martin Mathers, Contestant** I was no longer working on the show at this point but I was invited back to take part in a challenge on *Virtua Cop 2*. Me being an idiot pictured how it was in the previous series where I had all the time in the world to practise. I got to the set, they showed me the set-up, put me in a suit, and said, 'Right, so we're ready to go.' I was a bit taken aback because I thought I'd get a chance to practise. Obviously I'd played it lots, but not playing two machines at once. I'd never, ever done that because it's not a thing. Arcades don't have two of the same arcade machine side by side.

They were on a tight schedule so I just had to it there and then, which was absolutely petrifying. The weird thing is I genuinely nearly did it. I was so close to completing it. It actually featured on the final episode that a few years later then got distributed on a DVD and put on the cover of a national magazine.

You don't look at old gameshows like *The Price is Right* and get excited about the TV show where people guessed numbers and spun a giant wheel. *GamesMaster* was about people and reactions and the struggle to succeed. People loved it for those challenges and moments.

Martin Mathers, as well as being a lovely bloke, is the greatest games player in the history of the show as far as I am concerned. For that kid to get so close to that challenge without a single practice was astonishing. I wanted to give him another go so he could do it – and I was really opposed to doing things like that – but we didn't have time to reshoot.

IF IT MAKES YOU HAPPY

Contestant	John Regis vs. Tony Jarrett
Game	Athlete Kings (Sega Saturn)
Challenge	Compete in the 100m, long jump, 110m hurdles and the javelin

R.H.   John Regis and Tony Jarrett playing *Athlete Kings* was easily the best moment from series six. It was a show where everybody just laughed constantly from the beginning to the end, almost crying at time. They were fantastic and loved every minute of it. That makes a big difference. People being enthusiastic and enjoying themselves will always translate.

J.R.   **John Regis MBE, Contestant** It was hilarious. My character in the game with the big afro still makes me laugh out loud. Dominik was so funny and immediately put us at ease. It was just great fun and such a great concept for a show. It was so unlike anything else, with such a relaxed atmosphere, which made both Tony and myself enjoy the show even more.

What a glorious hour of life that was. Obviously, I am a huge athletics fan, so to have those two guys of that stature on in the first place is a thrill for me. They were so relaxed. They played along. And that in turn makes Rik and I perform better. So before you know it we are all making jokes about the size of our penises.Totally genuine. Totally unforced. Totally fun. A joy.

JUST A GIRL

Contestant	Zoe Ball
Game	Manx TT Superbike (Arcade)
Challenge	Complete the race in fifth position or above

R.H.   Zoe Ball was one of my favourite ever guests as well when she came on to play *Manx TT Super Bike*. Zoe was a really lovely person and just got into the humour of the silly show we were making.

Oh, I was utterly in love with Zoe Ball. Oh yeah. I mean, I say to so many guests on the show that I get them on because I fancy them, and it's a running gag. But I was genuinely in love with Zoe. I had met her a couple of times before and got on well. Even auditioned for the *Big*

Breakfast with her. She is responsible for my favourite celebrity line in the history of *GamesMaster*: 'I'm actually terrified of motorbikes but I like it up the back.' I almost wanted to stop the show filming right there and then, because that line? From Zoe Ball of all people? That is peak *GamesMaster*. That is peak nineties on-screen. That is all we could ever have dreamed of. We were never going to top that moment.

READY OR NOT

Contestant	Tetsujin vs. 100 Opponents
Game	Virtua Fighter 3 (Arcade)
Challenge	Beat 90 out of 100 opponents

R.W.   We'd heard about the Japanese 'Iron Men' and decided to try and stage our own Tetsujin challenge in the studio on *Virtua Fighter* 3. It was a major undertaking. I'm really proud of helping devise the running order that squeezed all that action into our little 24-minute show.

K.P.   There was a dial-up modem in the corner of the office, so as a contestant researcher I'd go to sites like Yahoo and just look online for gamers as a lot of them were the first to create websites. Through this research I found our Tetsujin. A guy who could beat anybody. So I told Jonny and we agreed to bring this guy in and have him beat 100 kids back to back. So I worked night after night trying to track him down to arrange for him to be on the show and fly him into London. I couldn't meet him at the airport so I asked one of the other researchers to go and take him to an arcade. I get this phone call back to the office saying, 'I've just had him play two people in the arcade. He lost both times.' Jonny paused for a moment and went, 'Great. Yeah, that's brilliant. Well done.' And I was thinking, *Shit*.

Slightly panicking, I made a dash to go and meet him myself. He couldn't speak any English but I made out he was saying he was basically tired. So then I took him to another arcade myself and I got all the kids around to play him. He beat every one of them and I was like, *Thank fuck*.

R.W.   Dave Perry did an excellent job as touchline reporter. Jane always said this was her favourite *GamesMaster* episode.

D.P.   I had no idea I was presenting that section until that day. I came in to do my bit as usual and was called in by Jonny who told me Jane had requested I present that section of the show that day. I don't know whether that was true or not but, of course, I was like 'Hell, yes.' It was my dream, especially after my taste for it on series three. It was the only time in the history of the show where somebody other than Dominik or Dexter actually presented. To this day I don't know why Dominik didn't present it, whether he had a dentist appointment or something. I always like to throw up as a point of contention that

I was the third presenter of *GamesMaster*. That's always good for an argument to get someone's back up. [Laughs.]

It was a memorable challenge and a great idea. Part of me isn't sure whether that guy was genuinely who he said he was. I mean, was he really flown over from Japan to do this challenge? It seemed strange to me that they would fly him in from Japan to take part in a challenge but hadn't taken the time, or didn't have the time, to find him opponents to play when he got here. It was a real anomaly.

Most of the challengers were kids from my mum's drama school. Thirty of them who played him a few times joined by 20 others.

R.D.   We tried to seed his opponents so that he faced the weakest players first. But as we all sat huddled in the gallery watching, the unthinkable happened. He took hits. His energy bar dropped perilously low. Thankfully he struggled through and won. But then with the next opponent it happened again. Frankly we were shitting ourselves. As the challenge went on and the quality of the opposition increased, the ease with which he dealt with them increased until eventually he won. It was only when he was being interviewed by Dominik we discovered what happened. The novice players were just smashing buttons at random, making it harder for him because it was impossible to predict their moves and counter.

AROUND THE WORLD

D.T.   Without doubt the most fun I had was flying over to Japan to shoot some features. I'd never been there before so to go across and shoot incredible stories and bizarre features was such a thrill. We shot these hilarious stories, like covering what was then the world's biggest indoor beach, The Seagaia Ocean Dome. It was awful. I mean, they built the world's biggest indoor beach right next to the actual, real beach. And because it was covered with a roof it was so humid. It was just this mass of people and tons of sweaty, massive bodies walking past all the time. Dominik hated it. [Laughs.] It was an unpleasant shoot to film but quite funny to do.

We also filmed at Sega's head office, which was this huge corporate office building with lots of corporate-looking businessmen walking in and out in full suit and tie. But you got up to the seventh floor or whatever, stepped out of the lifts and the whole floor looked like a jungle where all the programmers were working on the next big project. Every worker had customized their workstation and they were all interconnected. You know when you see those cool offices where they'll have a basketball hoop and table tennis? It was like that but totally over the top. A labyrinth of decorations and jungles and weird toys and all sorts.

The overriding memory I have of the trip though was Dominik being absolutely terrified of flying. I mean, like a fear of flying that I've rarely seen. Crapping himself, hands rigid, hating flying and then mostly hating Japan. Like basically just witnessing a misanthropic, sort of classic Dominik disgust for everything around him. [Laughs.] I was sort of culturally in awe of everything around me, telling him how amazing it all was and he just sort of grunted back in quite a grumpy way. Dominik did struggle on that trip. I don't think he enjoyed it very much.

The Japan shoot was really tricky for me. Completely different than the USA shoots, because literally three days before we flew out I met this girl called Phoebe. She had just started as a promo director at the Paramount Comedy Channel and was assigned to a promo for a 4th July Comedy Special I was hosting with page-three model Jo Guest.

When I saw Phoebe for the first time it was a huge big romantic cliche. I literally saw her bathed in sunlight across a crowded room. We filmed the promo the next day. Now if you are sitting in a bar with Jo Guest, you've both had a few drinks and all you can think about is the random girl who directed the promo? That is when you know you have been hit by cupid's cannonball.

So I phoned Phoebe from the pub that night and arranged a date for the next day, and boom. That was it. Utterly smitten. I told her afterwards that I had to fly off to Japan but I was going to marry her one day. So I spent all that trip in hotel rooms listening to Oasis's *Talk Tonight* in tears because I missed her so much.

I think I would have been OK if the trip had been with Jonny or Steve or The Dickster, cos they were all my best mates, and I could have cried on their shoulder. But I didn't know Tibbals as well, and our researcher Nicholas and our crew were all based in Tokyo. They were all top lads but I didn't know them and felt quite alone. It was a strange experience.

I was so wrapped up in my own emotions I think I actually flew out there First Class and left lovely Dave in Economy cos I wanted to be alone with my miserable, lovelorn thoughts.

D.T. [Laughs.] Yes, that's true. It wasn't a big deal. I thought that's what always happened with the talent. Man, that's funny. Whatever grumpiness there was, he was so engaging. A lot of people said he was difficult and a hard taskmaster and in some ways this was true but he was respected at being able to turn into presenter mode at a switch. We shot some amazing stuff so I was loving just being in Japan. Jonny let me stay out there for another five days exploring Japan.

I feel I didn't really pay attention to Japan. Which is a shame, because it is one of those places you are so lucky to visit. The Seagaia Feature with the fake beach is one of the best we ever did. And that Otaku cos-

play party in Tokyo with the weirdo wearing pants on his face. It's great stuff. Whereas other filming trips were drunken debauchery, this one was me saying to Tibbals, 'Sorry, I am not going drinking tonight, I have to spend a thousand pounds calling this girl I just met back in the UK. ' I don't feel Tibbals got the best version of me socially, which is a shame because he was such a lovely guy and a terrific director.

> D.T. It was a little disappointing he didn't enjoy it. I found it a little deflating at times but I didn't know what to expect to begin with. We went to a club one night which Dominik came to but aside from that everyone kept to themselves most evenings. I went out barhopping once he'd gone back home and was on my own. There's other shows where I've done plenty of evening boozing, especially back in the nineties. Doesn't really happen any more. Back then there were plenty of boozy productions, but this wasn't one of them.

The features are filmed some time after the challenges. So the Japan trip was the last stuff we filmed for that series. And it becomes weird that having filmed a series where the running gag is that I invite so many of the guests on because I fancied them that I actually end up falling in love with someone who was nothing to do with the show, hadn't watched an episode and didn't even know who I was. Even stranger is the fact that a quarter of a century later that very same woman – Phoebe – is my wife today, we have three amazing kids, and she still has never watched an episode of *GamesMaster*. Which is probably not a bad thing.

DON'T LOOK BACK IN ANGER

Contestant:	Kirk Ewing vs. Dave Perry
Game:	Super Mario 64 (Nintendo 64)
Challenge:	Achieve the best time on the ice slide

> K.E. Do you think the Christmas special is the single most famous moment from *GamesMaster*? It's unmistakably good television because it's an unexpected and genuine reaction.
>
> D.P. Dave Perry, Co-Commentator (Series 1–6) The clip from that show keeps being shown to this day on *When TV Goes Bad* on Channel 5. I'm somewhere between Oliver Reed and Shaun Ryder, which I'm quite pleased with. [Laughs.]

GamesMaster is rightly regarded as one of the most innovative and daring shows in the history of British TV. But the now infamous events of the Christmas quiz? That is what makes the show positively Shakespearean. And that is all down to Dave. Actually, I don't even think Shakespeare could have written something that epic.

D.P. We're none of us young men any more. We're not pretending to be something we're not or going anywhere particularly other than where life takes us. So many stories have built up over the years about this show and we've all been guilty, myself included, of perpetuating certain myths by not filling in the gaps. It's almost a shame to explain it.

R.W. I think the idea to do a quiz was mine, but I can't be 100% sure. I would have been pushing for something like that because by the time you got to Christmas all the games were out and we were broadcasting episodes that had been recorded maybe three months earlier. The plan was to bring the co-commentators together and test their knowledge of games with picture rounds, a bit of *Mastermind* thrown in based around their specialist subjects, some general knowledge and fastest-finger questions and then a final challenge between the two people with the highest score.

D.P. THQ, my bosses at the time, didn't want me to do the show. They thought I was finished with it all but I agreed to do it free of charge and against my employer's best wishes because Jonny begged me on the phone.

Dave had been filming with us the day before we shot it and that evening drew me aside and urged me in the most heartfelt way to secretly give him a list of the questions beforehand. Dave's argument was that he had a book on beat 'em ups coming out and that if he were seen to have anything other than perfect knowledge of the subject, it would affect the sales of this book. He went on to point out that he had done many favours for the show in the past, that he had come at short notice when other commentators dropped out, stayed late when shoots over ran, got up at ungodly hours to be on set when we needed him. And through all this he had never asked to be paid a penny other than his expenses. This was all perfectly true. I still believe to this day that Dave was an excellent commentator, so I was not about to argue that his contribution to the show hadn't been significant.

Dave no doubt knew that his final point would be the most persuasive for a producer – unless I gave him the questions, he didn't feel he would be able to come in the following morning and do the show. Bear in mind that at this point its about 8.00 p.m. after weeks of manic pre-production and ten days of actual shooting. I have had hardly any sleep and the thought of having to reformat the following day's quiz and then record something that wouldn't

> be nearly as good seemed horrendous. Dave's arguments about all
> he had done for the show and how hard he'd worked on his book, it
> all got to me. Call me a heel, but I agreed and duly handed over the
> questions.
>
> I was all set to take this secret to the grave, or at least to the end
> of the shoot, but Dave did a very foolish thing – he told someone.
> I have no idea who, but somehow it got to Dominik.
>
> Jonny Ffinch, Series Producer (Series 4–7), 2002

D.P. Why would I tell someone? I had no friends on set. They wanted to
bring me down and they hadn't been able to do it. So they had to
create a situation where they could. I smelt a rat. Jonny talked me
around and made promises to me that it would be fair. All those
promises were completely shat upon during the show.

I understand why Dave did what he did. He was all about his brand. His
brand was his livelihood. He wanted to protect it. And if he had come
up to me and said, 'Look, Dominik. I have this book coming out and
it's really important I win the quiz. Is there anything we can do?' then
maybe we could have worked out something funny. Maybe. Who knows,
eh? I guess it would have depended on what mood I was in that day.

> Within minutes Dominik came to see me and said, 'I've heard a very
> ugly rumour that Dave has asked for the questions for tomorrow's
> quiz and you've given them to him. That wouldn't be true would it,
> Jonny?' Now a bit of cloak and dagger with no-one the wiser is fine
> by me, but I make a point in life never to tell a direct lie, least of all
> to a friend. I admitted that it was true. Dominik responded, as I knew
> he would, by assuring me that unless the quiz was played absolutely
> fairly and I would promise that this would be the case, he was not
> prepared to present it. When Dave came in the next day I gave him
> the disagreeable news. I pointed out that it was his own fault for
> telling someone but that now, with things as they stood, I was going
> to have to write a new set of questions. He would either have to
> agree to play the quiz fairly or it would go ahead without him. Dave
> reluctantly agreed to go ahead.
>
> Jonny Ffinch, Series Producer (Series 4–7), 2002

Again I say: the key to the show was not taking ourselves too seriously.
So it's not like anyone would have given a fuck if, say, Rik was winning
and then got disqualified by the GamesMaster because of a bad mous-
tache. It would have been easily done. And Rik would have been happy
to do that. But no. It was all done behind my back. Dave was so scared
of losing he coerced my best friend to fuck with my show.

D.P.　It was the first time I'd ever taken anyone to filming with me. My girl-friend came along with me because it was the Christmas show and I thought this would be fun and we'd go to the wrap party afterwards and I'd introduce her to everybody. But we got there and I was just set upon from the off. Dominik pulled me out the caravan accusing me of cheating.

I think I actually had Dave up against the wall of the caravan and I was screaming at him, 'How dare you try and fuck with the integrity of my show, you little shit!' Which is ironic, given that we'd just filmed Uri Geller supposedly controlling a videogame using only his mind, which had in reality been played by a researcher, and we'd had this Tetsujin bloke supposedly play 100 challengers, which were actually 50 challengers who played twice, and 30 of them were from my mum's theatre school. I think it's all actually tied into what David Walliams and Matt Lucas had done to me on *Dom and Kirk's Night O' Plenty*. It is actually the exact same position I had Matt Lucas in about month or so before, using the same language. In retrospect, that can't be a coincidence. The idea that someone plans something sneaky behind your back. And I was like, *No fucking way am I letting that happen to me again*. So I think that's why I was so angry.

　　I was in a bit of a Christopher Walken in *True Romance* vendetta kind of mood. So from that point on I wanted Dave to lose so badly. He had tried to cheat my show. To protect a brand that by the very nature of him wanting the answers to a quiz beforehand is a fake brand. But when the cameras started rolling? The little bugger kept getting the answers to the new questions correct. And that is also the great irony. Dave didn't even need to cheat. He knew his stuff anyway.

> I won every single round on that show easily, despite them changing the endings around on certain questions. Obviously this was becoming predictable and the production team wanted to spice things up. So it was arranged that Kirk would come from behind to win. You'll notice that in the quick fire round that he gets a number of questions about *Earthworm Jim*. This is because he was working on developing a 3D version of the game at the time.
> Dave Perry, Co-Commentator (Series 1–6), 2002

K.E.　I wasn't personally involved in the set-up, if you can call it that. I didn't know what the questions were going to be, although when the *Earthworm Jim* stuff came up I thought, *Hmm, this is great because I'm working on this game at the moment*, so luckily I'd done a little bit of research on that.

R.W.　I can say with absolute certainty that nobody set out to set Dave up. I had a lot of time for him. He was without question the best of the co-commentators. Jonny liked and respected him too, though we both knew he took himself too seriously. We would have had to be the best TV producers in the world to have manufactured that. And we weren't that good.

There were two questions on *Earthworm Jim*. Two. That is all. Not enough to swing a quiz. I actually put them in hoping someone else would get them correct so I could rip the piss out of Kirk for not knowing about a game he was working on. So it wasn't set up. I can tell you for a fact that if you want to set something up? You don't involve Kirk. Because he is so unreliable he will fuck it up. As we came to see in the final round.

> The final game was originally going to be *Wipeout 2097*, but that is very difficult. And I was shit hot at it. The N64 had not been released in the UK at the time of filming, but Kirk had played on one for the past month, using *Mario 64* as research for the environments within *Earthworm Jim 3D*. It was a game they were sure he could play well enough. So the final was changed to *Mario 64* and I agreed to go along with it.
> Dave Perry, Co-Commentator (Series 1–6), 2002

I was so fucked off when Kirk utterly screwed up his run at *Mario 64*. I was like, *You twat*. Typical Kirk. Letting me down, just when I need him to win. So I was resigned to Dave coasting home and winning, which would have been unfair because cheats should never prosper. But then the final slice of hubris in this Greek tragedy is that Dave, rather cynically and cowardly, tries to slow Mario down as he slides down the slope so he can beat Kirk's pathetic performance by being pathetic for a sightly longer duration than Kirk. Losing all control, Mario then falls off the slope into the darkness, taking all Dave's credibility with him.

It was all so unnecessary. In the same way as he would have won the quiz without asking for the questions, he would have beaten Kirk if he had just tried to play the game like a proper Games Animal. But he didn't. And that is why the whole episode is Shakespearean tragedy. Dave is hoisted by his own petard, the tragic hero with the fatal flaw.

> The show was recorded as you saw it. Dave lost and had the most radical sense of humour failure I've ever witnessed. I couldn't believe that he didn't have the composure to realize that the best way of dealing with it was to be gracious. I felt a strange mixture of anger that he was being so bad-mannered and a kind of thrill at seeing someone bury themselves so comprehensively. We thought he was going to walk, but we just about managed to film the final minutes.
> Jonny Ffinch, Series Producer (Series 4–7), 2002

K.E. I remember the unmitigated joy I felt at winning. I was like, 'This is fucking great!' I'd done so badly at the *Mario 64* downhill slide that I just thought there was no way I was going to win and that Dave would smash it. But fuck him, right. He just assumed he was going to win. He was cocky as all hell at that point in time, and what with his greater knowledge and understanding of videogames he might have had some reason to be. [Laughs.]

D.P. What hurt more was the fact that Kirk was shit at it. It made me look even worse when I fell off. [Laughs.] But I had two options. The first was I smile and I be a good boy and quietly leave the stage. Nobody would have ever talked about it again. The second option, knowing I'd been lied to and bullied for years, was that I didn't let them get away with it.

And even then, even after all that, Dave has a chance to rescue himself by proving once and for all that he can have a laugh about his failings like everyone else on the show. But he can't. Rik, Kirk, Derrick? If it had been any of them they would have made a joke about it. But they hadn't spent this series, and all the others, saying stuff on air like, 'I am the best games player in the country.' Dave did. And whenever he would say stuff like that I would think, *Oh Dave, this is just so not what this show is about now.*

So Dave has painted himself into a credibility corner, and so he, understandably, tries desperately to protect his Games Animal brand by claiming he has been set up. He could have even done that and got away with it if he had done it with a smile on his face. But he has a face like a smacked arse. And so instead he comes across as a completely huffy, petulant child. I can only thank him for introducing me to what huffy, petulant children would be like years before I had them myself.

K.E. The cameras stopped rolling. It was deathly silence. Dave walks to the end of the church, walks out the door and as the door is closing Dominik shouts, 'Yeah, see you, Dave. You made yourself look like a right fucking cunt there, didn't you?' which echoed across the church. Then silence as the door shut. Followed by laughter. The idiots had won this round. But there wasn't much gloating about it afterwards. It was clear that we, that Dominik, had crossed a line. And then we all went to a party that night which Dave didn't come to. He'd obviously had enough at that point. And right too, you know. You don't want to be called fucking horrible names on the way out of the door, it's not nice.

D.P. It was cowardly. It wasn't one on one. It wasn't resolved over a beer. It was a gang of people that were all rolling over to him. To this day I can join any conversation, any games forum and within five posts somebody will mention *Mario 64*. The industry that I was passionate about and cared about, I can't enjoy. I don't still have a problem with it but I refused to accept the bullying. It's not right. I'd worked very hard for years in magazines and on TV to get where I was. The years and years that I'd been a high-profile personality in the games industry, how many people ever came out in my corner? Not many.

I think it was just a big release of tension from me. That day had been so fucked up. And it's pressured enough filming a TV show, let alone one where someone tries to cheat and you have to rewrite and replan stuff because of it. And throughout every piece of challenge filming on the show there is a part of my brain that tries to see it from the point of the viewer. How the story is going to play out to them. And that shapes my chat. And this was such a tricky one to do that with so that added to the pressure on me. Plus it was the last bit of challenge filming on the last day of what was, as far as I was concerned, going to be the last day of *GamesMaster* challenge filming ever. So I was stressed to the tits.

And while I was the loveliest, nicest, most supportive and loyal person to my pals? If you were on the other side? I could be the biggest bastard in the world. I was a nightmare. So, yeah, I probably shouldn't have been quite so aggressive to Dave afterwards, although I don't remember his girlfriend being there. I am not sure I ever knew that.

That said? I wish we had kept the cameras rolling while Dave left the church. To have me screaming, 'You made yourself look like a right fucking cunt there' as he traipsed out. Wow. Now that would have been the blooper reel to end all blooper reels.

> D.P. I went home in the car thinking, *What the fuck just happened? How did that just play out, and how have I looked in that moment?* I couldn't watch it on broadcast because I felt it would be too raw for me, but I did watch it at a quieter point soon after, purely so I could prepare myself for what was going to come. I was aware of colleagues having watched it and others within the industry because at that time I'd left journalism for a marketing role at THQ International. I was visiting all the publishing houses like EMAP and Future, all the places who had been my historical enemies in the magazine years because I'd been competing against them. Those people hated me for being this trumped-up, egotistical magazine editor. Now I was having to go to them with product to present, so I was having to mend bridges. Suddenly they were given all this ammunition by this show. It was very hard and just so very, very raw for me.
>
> K.E. The tension between Dave and Dominik had been bubbling under all series. You know, Dave probably saw himself as a natural television presenter so there was a rivalry on that level. It was probably disappointing for him to be relegated to this sort of ridiculed character on set. But at the same time it gave the audience what they wanted, didn't it, which was some kind of conflict.
>
> D.P. I was wild as a young man and enjoying what my quota of fame was giving me. But I was brought up well. I was always polite and treated everyone respectfully behind the scenes, which was why I was so butt hurt over the whole thing, because not one person stood up for me. You try and be good to people and you try and be a good

guy but the way it ended for me, I never knew if I was or not. When I walked out the door and Dominik started shouting and swearing at me, you feel like the whole show hates you. You don't know who likes you or who doesn't. You just feel like everyone fucking hates you.

Something that stuck with me afterwards for years was that not one person from Hewland contacted me afterwards. After six series and my association with that show and the company, not one person contacted me to see if I was OK or to ask why I acted like that. It just went very sour in the end, which was a shame. It was almost like, 'Yeah we've fucking got him. Now let's go and have a party'.

It's a shame because *GamesMaster* always worked best when Dominik and I were on screen together. Me, the short, handsome guy in the bandana. [Laughs.] The guy with outrageous clothes that was so fucking into games he called himself the Games Animal, alongside Dominik, who was this cynical, Scottish guy handing out the witticisms. It fucking worked. It was a great formula but he didn't want it. I wanted it but he didn't. If we'd been straight with each other over a few beers we could have played up the hate and played up the conflict. That could have been an angle. The contrast that ultimately led to the conflict was actually a result of the show's strongest element. It all led to that great moment. That great shitty climax.

The problem was that by series six the show was a very different beast. It was a comedy show. The number one rule was: Do Not Take Anything Too Seriously. So Rik is very self-effacing. Kirk almost celebrates this air of being the stoner who knows how ridiculous the whole thing is and then there's Derrick who occasionally gets tongue-tied and just laughs and is obviously having the time of his life.

Dave didn't evolve. Dave was still taking games far too seriously. There was no self-awareness. There was no humour. And as a result it jarred more and more. He knew a lot about games and could talk about them at length but without any sense of humour. And that is a shame. Because I think back to the Take That challenge of series two, with him calling them all Ken and that was great stuff. And I have no doubt at all that I could have worked with him like I did with Derrick and Kirk to help evolve his on-screen personality into something more akin what the show had become. But I didn't. Because I didn't like the guy he had become. Or maybe it is more fair to say the guy I had become did not like the guy he had become. And that's on me. But somewhere along the line he took himself too seriously. And that was the biggest mistake you could make on *GamesMaster*.

K.E.   I had plenty of other conversations with Dave where he was perfectly nice and perfectly reasonable to me. He never made me feel bad on set or would give me any trouble whatsoever. I drifted in and out of a couple of series but Dave was an integral part of the show coming into being from series one. The Christmas special was just his demise.

He brought game authenticity to the show and he absolutely knew his subject brilliantly – as a journalist, not a marketing manager.

The fallout lasted years, and Dominik and I went through a phase of trolling him online. Dave fell into that trap a bit as well by virtue of pushing his slightly odd agenda. It was just fuel to a fire. But ultimately it stopped and there's no bad blood now. I hope Dave doesn't feel any bad blood because it was all pantomime and ludicrous. Dave was a relatively serious individual who took his work seriously, so it was easy to poke fun at him. Basically, you've someone in a fucking Union Jack bandana and leather pants taking themselves seriously. It was like, 'Well thank you, God!' [Laughs.]

Some people might say that behaving as he did on the Christmas quiz was the biggest mistake Dave made. But it wasn't. And trust me here, because I have clawed out a living in the media for 30 years now on two continents. My career has been up and down more than the FTSE 100, and I have made more mistakes than anyone. I know mistakes. I am the MistakeMaster. This was actually the second biggest mistake Dave made. The biggest mistake was lying about it over the years. Every time he was asked about it, still peddling that crap about being set up or deliberately throwing the *Mario 64* round. That is his biggest mistake. If at any point he had said, 'Yeah, I fucked up, but here is why' as I have done, many many times in my career? Things would have been better for him. But then again, he is responsible for the most famous moment on the show. So maybe it's all been worth it for him.

D.P.   That moment damaged my career so badly. But I made sure I am synonymous with that show and with *GamesMaster* forever. The show in which Dave Perry throws a tantrum. There's been years of great, convoluted scenarios explaining what happened but it's only ever reduced to that reaction. I'll never know what it cost me long term because – and this will sound such a contrived thing – with the damage to my brand and name, I'll never know what I could have done after it if I hadn't behaved in the way I did. But the way I behaved was me being honest. I could have walked and smiled or I could stand there with all those cameras on me and all those people – none of them batting my corner – and say, 'I feel I've been set up pretty badly here'.

The thing that's made it bearable all these years is the moment actually made me legendary. I would never be forgotten in the history of the show. Although it's not the way I'd have liked, I acknowledge that I gave *GamesMaster* the most memorable moment on screen in all seven series. But look, there's a lot of *GamesMaster* to get to that point and within those years were a hell of a lot of happy moments for me.

J.H.   Jane Hewland, Executive Producer Boys will be boys, what can I say?

J.F.   We felt we were running out of steam with Channel 4 because the ratings were going down. The executives thought videogames were a social menace, Dominik was a loud-mouthed git, and the attitude of the show in general was utterly reprehensible. The ratings weren't what they used to be, but that's true of all long-running TV shows. So, we got to the end of series six by which point Jane had me lined up to work on the Computer Channel, which was just starting up. It was such a comedown. God, it was shit. There was no money so we employed absolute children. It was actually quite hard work getting them to do the job. I was thinking, *I can't believe I was having so much fun on GamesMaster and now that's all over.*

T.T.   I didn't realize at the time that *GamesMaster* would become such an iconic programme remembered all these years later. I've done a lot of TV and this is about the only thing that people get excited by. It seems to have stayed in people's minds and reminds them of their youth. Like *Grange Hill* for techies.

R.D.   I've worked on a lot of shows and *GamesMaster* is still on my CV. I've cut out years and years of stuff but it's there because people still remember the show. For a long time after I went on to work on various Hewland productions, stuff nobody gives a fuck about and rightly so, but *GamesMaster* spoiled me. I expected all TV to be like that. It had a budget and it was one of the last great youth shows. Everything I worked on subsequently we had to do all our own camera work. It was the dawn of the multi-skilling age. With *GamesMaster* I thought *this is what TV looks like.* A huge church that looks like Atlantis on the inside and loads of people turning up and loads of buzz. Hewland felt like an eccentric place to work. Everybody in there – and I mean this in the best possible way – was crackers. Some people were wankers, some were lovely but it was always a fun place to work.

It's the perfect series with the perfect last episode. We literally cancel our own show. On air. No one does that. The idea of having an Offence-O-Meter running throughout the show because you are on your last warning from Channel 4 is pretty ballsy. But we go one step further. We deliberately go out of our way to have more and more innuendo so it fills up, we pretend we are getting calls from Channel 4 warning us throughout the show and by the end I am one naughty word away from getting the show cancelled.

So what do I do? I look directly into the camera and say, 'I don't give a f—' And we cut to credits. And can I remind you at this point in time that we are still officially a kids' TV show going out at 6.00 p.m.? I mean what a way to go! I don't remember them doing that with *Live and Kicking.*

SERIES SEVEN

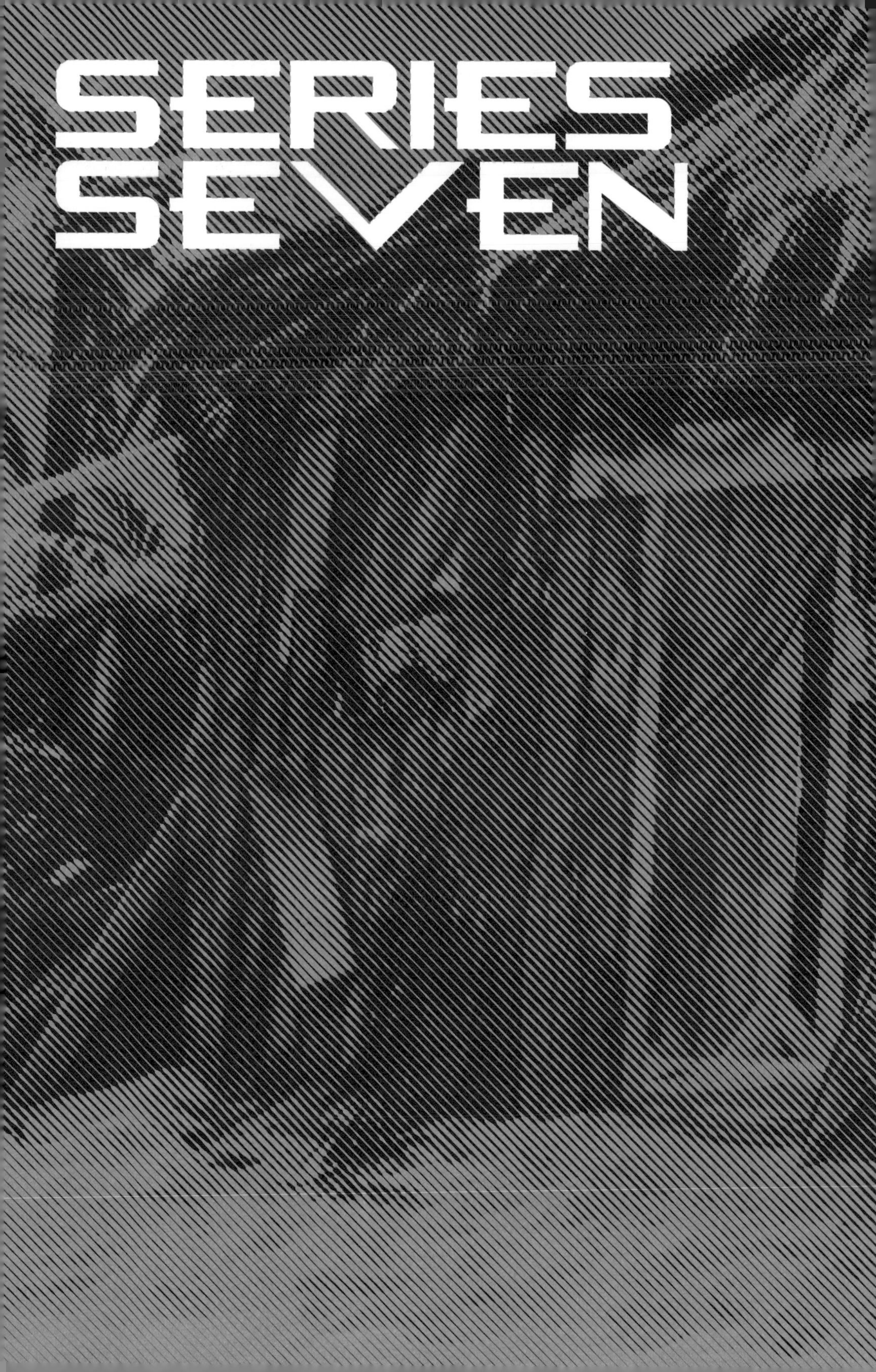

NOVEMBER 1997

o by 1997 I was becoming a slightly different Dominik Diamond because of Phoebe. I was so besotted, everything was Phoebe Phoebe Phoebe. She wasn't a party animal at all. In fact, I used to call her Phoebe Two Beers because that was her limit. She was very grounded and spiritual, and had this big posh family who were all the children of alcoholics so didn't really cane it.

As a result there was no way I was flying anywhere to film anything again, because I didn't want to go through a) the fear and terror and b) the getting blind drunk and possibly causing another case of air rage. That was bad enough when I was a poster boy for nineties excessive behaviour, but not as I was attempting to insert myself into this lovely new posh well-behaved family. I couldn't be the twat of yore.

Phoebe's family reminded me of Myf's in many ways. Stable. Calm. Happy. Refined. And I wanted to be part of that. I wanted all that grown-up stuff. I didn't want priapic excess anymore. I wanted a family. Wife. Kids. And I wanted to do more grown-up things in general.

I distinctly remember telling Jonny and Jane in series six that it would be my last, and them agreeing that they weren't going to risk a Dexter situation again so we would just end it. I had moved on to not just another TV show but another channel. When Channel 5 launched in March 1997, I was one of the launch personalities, hosting their late-night sports strand *Live and Dangerous*. So I had posters of my face up all over London on bus stops, which was very exciting. I was doing that show four nights a week, then travelling to Southampton on Fridays to do their Saturday lunchtime sports show *Turnstyle*, then hammering back to London to do my BBC Radio 5 Live show *Sportscall*. So I was like: *I'm the Sports Guy now.* I didn't actually have any time to do another series of *GamesMaster*.

This was the first time I felt that I had managed to escape the career pigeonhole of the show. I was treated as a bona fide sports presenter. I worked really hard to become that. Probably harder than I swotted for my A levels.

But luckily, by the time it came to actually sorting out filming this Series That Never Should Have Been I had fallen out with the head of Channel 5 sport, Robert Charles, because he wanted me to be less dangerous. On a TV show called *Live and Dangerous*. Which didn't make sense to me. So I was wondering what to do about all this and then Jonny calls about *GamesMaster* and I thought, *Well isn't this just wonderful timing?* So I told Channel 5 to stick their sport shows up their bum because I was off to play with my mental videogames pals again.

J.F. Jonny Ffinch, Series Producer (Series 5–7) I was in an edit quite late one evening working on shows for the Computer Channel and I suddenly got a call from Channel 4 publicity saying, 'Hi, we're about to publish the autumn schedule and we just want a run-down of what's in *GamesMaster* this year.' And I responded, 'Sorry, what's in *GamesMaster* this year? Well, I don't know because it hasn't been commissioned.'

Series seven of *GamesMaster*: the TV Series That Never Should Have Been! There is something wonderfully, gloriously *GamesMaster* about the events of 1997. In series six we nailed it and it had the perfect ending. So to have that show come back for one more ride because the channel forgets to cancel it? That is brilliant.

They told me it was in the schedule. I called up the commissioner the next day and he was like, 'Oh yeah, *GamesMaster's* happening.' Well, nobody fucking told me. [Laughs.] That said, I was delighted because I thought *Great, one more run around the block.* And that's why the last series was 10 shows, because we just couldn't get 18 shows together in time. It just showed the bizarreness of Channel 4 at the time that they just assumed it was happening but didn't bother to tell the people in charge of making it. Nobody called. That's how the last series got commissioned, basically by accident.

That is not just wonderfully *GamesMaster* but it is also quintessentially nineties. The decade of all that wonderful bad behaviour and excess and big mistakes ends with a major TV channel somehow not reading the memo we sent saying: 'We have ended the show.' Or maybe we forgot to even send the memo. Who knows, eh? It was the nineties! And then the presenter having moved on to other things in what was probably a really smart career move decides to blow that all up to have a laugh with his mates again.

BITTERSWEET SYMPHONY

J.H. Jane Hewland, Executive Producer We were developing the Computer Channel in collaboration with Sky, and that's where our focus was as a production company. That said, it was just a ridiculous experience. I tried to persuade Sky to call the channel 'Tomorrow' because I felt the pitch and programming needed to be about future technology. It could have been fantastic but they didn't go for it. Really we should have walked away, but we didn't. The point is we were thinking of other things by that point. Reaching seven series of any show in television is an achievement, but it was the right time to end the show.

J.F. Jane didn't want to be cancelled so she said this really would be the last one we'd do. And I think she was right. As an ongoing production, it was starting to feel like we'd peaked the fun and silliness of the time. Dominik was calming down by this stage because he was with Phoebe, who was a very good influence on him. I think we probably would have been cancelled. But we didn't give them the chance. We cancelled ourselves.

M.M. Mike Miller, Head of Sport, Channel 4 It's always a difficult decision for either the production company or the channel to end a show, but things have a natural lifespan. Other broadcasters begin to pick up on what you're doing and take over, so a show that was once unique is no longer new and fresh. And because our remit at Channel 4 was to constantly look for different ways of showing things that others weren't, you had to let the likes of the BBC, ITV or Sky take over once something became mainstream. That's one of the dilemmas for Channel 4 these days. Now that there's so many channels and so much content, how can they be different? You never like to see something go but you also need to have the money to put into new things. You can't just keep doing the same thing again and again.

J.F. One thing I do think is sad about the last series is that at the point we approached filming Dominik decided he couldn't fly. It was a shame because we definitely would have enjoyed one more big trip abroad. I think it impacted the series to be honest, and it would have made it better. Everything else about that series I really like, though.

The lack of those features gave us more time to let the review section breathe, and that coincided with the debut of Richard Pitt. I don't know who was responsible for finding him but he is my favourite 'other voice' on *GamesMaster* ever. He just has a totally different voice to anything we'd had on the show before. Unashamedly intelligent words, camp delivery, and he looks like David Bowie à la Thin White Duke. He was the coolest reviewer we'd had since Frank O'Connor. Honestly. Every word he says is so charismatic, almost hypnotic. Such a presence. That review section is superb in this series. We have the biggest games like *Final Fantasy VII*, and Richard and Rob discuss controversial releases like *Postal* in a very intelligent way. And actually, in a weird way, I think more than anyone else that appeared on the show, Richard Pitt could have presented a really interesting future version of *GamesMaster*. Sadly, we will never know because he died in 2009. Which is a bizarre and tragic footnote to this final series. And for me a real cautionary note: that not everyone got out alive from this show that was so utterly enmeshed in nineties behaviour on and off screen.

J.F. Going into production, the biggest worry I had was that The Dickster was committed to another TV show. He was so integral to the success of the show and such a brilliant person to work with that the thought of doing the show and thinking up the challenge events on my own, I was really quite alarmed about it. As it was, we had an established method for creating challenges by this point, so I did manage to implement more or less the same process we'd undertaken on the previous series. So I'd eventually worked out what Jane had desperately been trying to explain to us about events. [Laughs.]

What's quite funny is that as the producer you don't have that much to do with the crew. When you're dealing with content and the editorial your whole focus is on what you're shooting and on Dominik. Even by series seven, it used to amaze me walking on to set because as the producer you think you're across everything, that you know everybody. I'd turn up and look around thinking, *Who the Hell are all these people?* I had no idea. They all looked so busy.

R.H. Rik Henderson, Co-Commentator (Series 5–7) It was a hard series to film because we knew it really was going to be the last. So I think a lot of us tried too hard. It's not my favourite series, to be honest. I'm very critical about myself and I'm not pleased with my performance at all. I think it might have been the animosity between me and Dom.

A few years prior we'd set up a Sunday league football team called 'Diss United'. For the first season Dominik had a column in *FHM* about it. I was always referenced as Rik Big Bum. It was brilliant fun for a year and then it suddenly wasn't, because getting people to turn up and pay their subs was hard work. I co-managed it the first year and then Dominik took over for the second year and just hated it. And eventually me and Dominik really fell out over it, like properly fell out. Between series six and seven we hadn't spoken once. When I got the call to come back for series seven I was surprised, to be honest, because the first words I spoke to him were on set. Literally within that moment though we were best mates again. Before then I just didn't want to speak to him at all. And he didn't want to speak to me. Over a football team. [Laughs.]

I don't remember what Rik and I fell out over. I do remember that team being an utter catastrophe. I would get a team sorted out. Eleven players and three subs. Mostly from the games industry. And then I would turn up on a Sunday morning, with a raging hangover from all kinds of stuff that had entered my body the night before, and we'd have maybe eight players turn up, every single one of them either hungover or still high from the night before, except this wonderful Frenchman called Bernard from Infogrames who was probably the best footballer I have ever played with. He took it very seriously and would be there an hour before, stretching and whatnot. He would get even angrier than me when no one turned up.

R.H. We were not good. We barely ever won a game. There was one match though where this amateur referee went up to Dominik as captain to do the toss-off and he just went, 'Can I have your autograph?', to which Dominik responded, 'After the game, pal', and all through the game we got away with the most outrageous behaviour without a single strike.

And I had to keep this whole disastrous thing going because I had a column in *FHM* about the adventures of my Sunday league team. To be fair, the disastrous nature of the team did mean it was a wonderfully hilarious column, but it didn't make for great friendships.

So Rik and I fell out. But again, that is another wonderful thing about series seven. Without it I probably wouldn't have patched things up with Rik. But when Jonny called me and said that Channel 4 forgot to cancel the show so did I mind coming back for a shortened series I was like, 'OK, but only if all my pals are there again!'

All the commentators have my favourite moments ever in series seven. When we had Catalina Guirado from *TFI Friday* on playing that *Rosco McQueen* firefighting challenge, I say to Rik, 'Did you ever want to be a fireman when you were little?', and he replies, 'No, but I did want a big hose.' That is peak *GamesMaster* there. And by this stage I had encouraged Derrick to just open his mouth and say whatever the fuck he wanted without thinking. Which is why we have him talking about how he will be flying a spaceship around in the year 2000 and how in beat 'em ups heads pop off 'like juice from a lemon'. You can't script that surreal brilliance. And Kirk as well, has so many brilliant lines.

> K.E. I only had a couple of challenges to do in this series. I don't know if somebody had just woken up and realized that I wasn't that good but they had less of those silly, random-style challenges for me so I was probably less involved in that series than any of them for that reason.

Every time Kirk is on in series seven he says something utterly brilliant. I don't know if that's because he was less stoned and more focused. Or maybe he was the opposite. Either way, he is top level. When we have the celeb boxers on and I say he has been in many rings himself, he replied with the words, 'But never yours, you deviant!'

In the Christmas show I ask what he is going to find in his sack this year and he says, 'Nothing because I am barren.' And obviously there is nothing funnier, for me anyway, than having Kirk wear a *PaRappa The Rapper* mascot head. Best of all, he has my favourite co-commentator moment ever – in the first episode where he and I have just given Jo Guest a big kiss and then Kirk grabs me and kisses me full on the lips and says, 'Just wanted to catch the tail end of Jo Guest there.' Kirk is basically Seth Rogen in series seven.

And they all made me so happy. Just hanging with them. I absolutely love series seven. In many ways it's my favourite of them all. It's not quite as good a piece of television as series six, but I am actually smiling in it. Seriously. If you watch it back, it is amazing how chilled and smiley I am. My disposition is as sunny as the desert island setting itself. Because I was finally in this little pocket of harmony in my real life, and this was just like being allowed to go out and play with your mates and then come home for your dinner at the end of day. For money. It was such a wonderful bonus.

SERIES SEVEN

WHAT A BEAUTIFUL DAY

If anyone out there can tell me what the opening title sequence of series seven is about, I would love to know. I guess this is the problem of having a tiny amount of time to get a show together. I suspect there was a grand idea. And for some reason I have stuck in my head the idea that the dream sequence was supposed to be me running through the settings of the previous series of *GamesMaster* in a nightmarish way. I mean that would make sense, wouldn't it? But why didn't we do that? Probably because someone decided we couldn't spend £50,000 on opening title sequences any more. So it just becomes these vague nightmarish tropes of corridors and tunnels and forests and, for some reason, a fruit and veg market. I just remember having to run everywhere in pyjamas and getting sore feet from running through the forest. And if it is a dream, does this mean that the desert island is part of the dream? Is the whole of series seven a dream?

> **D.M.** The desert island set was a lot of fun. It worked well because the island was a full studio build where it was all containable. You could really concentrate all of your love into a reasonably small surface area. But it was a total bitch to build. We built a vast tank for the water and then we built the island. We got tons and tons of kiln-dried white sand from a place in Surrey, and we got the rustication and the texture of something that had been sun bleached pretty well.

The desert island allowed us to come up with what was probably our best role for the assistants, this time as Girl Fridays. What I love about this last series is that Helena and Leigh Ann have Dominik Diamond/Jonny Finch lines to say. And that works brilliantly. To have these sweet, innocent-looking women saying Dominik Diamond innuendo is like that great comic theory by Dr Jonathan Miller that I learnt alongside Simon Pegg at Bristol University: 'Comedy is the rehearsal of alternative categories.' So Leigh Ann teases a challenge involving boxers by saying, 'Ryan Rhodes and Kalif Shafeeq beat each other's meat' while Helena leads into a challenge involving marines by saying, 'But we begin with an event which we like to call "Three Big Men Get Hard"'. And they both deliver those lines brilliantly. Totally deadpan. By this stage, that is far funnier and more shocking than me saying it.

> **H.T.** Helena Tepper, Girl Friday (Series 7) That desert island set was something else. The sand was gorgeous, and the way they lit it was like being taken into a different world. We were literally the Girl Fridays washed up on this beach with little tiki huts and boats. Speaking of which, I was meant to row the guests in from the sea on to the beach.

Problem was I couldn't row, so I kept going round and round in circles. [Laughs.] All Saints came on as guests and I had to row out to pick them up. I just kept going round and round in circles. It happened with all the guests. We were just all crying with laughter. Eventually they had to come up with an idea of someone literally pushing the boat while I pretend like I'm rowing. They just thought it would be easier. Probably thought, 'Helena's wasting our valuable filming time here.'

GamesMaster wouldn't be *GamesMaster* without some form of set disaster, but we thought we'd got away with it this time because it was a proper studio. Drogo wasn't having to cram Hell into an old church or whatever. He could plan everything meticulously, which is why the desert island is genuinely a proper movie set. Unfortunately, it was also the first time we had tried to bring the guests on via boat. Sure we had them coming on that way in series four, up the River Styx, but that was a boat on rails underneath the water. This time it was a proper sea, with wave machines, and a wibbly wobbly boat that poor Helena had to try and row, which is basically impossible. And we didn't realize that until we had the guests there, so there was an inordinate amount of delays while we tried to fix that until we realized we would have to get someone to push the boat just out of shot so Helena wouldn't have to row.

That set was ace, though. Especially the little tiki hut, which has that great sign outside saying 'House of Pants'. And I love those bits at the end of the show where I go into it with the girls and then Jonny throws on a comedy sound effect at the end. Jonny's sound effects throughout the series are brilliant. From toilet flushes to farting noises to chainsaws, they are like little sprinkles on the top of a cupcake.

MY FAVOURITE GAME

In spite of the last series being cobbled together really quickly, we have some of our best challenges ever. Sure we have self-indulgent, less-than-A-list celeb appearances on occasion. The band Kaleef came on because I had seen them live a month before and got drunk with them and liked them. And Ryan Rhodes the boxer came on because I had actually sparred with him on my Channel 5 sports show. But it works because these guys are fans of the show and they love coming on, so they are also really chirpy and positive and energetic and sunny. We also have some great stuff in there for hardcore gamers: specially designed levels on brand new games like *Tomb Raider 2*, top-level players finding out special moves on the very latest *Mortal Kombat* arcade game and – in what was possibly the best hardcore gaming challenge we ever did in the history of the show – we genuinely have the four best *Tekken 3* players from all over the world flying in for a tournament. We just wanted to spend all this lovely money one last time on the biggest and best shit we could think of.

> **J.F.**   We had the budgets to do that. I mean, they'd be coming over in Economy and we plonked them in some roach-infested hotel while they were here, but we did fly them over from Japan and the United States. I'm sure they barely understood what was going on, finding themselves bussed on to set, ordered about for a few hours and then sent flying back home. The *Tekken 3* tournament was a great final event to stage. I liked the name of that event too, 'Oi, Bloke From Another Country, Are You Starting?'. Giving each event a typically silly name was a great thing we stumbled on, as it immediately built a sense of occasion.
>
>   I'm particularly fond of the event name, 'Is the Net Full of Cak?'. I was with Dominik near the end of filming saying, 'Yeah, it's just bollocks. It's never going to go anywhere' and Dominik was like, 'I don't think I'm ready to say that. We need to say something more nuanced'. Anyway, that was my amazing prediction for what was going to happen. And to be fair, it is full of cak.

The last series also features my best writing ever. Mostly in the challenge titles. We have a game featuring motorbikes? Let's call it 'Buff My Helmet For Extra Speed'. We are having a challenge on an arcade skateboard game? Let's call it 'Oi Bloke, Get Off My Halfpipe'.

And then we have the intros and outros for the show. In every closing link I list a reason why Channel 4 is going to be shit when we are not on it. That is pretty ballsy. That is not something any other show did at that time. And the opening links are superb. The one where I complain about the girls giving me crabs again, then it turns out it's a gag about the monotony of crustacean cuisine? That is as good as the innuendo ever got. And you can tell how confident I feel about the comedy I am writing that I am prepared to force my, by this time, sizeable hideous body into a tiny pair of Speedos and lie in freezing cold water for a *Baywatch* gag. That one is my favourite show opening links of all time.

Making the series was liberating. We had cancelled ourselves so we have no fear of failure, no need to please an audience or Channel 4 or anyone really, other than ourselves. You don't get that freedom in TV, ever. We give absolutely no fucks about complaints so we basically have celebrity women wearing as little as possible playing arcade games that require them to jiggle around constantly. Which they do with gay abandon in the case of Emma Noble and the utterly out of control Emma Harrison. I still see her playing that *Rapid River* game every time I close my eyes to this very day. All the celebs are playing these huge silly arcade games – it's basically *It's A Knockout* with breasts.

> I don't want to bother working myself up about it. As far as I can make out, the root of the problem lies in the fact that the show doesn't appear to believe games are at all interesting. Symptoms of this include the obligatory 'ho-ho-ho-lads-eh?-eh?' glamour girls, the relentless parade of 'oo-we-are-impressed!' celebrities. As a games player, I find *GamesMaster* insulting. As a woman, I find it misogynistic. As a television professional, I find it mediocre. Oh damn, I didn't mean to say all that. Er, the first series was good, though. A breath of fresh air.
> Violet Berlin, *The ZX Files*, 1997

V.B. **Violet Berlin** I stand by it. I may have said it more calmly if Dominik hadn't slagged me off to the press, and yes I may have been a little untactful, but I found the interactions with the women so demeaning. My anger went further than Dominik and the show, though. To me the attitude and humour was reflecting sexism I encountered in the games industry, which at the time was massively insecure about what it was. Society up until this point said if you play games then you're a nerd and uncool, more so if you're a woman. It was still not considered a cool thing for a television to cover either, less so if you're a woman. It was all one big boys' club.

I was interested in reporting about games and future technology so I was speaking in a very different language to Dominik. I could see what *GamesMaster* was doing in taking the piss out of itself, which allowed it to become mainstream in a cool way. However, I just thought the tone of it all was such a shame considering how innovative and fresh it all felt just a few years earlier. I'll always look back fondly on the first series though, as *GamesMaster* truly allowed gaming to come out from under its rock and take its place as an established part of youth culture.

J.F. We were setting up some ridiculous challenge with a couple of models on *Final Furlong* and I could hear on the feedback that one of the runners, Millie, was lightly expressing that it was absolutely pitiful the way these women were being brought on to ride horses on some daft arcade machine. I said to her, 'Look, our audience is young men, we are just monkeys and this is just male, monkey entertainment.' It's probably hard to defend now, but it's what it was. This discussion with Millie led to us beginning to interact and getting to know each other. And that's how I met my wife.

E.H. **Emma Harrison, Contestant** I just remember laughing from start to finish. I got invited to a lot of TV shows around this time after leaving *Neighbours*. And you know, you arrive and do your bit and leave. But my abiding memory is just how immediately welcoming and respectful Dominik and everyone was, and the sense of fun on set. A lot of TV wasn't like that and I wish it had been. I just have so many happy and fun memories of my life back then, but honestly I can say that was one of the happiest, peak moments of my career.

SERIES SEVEN

R.H. I was really looking forward to All Saints coming because they'd been on *The Big Breakfast* guest presenting that week. But they came on with an absolute attitude before the cameras were rolling. Dominik stood there and they were really stroppy, which he took an instant dislike to. Not to them necessarily but to the fact they were stroppy. They were saying, 'We're so tired, we don't want to do this' out loud. Dominik asked them why and they said they'd been presenting *The Big Breakfast*. And brilliantly, Dominik responded, 'You do realize we get three times the viewers of that?' And bang. They were suddenly on board. We were all laughing in the background thinking that put them in their place.

We were always the show that didn't take ourselves too seriously, but this time I went out of my way to chat more to the celebs who were coming on, to make utterly sure they realized we were just out to have the most insane amount of fun and no one should give a fuck. So, All Saints, who were a serious business and commercial titan at the time, with a lot of pressure on them to be the next Spice Girls, were a little bit serious when they came on set. I had to let them realize this was not a place for egos. That it was a little safe space where careers could be put on hold in the name of having a laugh. And they turned out to be brilliant guests. Great chat.

M.M. Martin Mathers, Co-Commentator (Series 7) It's very surreal that I went from being first series failure to working on the show via *Games World* and then building up enough of a rapport to be invited to commentate on a challenge. I walked on to set and Dominik saw me and literally enveloped me in this gigantic hug that was just so comforting. I was like, *Wow, this is really cool that they want me here again.* I'm not one of those people who thinks they're memorable.

I felt very stilted stood next to him commentating while two children played some shit dinosaur shooter. But I spent the day down there and caught up with old friends. It was just really nice to be closing the loop from being on the first series and going all the way around to being on the last series.

I think from day one Jonny and I wanted Martin back on for the final series. He was one of us, one of the team, one of the researchers. As I've said, he was also in my opinion the best games player we had ever had on, just shading Danny Curley. So of course he is coming back on. But you know what? This time? Let's have him in the top tier of the pecking order. Let's promote him to co-commentator. Because we can do what the fuck we want! It's like the Mafia opening the books. It's Martin's graduation!

CLOSING TIME

So, that's it. I would like to personally thank the many talented people that have worked on this show. They will all go on to bigger things but somehow none of them will seem quite as self-indulgent as *GamesMaster*. I know some people might have thought it's been flippant. To some people it might seem as if it's been in bad taste. But it was made with the total conviction that, to you, the viewers, it meant something. So I guess really now with the last link of the last series I should come up with the funniest gag in the history of *GamesMaster*, but ... I can't.
Dominik Diamond

J.F. We didn't have a huge amount of time to put this series together, and I'm afraid to say that in deciding to make the last show a clips show it got rid of 10% of our problem when trying to shoot 10 shows in a studio. We thought we could get away with it and intersperse some nice links of the crew dismantling the set. It felt like a great way to wrap things up, so we made it work without it feeling too inappropriate.

If I had my time again I would have done something really big and gone out with a bang. I mean, we'd already had a clips show in series five as a Christmas show just two years earlier, so we went out with a slight whimper really. That was a practical decision but probably a rather cowardly one. The trouble with doing a clips show is what you're really doing is transferring your problem to a future date. Yes, you don't have to shoot anything in a studio, but when it comes to editing the thing together you're then facing the task of quickly looking through seven series of material and 126 tapes to try to find the best bits. It turns into a horrible post-production nightmare.

R.W. Richard Wilcox, Programme Consultant (Series 7) Although I wasn't working on the series I did head down to the studio for the very last day of filming. It was all very strange to be back but to have no role. I was itching to get involved, to help things along but it wasn't my job any more. Dominik suggested that for one of his final links I be the one who is switching off the screens in the gallery right at the end of the episode, but for some reason it didn't happen.

I think one of the reasons *GamesMaster* is so fondly remembered is precisely because I *didn't* have another success like it. Not in TV anyway. If Ant and Dec hadn't gone on to do *I'm a Celebrity* we'd all be waxing lyrical about *Byker Grove* and *Let's Get Ready To Rhumble*. But no one mentions those works of cultural genius because they did other bigger things. Don't get me wrong, I have managed to keep some form of media career going which has supported me, and it has been far better than having to get a proper job. Newspaper columns for *The Star* et cetera are far more fun and lucrative than working in a bank. And I have done OK in radio since. An award-winning run on XFM Scotland helping launch the most wonderful wave of Scottish indie music like Biffy Clyro, The Fratellis and Glasvegas – that was great. I came out to Canada to retire and be a farmer and ended up hosting the biggest radio shows in the country. But that's radio. No one really cares about that stuff. No one goes on YouTube to listen to clips of a radio show from 30 days ago, let along 30 years.

TV is different. It's a bigger deal. And while I tried to do other telly stuff, it just didn't work out. I worked with some lovely people but it just wasn't as much fun as *GamesMaster*. Making TV is actually really boring. You spend ages hanging around for stuff to get set up and then you finally say something. It's not like doing a breakfast show on the radio where you think of something during a song and then just do it. And then play another song and come up with another daft idea and just do it again. And also, the older one gets? Especially someone like me who hates the way they look? The worse one feels one looks on screen. And that's what is great about radio. No one sees your fat, bald, ugly face. Apart from the times some idiot boss makes you do videos for the station's Facebook page or go out simultaneously on YouTube or ghastly shite like that.

So I think what makes the last show in particular so poignant today, the dismantling of the set and whatnot ... is that it is not just the dismantling of the *GamesMaster* show, but also the dismantling of my TV career, if that doesn't sound too overdramatic.

> **R.H.** My favourite episode is the last episode, purely because of Dominik's speech at the end. It was beautiful, so moving. It summed up everything about how much fun and special the show was.
>
> **R.W.** If you want to know how good a presenter he is, just see what a mess Jeremy Clarkson makes of his similar final link in *The Grand Tour*. I still think it's such a shame Dominik didn't find another great vehicle for his talents on TV. They don't come along very often. Dominik had *GamesMaster* and we knew it was special, so we all worked our little socks off to try and make it the very best it could be.
>
> **J.F.** Dominik's last link was pretty heartfelt, and although we still had several months of editing, that was the last studio shoot. We'd still see each other in the weeks afterwards recording the voiceovers. But in the studio we were quite teary. When the cameras stopped Dominik and I were just stood cuddling at the end. People like Millie were looking on, and were just like, 'What's up with these guys? One minute they're making smutty jokes about page-three models, the next they're cuddling each other crying.' [Laughs.]

Lost In Translation
I was so sad in Japan because I had just
fallen in love with the woman I would
marry and I missed her. So in a shocking
move I consoled myself by smoking fags.

ARCHIVE VI

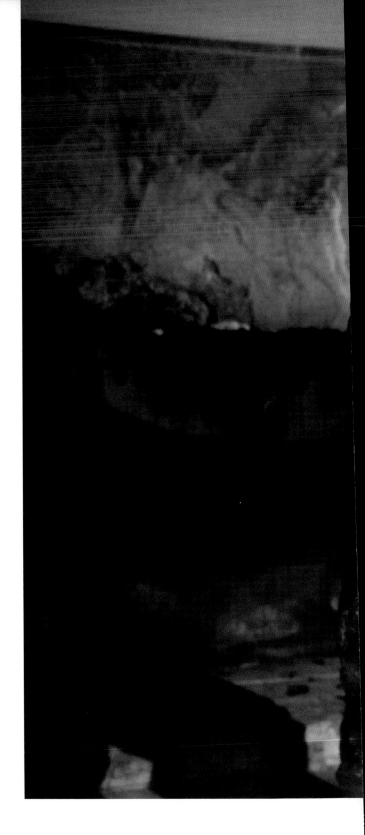

Bosom buddies
I am obviously laughing at something Rik
is saying here. That happened a lot, on
and off screen. We giggled and drank our
way across Camden regularly, once
laughing so much while peeing outside a
pub we fell down an embankment
mid-stream. What a death THAT would
have been!

ARCHIVE VI

The A-Team
We genuinely were as close as this photo shows. Notice Kirk lurking at the back, up to no good. That fits.

The Waterboys

Series one and two I would hurry off
the set between takes. By series six
I just hung out there all the time because
without a live audience there really
wasn't any difference between on and
off screen. We were just messing about
playing games and now and again we'd
roll the cameras.

A

A
Lovely Ball
See that face? That is the undisguised joy of having the most attractive person on telly pressed up close to you. My face looks chuffed too.

B
Fishy
See that face? That is the undisguised joy of having he most attractive person on telly pressed up close to you. Michael Fish's face looks chuffed too.

Besties
Kirk and I on the set of *Night O' Plenty*.
A complete riot of a show for the
wonderful Paramount Channel. The
show's sign was made by Leigh Francis,
or Keith Lemon, as he is known now.

ARCHIVE VI

Paradise found

What do you do when Channel 4 forget to cancel the show and you have to make it at a couple of weeks notice? Build a complete desert island and ocean in a TV studio, obviously. Drogo Michie, genius set designer once again.

ARCHIVE VI

A

B

A
Series three
Sir Patrick looking understandably
bemused.

B
Series four
Sir Patrick realizing millions will remember
him for this rather than Uranus.

286/287

C

D

C
Series Five
The best Sir Patrick ever looked as The
GamesMaster. And the dude knows it.

D
Series Seven
The sun sets on the most remarkable bit
of casting in the history of UK TV.

A

B

A
Tear jerker
Is this the greatest ending speech on a TV show ever? I couldn't possibly comment. But it is. It really is.

B
Taxi for Sir Patrick
This was the day Sir Patrick and I met for the first and only time. His last bit of filming. That's wonderfully poetic. It meant there was no chance of us ever having a fight.

Everyone talks about that last link. And I actually had it written before anything else for that series. I knew those were the last words I wanted to say. To completely step out of any form of character, any form of innuendo, have no videogames on set and be wearing my normal clothes and just speak from the heart. It's very special. I also love the link just before when Helena and Leigh Ann walk out, also wearing their normal clothes, and we give each other a kiss goodbye and it's all totally natural. This show that was so heavily constructed in terms of the massive sets and bizarre locations and the virtual world of videogames themselves, ends with everything being stripped back and natural. It's very postmodern. Thank you Bristol University Department of Drama – I got there in the end!

And also – just to add to the poignancy – a couple of months after all that, I finally meet the GamesMaster after all this time. It wasn't even planned. I was heading into an edit suite to do my last batch of voiceovers, and Patrick Moore was in there before me. For once, I was early rather than late. So I am sauntering into reception, and lo and behold there is Patrick Moore. Totally surreal. I literally screeched, 'Patrick!' And he just looked at me a little confused. So I said, 'Dominik Diamond!' And he replied, 'Upon my soul, we finally meet at last!' And there was an awkward silence. I mean, what do you say to each other? You have shared the screen of this huge TV show for seven years without meeting. What are the words?

So I said, 'Where are you off to now?' And he said he was off to watch the cricket on the telly. And I loved cricket. So we spoke about cricket for about 10 minutes until his taxi arrived.

Again, isn't that wonderfully *GamesMaster*? That when Patrick and I finally meet we don't talk about the show or videogames or anything. We talk about cricket. My only regret is that I didn't make a Uranus gag with him.

J.F.   The last time I filmed with Patrick I just said something anodyne like, 'Well you never know, Patrick, we might get together for some other reason one day.' And he went, 'Oh yes, absolutely, marvellous', and that was the last I saw him. To be honest, I used to dread my filming days with him. He was too comfortable in making dodgy comments around people that were definitely designed to provoke. And it just seemed a bit lazy to me really. They were kind of funny for a bit but they were also quite boring. Then you had to go out to lunch with him where he'd go through this shtick of being very eccentric while saying lots of crazy, racist, right-wing things designed to shock. But, God, I wasn't shocked or entertained. I was just bored, quite frankly. I know that sounds terribly mean but I just wasn't so enamoured with him, I'm afraid. I think he was quite an old, kind man in his own way in life. During filming he did once say to me, 'What is an N64? Does it have wheels?'

I know people who worked with him said he was a reactionary right-wing chap, so I am glad I only had that one meeting with him. I can look at him purely as the GamesMaster and still appreciate what a truly brilliant choice he was and what a truly brilliant job he did. He is an icon and our relationship was never sullied by getting to know each other. And it is a relationship. We are linked. Forever. I didn't realize how much until one morning some years ago when I woke up in Canada to a slew of messages on Twitter and Facebook saying sorry for my loss.

Patrick had died that day. And people were genuinely concerned. They wanted to know if I was OK. They were sad because the show meant so much to them and they sort of transferred their feelings of loss to me. And then I suddenly felt sad. I felt genuine intense bereavement over this man I had only ever spent 10 minutes with in real life. And that is the legacy of the show at the end of the day. Feelings. Good TV creates feelings. Brilliant TV keeps those feelings in you forever.

GOOD RIDDANCE [TIME OF YOUR LIFE]

J.F. *GamesMaster* ended at the right time for us as a team but it had life still in it. Really it ended just before serious money started pouring in through coverage of games, just as sites like IGN were starting up. If we had still been on air and had a presence, we could absolutely have done all of that. We could have been huge and be absolutely rolling in money now. [Laughs.]

Oh my God, don't even think about mentioning how much money we'd have made if we'd just kept going another few years. Holy shit. I'd be a multi-millionaire. If we'd have kept going to the end of the millennium? And then really whored ourselves out on the internet? When I see how much money the likes of PewDiePie and those other witless morons make? I weep. I truly do.

J.F. Jane always says you don't want to be ahead of your time, you want to be at the time. When you're ahead of your time people come along and copy what you're doing. Games coverage and watching people play games is absolutely huge now so it's a shame we stopped when we did.

R.W. I loved my time on *GamesMaster*. We all did. We knew we were making something that people loved. We knew we were breaking new ground in showing how games were developing as an entertainment medium and how playing them could be a compelling TV spectacle. The show had a confidence and an attitude that was unique. It wasn't edgy for the sake of it. It was intelligent and informed and bloody funny. The combination of my research, Steve's visual flair, Jonny and Dominik's writing and, of course, Dominik's unmatched delivery meant you were in a world that you wished you could spend your life in.

J.F.   Nobody else could have done with that show what Dominik did. He was a forceful character and a voice like no other.

D.W.   Danielle Woodyatt, Virgin Games There'll never be another Dominik Diamond. He was an absolute one of a kind. Thank God. [Laughs.] But he was so passionate about what he was doing and wanted everything about the show to be perfect. Jonny and Jane were great ambassadors for him.

D.F.   Dexter Fletcher, Presenter That was a huge part of the show's appeal, the punk attitude of Dominik Diamond. He was a bit of a 'fuck you' kind of guy and that's why the audience loved him. The show needed that. There's an element of videogames having always been viewed as a bit nerdy and it's bollocks. They're some of the coolest fucking things around. This was a show that was bringing a bit of coolness and credibility to games. I'm happy to have been a small part of something that people remember so fondly and likely want to see another series of. There's probably more call for it now than there even was then.

D.M.   Retrospectively, in a sort of trashy, throwaway way the show represented the niche cultural zeitgeist of its time. You don't think about it when you're doing it but it had a look, a feel and a language. It had all sorts of things that with the benefit of history probably tick a lot of boxes for cultural anthologists about that boom period for videogames. The internet hadn't swamped things so it was a really important tool of communication.

A.W.   Adam Wood, Series Producer (Series 1–2) Something I underestimated at the time was it's actually quite hard to have a TV show that's a hit. I underestimated too the fact that it's quite rare that you have that much fun on a show. My enduring memory of GamesMaster was just a happy time being given creative freedom and to let one's imagination run wild without fear. It's lovely that people remember and liked it but that's just a bonus. That's luck in a way. You make these shows and you put the same amount of love and dedication into making every show. By the time it goes out you've long moved on to another production. Often you get the overnight viewing figures the next day and it's not the number you want. And it's incredibly disappointing. But you must never forget the emotional journey you've had with the show. Even if GamesMaster hadn't been successful it wouldn't have changed my experience. Most shows really involve thinking about it and digging deep. Back then we were young and hungry. We put a lot of thought and care into it. And if it did feel fresh I think it's because we were fresh and unhindered. It meant something.

J.F.   There's a funny thing about geek culture – whether it's comics, superheroes or videogames – in that fans cherish their origins. People adore the magic of those early videogames because living through that time was all about innovation and looking to the future. GamesMaster was loved in part because of its subject, but more so as a show celebrating the culture and fun of playing videogames. It's a document of an industry as much as anything.

H.H. **Harry Hewland** I have a lot of nostalgia for the format of television, and it's weird to see it morphing into a shape that nobody really recognizes anymore. We're streaming but also hanging on to the dying broadcast world we know of old. And commercial breaks are slowly dying too. Look at the commercials of our youth and you're immediately hit with this wave of nostalgia for big ad campaigns. Now we can't wait to fucking skip them. It's not a world that resembles the one I used to know. But what I do know is that hopefully the storytelling skills that I learnt from my mum, either through nature or nurture, made me at ease with keeping faith in good ideas.

M.M. **Mike Miller, Head of Sport, Channel 4** For *GamesMaster* to come back and work it's got to be situated in today's era, not try and replicate something from 30 years ago. You need to have people like Jane and the people she had around her who understood that by putting together the right mix of genres with the right vision you can create something interesting, unique, fun and serious at the same time. There aren't many people around like that. There's a lot of creative people but they don't necessarily think in those terms.

J.F. It's really very simple. You put on a show like *GamesMaster* and you will get young people from all different cultures interested. In fact, something we didn't ever really receive any recognition for was having lots of young Black and Asian kids on to the show as contestants, far more than you would see on other TV shows of the time. Videogames have that cultural appeal. There was no barrier to anyone coming on to *GamesMaster* because it just wasn't a polite, middle-class show.

So, how do I sum up the show after all that? All those amazing words from all those amazing people? I feel like I did during the last link on the last show. But 25 years on. As a proper grown-up, with maturity and wisdom and cardigans and stuff like that. What do I say at the end of it all … again?

Legacy can be a pretentious word because people use it when it's not merited. But those lovely memories you have of the show? That is legacy. Genuine, proper, all-singing, all-dancing legacy. *GamesMaster* is in part the show you remember so fondly because yes, it was funny and yes, it had videogames which were popular, but there have been other TV shows with videogames and funny bits. What set *GamesMaster* apart was that it was dangerous, but dangerous without being contrived. That may seem a strange thing to say about a show that featured the world's most famous astronomer as a floating overseer, Uri Geller controlling a game using only the power of his own mind, and a Scottish bloke flying to Japan to ask people on a fake beach if they've copped off with anyone. But we never seemed to have to try too hard to produce that stuff. There was more originality in one episode of *GamesMaster* than most shows have in a lifetime, but those ideas just gushed out from a bunch of ridiculously talented young people who didn't have anyone telling them to stop. Luck played a part; I won't deny that. Two great strokes of luck in particular. To launch the show when the videogame world was exploding, and to broadcast it on a channel whose management team didn't bother us because they didn't really understand the show. Those things were huge. Mike Miller was the only person working in Channel 4 management who ever watched it, and he was a bit weird like us. Thank fuck for that.

That allowed us to break rules. To fuck around with stuff. But, again, we never tried too hard. With the exception of the late-night special, we never had a single swear word on the show. We were dangerous with innuendo and disrespectful to authority, even to the channel that broadcast us. And we snuck it in under the radar of the grown-ups. Kids love behaving badly. And we did. We were punk and we were cool, and the cool, punk stuff is what you remember most from your childhood.

When each show aired during those glorious seven years, WE knew it was dangerous. YOU knew it was dangerous. But Channel 4 didn't. And neither did your mum and dad. It was the TV equivalent of smoking a cigarette behind the bike sheds. And we were never cancelled. We got away with this for seven years! 126 episodes! Game of Thrones only had 73, and unlike them we didn't screw up the ending. With the exception of the occasional fast food sponsorship, we never compromised on anything, and we went out on our own terms. Twice.

The wee kid I was at the start of the nineties wanted to be famous and do something different, something funny, something dangerous, something they would be remembered for. And it happened. It really did. Not in the way I dreamed it would, because it involved Sonic the Hedgehog rather than standup comedy, but that's OK. The 21-year-old Dominik Diamond wanted to do something that shook the world. Not sure he did that, but he certainly shook some pants.

J.F. *GamesMaster* came from Jane. No other owner of a production company would come up with that kind of show and let it evolve the way it did. The amazing freedom and energy of that show is all down to her. She is just the most amazing person. Anyone that ever worked with her would say they never had a boss like her. When she decided to retire there was a small window where I could have got another job in TV but I just didn't want to go anywhere else because I knew it would never be as fun. There will never be anyone like her in TV again.

A.W. She's anti-establishment and a naturally rebellious person. She isn't someone who goes with the flow.

C.M. Cameron McAllister, Series Director (Series 1–2) The concepts always came from her and the inspiration for doing it. She came up with so many brilliant ideas and took a great punt on people and me, giving me the most incredible opportunities that I wouldn't have got anywhere else. I was very lucky.

S.C.   **Steve Carsey, Researcher (Series 1–2)** You go through your career with mentors and opportunities. Thanks to not taking no for an answer, Jane gave me my first break in television and I've never been out of work since. I'm forever grateful for whatever she saw in me. My life would have been very different.

K.P.   **Kyle Prince, Researcher (Series 6)** I was a working-class kid who just wanted to work in television and make great shows. It's only when you're older and go to places like the BBC you see how class ridden it is. It wasn't like that working for Jane. She was tough but she was straight up and would say, 'I'm giving you three months and then you're out', but she'd give you that opportunity and the credit. A lot of production companies aren't like that now. This was a time where you were thrown together with people from all walks of life, spending hours in edit suites talking about a shared love of movies until three in the morning. With people like Gareth Edwards, who was the graduate trainee at Hewland. He went on to direct *Star Wars: Rogue One*.

L.O.   **Luke Owen, Under Consoletation: The *GamesMaster* Podcast** *GamesMaster* was my favourite show in 1992, and it's still my favourite show 30 years later. The older I've become, the more I love and understand what it was. A show reflecting gaming culture with its own language and humour, where describing something as 'pants' or 'cack' became part of my own lexicon. Indeed, I once got in trouble at school for calling a book 'pants' and pleading with my teacher that Dominik Diamond had said it on *GamesMaster* so surely it was OK for me to say it.

I've slowly become obsessed again, which led to me reaching out to Ash Versus about starting a podcast reviewing every episode of the show in order in 2019. Never did I think that tweet would lead to me speaking with several people who worked on the show – including Dominik.

A.V.   **Ash Versus, Under Consoletation: The *GamesMaster* Podcast** As we've looked back with a more critical eye, it's been fascinating to see how quickly technology was moving at this time. In six short years *GamesMaster* moved through three generations of Nintendo consoles, two and a half consoles from Sega, a successful debut from Sony, less successful debuts from 3DO and Philips, and bore witness to the death spasms of Atari and Commodore. Despite the technological rollercoaster the series helped to highlight, it has become apparent that it was the other aspects of the show that have had a more lasting impact on me: the hosts, the humour, the use of language and wordplay, and the fact that above all else the show never talked down to its audience. We were always treated as adults – albeit adults with an occasional taste for joystick-related euphemisms.

Thirty years on from its debut, and I'm a fair bit older, and occasionally a little bit wiser. *GamesMaster* has aged too – some parts better than others – but it still stands head and shoulders above its contemporaries in one important regard. It's still steadfastly not cool; and that, to me, makes it the coolest show of them all.

J.H. I'm very grateful people remember *GamesMaster* so fondly. There's no show without an audience and we were very lucky people held it so dear at the time and all these years later. It was a big investment and a big risk to get it going but it was very exciting and an incredibly fun experience.

H.H. It was the first real television programme to acknowledge and celebrate the hysteria and excitement around videogames globally. My mum was quick to strike. She got the show on air and it hit the crest of that wave. The sense of nostalgia and of people looking back at their childhood and teenage years is why we remember it so fondly, myself included. It goes hand in hand with the excitement that people like us had at that time about videogames. It was like being there for the first motor car. Videogames really were something that changed the world.

I'm a dad now. I recently dusted off the NES, the same one mum gave me for Christmas all those years ago. The one that inspired the show. I've had it this whole time. I got it out of the attic for my six-year-old son to play with. It was a real bonding moment. And it lasted five minutes before it packed in. Typical. [Laughs.]

LET FOREVER BE EPILOGUE

The nineties couldn't last forever, could they? About a month after the last *GamesMaster* aired Phoebe told me she was with child. So I had to put aside foolish things like fun. I set up my own production company to make my shows for BBC Radio 5 Live and by the end of the decade I had a staff of 13 in London and the first of three children. I wasn't going to games industry parties any more because I was too busy trying to schmooze TV execs for commissions and watching *Buffy the Vampire Slayer* with my new baby daughter. I would like to say I kicked all the drugs and booze, but that sadly took a bit longer. That is the one bad thing that happened because of *GamesMaster*. Too much success too young and too much partying did create addictions I battle with to this day.

But I don't think you can take that aspect out of the nineties, I don't think any of us can. The nineties are not the nineties without strong lager and cocaine and bad behaviour. Sadly. I just wish that decade hadn't whizzed by so damned fast as a result of them. I was so lucky to not just live through it, but to be at the epicentre, to help create it. But it was a total whirlwind. I think of how time drags so slowly these days, and how boring most of life and work is. To be surrounded by that level of talented people, all working together, all believing in what they are doing and kicking the arse out of it partying and having a laugh? Whether that is us on *GamesMaster* or Robbie Williams or Noel and Liam. You are lucky to get a moment like that in your life. And I had it for a decade. And I am lucky that Jane Hewland remains a mentor to this day, and I am even more lucky that Jonny Ffinch is still the most intoxicatingly interesting human being I know. I love him to bits. His friendship has been one of the most enriching things in my life. And Kirk. Kirk is still Kirk, thankfully.

In terms of the legacy of the show itself? People say it was the last great youth show, and it probably was, but I also think it was the first great 'challenge' show. They reinvented *Top Gear* to include challenges. That was obviously our influence. And these days, what is *The Great British Bake Off* and *Sewing Bee* and *Art Whatever*? They are *GamesMaster* events with sugar and flour instead of Sega and Nintendo.

The legacy of the show lives on for me personally today and every day. Here's how it goes: No matter where I am in Canada – and I am lucky to have lived and worked coast to coast now – no matter where I am, there will be pockets of British expats who listen to my radio shows and will call up and go, 'GamesMaster!'

Or there will be a Canadian who I work with who will come up to me and say, 'I have a mate in the UK, and I was talking to them about you, and they can't believe I'm working with the guy from *GamesMaster*.'

I will always be synonymous with the show; the show will always be synonymous with me. And that's fine. Actually, that's more than fine. That is brilliant. People often ask me, after they've met me and asked loads of questions about *GamesMaster*, they will say, 'Sorry, I bet you get sick of talking about that show.'

But why would I? Does Paul McCartney get sick of talking about the White Album? Does Coppola get sick of talking about *The Godfather*? Millions of people dream about appearing on telly. A tiny fraction do. An even smaller fraction do a show that is a hit, and virtually none do a show that people still care about 30 years on. And I get messages from people who tell me how *GamesMaster* was the best part of their childhood, and that makes me happy. Because it was the best part of my childhood too. It's just that the best part of my childhood happened when I was in my twenties.

I just wish my kids realized what a big deal it was, then I might get more respect. But they are teenagers weaned on horrendous YouTubers shouting at each other over videogame footage. And they think that is videogames TV.

It's also ironic that I was worried about *GamesMaster* suffocating my career, when in fact it helped the only other part of it that was as much fun. The only time I ever felt I was working with similarly talented people smack bang in the middle of the zeitgeist: XFM Scotland a decade later. We were a brand new station, with a tiny budget, and yet we had every single big indie music star of the time appearing on it. Why? Because of *GamesMaster*. Because all those kids who watched the show ended up forming bands a decade later.

So you have this crazy situation of Arctic Monkeys playing Glasgow Carling Academy in 2006. Their tour bus is outside, surrounded by screaming fans, and every DJ from every radio station in Scotland is clamouring to get a few words as they exit. Meanwhile, I am actually in the tour bus. With them. And they are begging to play *Street Fighter 2* against me. That is how I ended up getting all those great interviews for XFM. That is how my pregnant wife Phoebe ends up sitting on Kaiser Chiefs' tour bus in New York City sipping apple juice in air-conditioned comfort while I sit interviewing Ricky Wilson on the street. That is how I become mates with The Fratellis and Glasvegas and Biffy Clyro. That is how I get Scottish Radio Presenter of the Year for that show. That is how I get a Sony Nomination for UK Music Personality of the Year. It's all because of *GamesMaster*.

So I am eternally grateful to it and all these truly brilliant, magical people who made it happen. Even Cameron.

EPILOGUE

EVENT	GAME	FORMAT	CHALLENGE	JOYSTICK
Challenge	Super Mario Bros. 3	NES	Collect 50 coins and exit level in 2 minutes	Win
Celebrity (John Fashanu)	Manchester Utd Europe	Amiga	Beat the opponent by scoring the most goals	Win (Opponent)
Challenge	Mad Dog McCree	Arcade	Rid the town of outlaws	Win
Challenge	Sonic the Hedgehog	Mega Drive	Collect 150 rings on Green Hill Zone, Act 2 within 2 minutes	Win
Celebrity (Gary Mason)	Sonic Blastman	Arcade	Beat the opponent with the highest combined score	Win (Opponent)
Challenge	Lemmings	Amiga	Save 91% of Lemmings within 2 minutes	Lose
Challenge	Mega Man 2	NES	Complete the level within 3 minutes	Lose
Celebrity (Annabel Croft)	Pro Tennis Tour 2	Amiga	Beat the opponent in a best-of-three tennis game	Win (Annabel)
Challenge	Zoom!	Mega Drive	Beat the grid within 1 minute	Lose
Challenge	Road Rash	Mega Drive	Complete the race in first place	Lose
Celebrity (Eric Bristow)	Helmdall	Amiga	Free the maiden within 2 minutes	Win (Opponent)
Challenge	Panza Kick Boxing	Amiga	Beat the opponent by knockout	Win
Challenge	Duck Tales	NES	Complete the level within 2 minutes 30 seconds	Win
Celebrity (Jimmy White)	Jimmy White's 'Whirlwind' Snooker	Amiga	Beat the opponent with the highest score within 1 minute 30 seconds	Win (Archer)
Challenge	Neighbours	Amiga	Complete the race in first place	Lose
Challenge	Top Player's Golf	Neo Geo	Achieve three holes in par	Lose
Celebrity (Pat Sharp vs. Mick Brown)	Ski or Die	Amiga	Beat the opponent with the highest combined score	Win (Mick)
Challenge	Brat	Amiga	Complete the level	Lose
Challenge	James Pond: Codename Robocod	Amiga	Complete level within 1 minute	Lose
Celebrity (Kendo Nagasaki)	WWF WrestleMania Challenge	NES	Beat the opponent into submission	Win (Opponent)
Challenge	Thunder Force III	Mega Drive	Complete the level in mania mode	Lose
Challenge	Strider	Mega Drive	Complete the level within 3 minutes	Win
Celebrity (Pat Cash vs. Emily Cash)	Baseball Stars Professional	Neo Geo	Beat the opponent by scoring the most goals	Win (Pat)
Challenge	Terminator 2: Judgment Day	Amiga	Reassemble the Terminator's face in 1 minute 40 seconds	Lose
Challenge	Zany Golf	Amiga	Complete the most holes without running out of shots	Win
Celebrity (Barry McGuigan)	Final Blow	Mega Drive	Beat the opponent into knockout	Win (Opponent)
Challenge	Shadow Dancer: The Secret of Shinobi	Mega Drive	Guide the warrior through the second and third levels within 2 minutes 30 seconds	Win
Challenge	Duck Hunt	NES	Shoot 8 out of 10 ducks / Shoot 9 out of 10 clay pigeons	Lose
Celebrity (Emlyn Hughes)	Emlyn Hughes International Soccer	Amiga	Beat the opponent by scoring the most goals	Win (Opponent)
Challenge	Decap Attack	Mega Drive	Complete the first two levels within 2 minutes	Win
Challenge	Street Fighter II: The World Warrior	SNES	Beat the opponent in a best-of-three fight	Win
Celebrity (Tony Slattery)	Who Shot Johnny Rock?	Arcade	Complete the level within three lives	Lose
Challenge	Dragon's Lair II: Time Warp	Arcade	Complete the first level in a single life	Lose
Challenge	Chuck Rock	Mega Drive	Complete the level within 1 minute 45 seconds	Lose
Celebrity (Frank Bruno)	Sonic Blastman	Arcade	Beat the opponent with the highest combined score	Win
Challenge	Zool	Amiga	Beat the opponent on a speed challenge	Win
Challenge	Super Mario World	SNES	Collect 200 coins and exit the level in 1 minute 15 seconds	Win
Celebrity (Vinnie Jones)	Soccer Brawl	Neo Geo	Beat the opponent by scoring the most goals	Win (Vinnie)
Danny Curley Challenge	Sonic the Hedgehog 2	Mega Drive	Beat Danny Curley on a speed challenge	Lose
Challenge	Fire & Ice	Amiga	Complete the level in 2 minutes	Lose
Celebrity (Rory Underwood)	Navy helicopter flight simulation	Amiga	Land the helicopter on a moving ship	Win (Opponent)
Danny Curley Challenge	Mario Lemieux Hockey	Mega Drive	Beat Danny Curley with the most goals	Lose

EVENT	GAME	FORMAT	CHALLENGE	JOYSTICK
Challenge	Pilotwings	SNES	Beat the opponent with the best landing	Win
Celebrity (Take That)	Dyna Blaster	Amiga	Beat the opponents to be the last player standing	Win (Robbie)
Danny Curley Challenge	Arch Rivals	Mega Drive	Beat Danny Curley by scoring the most goals	Win
Challenge	Mole Patrol	SNES	Blast 17 moles in 1 minute	Lose
Celebrity ('Hacksaw' Jim Duggan)	WWF Super WrestleMania	SNES	Beat the opponent into submission	Win (Opponent)
Challenge	King of the Monsters	Neo Geo	Beat the opponent in a best-of-three fight	Win
Challenge	Myth: History in the Making	Amiga	Complete the level in 1 minute 30 seconds	Lose
Celebrity (Jet vs. Shadow)	American Gladiators	Mega Drive	Beat the opponent in a speed challenge	Win (Shadow)
Challenge	Super Tennis	SNES	Beat the opponent in best of five games	Win
Challenge	The Addams Family	SNES	Collect 50 dollars and exit the level within 2 minutes	Lose
Celebrity (Kristian Schmid)	Space Pirates	Arcade	Rescue colonists	Lose
Challenge	Agony	Amiga	Complete the first level without losing a life	Lose
Challenge	Joe & Mac	SNES	Complete the first level within 1 minute 30 seconds	Win
Celebrity (John Parrott)	Archer Maclean's Pool	Amiga	Amass the highest score within 1 minute 30 seconds	Win (Opponent)
Challenge	Fatal Fury	Neo Geo	Beat the opponent in a best-of-three fight	Win
Challenge	Super Mario Kart	SNES	Complete the race in first place	Lose
Celebrity (Richard Norton)	Catch the Flag	Arcade	Inflict as many hits on opponent as possible within 3 minutes	Win (Draw)
Challenge	Pinball Fantasies	Amiga	Beat the opponents with the highest score within one ball	Win
Challenge	Palm Springs Open	Phillips CD-I	Complete the first three holes in level par	Lose
Celebrity (Johnny Herbert)	Lotus III: The Ultimate Challenge	Amiga	Complete the level in 1 minute 30 seconds	Lose
Challenge	Street Fighter II: The World Warrior	SNES	Beat the opponent in a best-of-three fight	Win
Challenge	The Humans	Amiga	Rescue the baby dinosaur in 1 minute 30 seconds	Win
Celebrity (Todd Carty)	Baseball Stars 2	Neo Geo	Beat the opponent with the highest score of runs	Win (Opponent)
Challenge	Street Fighter II: The World Warrior	SNES	Beat the opponent in a best-of-three fight	Win
Challenge	Christmas Capers	Amiga	Collect 20 presents within one life	Win
Celebrity (Bob Holness)	Volfied	Amiga	Fill in the screen within 1 minute	Win (Opponent)
Challenge	Street Fighter II: The World Warrior	SNES	Beat the opponent in a best-of-three fight	Win
Challenge	To the Earth	NES	Reach Uranus within one life	Lose
Celebrity (Linford Christie vs. Colin Jackson)	Quest for Gold	Neo Geo	Beat the opponents with the fastest possible time	Win (Colin)
Challenge	Streets of Rage 2	Mega Drive	Beat the opponent in a best-of-three fight	Win
Challenge	Taz-Mania	SNES	Complete the level within 2 minutes	Win
Celebrity (Ian Wright)	Super Kick Off	SNES	Beat the opponent by scoring the most goals	Win (Opponent)
Challenge	Nigel Mansell's World Championship	Amiga	Beat the opponent with the fastest lap time	Win
Challenge	Terminator 2: Judgment Day	SNES	Destroy T1000 within 1 minute 30 seconds	Win
Celebrity (Mark Wingett vs. Huw Higginson)	Gallagher's Gallery	Arcade	Beat the opponent with the highest score	Win (Mark)
British Nintendo Challenge	NCAA Basketball	SNES	Beat the British Nintendo champion with the highest score	Lose
Challenge	Road Rash II	Mega Drive	Win the race in first place	Lose
Celebrity (Cathy Dennis)	Global Gladiators	SNES	Complete the level within 2 minutes	Lose
British Nintendo Challenge	Super Soccer	SNES	Beat the British Nintendo champion by most goals scored	Lose
Challenge	Alien 3	Mega Drive	Rescue eight hostages and exit level within 2 minutes	Win
Celebrity (Ulrika Jonsson)	World Heroes	Neo Geo	Beat the opponent in a best-of-three fight	Win (Opponent)
British Nintendo Challenge	Pilotwings	SNES	Beat the British Nintendo champion with best landing	Win
Challenge	Disney's Magical Quest	SNES	Complete the level within 1 minute 30 seconds	Win

APPENDIX/CHALLENGES

	EVENT	GAME	FORMAT	CHALLENGE	JOYSTICK
SERIES TWO	Celebrity (Vic Reeves)	Sleepwalker	Amiga	Complete the level without waking Lee	Lose
	Challenge	Starfighter Ace	PC	Dock the mothership	Lose
	Challenge	Kid Chameleon	Mega Drive	Complete the level in 2 minutes	Win
	Celebrity (Gordon Burns)	Blastris	SNES	Construct five lines	Win
	Challenge	Football Frenzy	Neo Geo	First person to reach 10 points	Win
	Challenge	Bill's Tomato Game	Amiga	Complete the level within 1 minute	Win
	Celebrity (East 17)	Contra III: The Alien Wars	SNES	Complete the first level within four lives	Lose
	Challenge	Evander Holyfield's 'Real Deal' Boxing	Mega Drive	First knockout wins	Win
	Challenge	Lemmings 2: The Tribes	Amiga	Save 50 lemmings within 2 minutes	Win
	Celebrity (Josie Lawrence)	Mad Dog II: The Lost Gold	Arcade	Rescue the hostage within three lives	Win
	Multi-Format Magazine Challenge	Sonic the Hedgehog 2	Mega Drive	Beat the opponent in a speed challenge	Win
	Challenge	Captain Dynamo	Amiga	Complete the level within 1 minute 30 seconds	Win
	Celebrity (Tony Daley)	Strikerz	SNES	Beat the opponent by scoring the most goals	Win (Tony)
	Multi-Format Magazine Challenge	Sonic the Hedgehog 2	Mega Drive	Beat the opponent in a speed challenge	Win
	Challenge	Super Mario World	SNES	Complete the level in 1 minute 15 seconds	Lose
	Celebrity (Steve Backley)	The Games: Summer Challenge	PC	Beat the opponent with longest possible throw in javelin event	Win (Simon)
	Multi-Format Magazine Challenge	Sonic the Hedgehog 2	Mega Drive	Beat the opponent collecting most rings in bonus stage	Win
	Challenge	ActRaiser	SNES	Complete the first level within 1 minute 30 seconds	Lose
	Celebrity (Arm Wrestlers)	Arm Champs 2	Arcade	Beat the opponent with highest scoring arm wrestle	Win
	Challenge	Fiendish Freddy's Big Top O' Fun	Amiga	Complete four successful dives	Lose
	Challenge	Shadow of the Beast III	Mega Drive	Complete the level within 1 minute 30 seconds	Win
	Celebrity (Ice Hockey Players)	NHLPA Hockey '93	Mega Drive	Beat the opponent by scoring the most goals	Win
	Challenge	Mortal Kombat	Arcade	Beat the opponent in a best of three fight	Win
	Challenge	Mortal Kombat	SNES	Beat the opponents in a round-robin tournament	–
	Celebrity (Sonya Blade vs. Johnny Cage)	Mortal Kombat	Mega Drive	Beat the opponent in a best-of-three fight	Win
	Challenge	Mortal Kombat	Mega Drive	Beat the opponent in a best-of-three fight	Win
SERIES THREE	Challenge	Ultimate Soccer	Mega Drive	Beat the opponent team with the most goals	–
	Celebrity (Gabrielle)	King of the Monsters II	Neo Geo	Beat the opponent in a best-of-three fight	Win
	Challenge	Super Bomberman	SNES	Beat the opponents to be the last man standing	Win
	Challenge	James Pond's Crazy Sports	SNES	Beat the opponents in the fastest leapfrog record	–
	Gladiator's Supreme Challenge (Shadow vs. Falcon)	Clayfighter	SNES	Beat the opponent in a best-of-three fight	–
	Challenge	International Tennis Open	CDi	Beat the opponent in best of three rounds	Win
	Challenge	Mr Nutz	SNES	Beat the opponents in speed challenge to complete level	–
	Gladiator's Supreme Challenge (Cobra vs. Scorpio)	Clayfighter	SNES	Beat the opponent in a best-of-three fight	–
	Challenge	Muhammad Ali Heavyweight Boxing	Mega Drive	Beat the opponent in two rounds of boxing	Win
	Challenge	Streetfighter II Turbo: Hyper Fighting	SNES	Beat the opponents in a round-robin tournament	–
	Gladiator's Supreme Challenge (Shadow vs. Scorpio)	Clayfighter	SNES	Beat the opponent in a best-of-three fight	Win
	Challenge	Art of Fighting	Neo Geo	Beat the opponent in a best-of-three fight	Win
	Challenge	Micro Machines	Mega Drive	Beat the opponent collecting the most bonus points	–
	Celebrity (Utah Saints)	WWF Royal Rumble	SNES	Beat the opponent into submission	Win
	Challenge	Super Q*Bert 3	SNES	Colour the in-game pyramid within 1 minute	Win

EVENT	GAME	FORMAT	CHALLENGE	JOYSTICK
Challenge	Cosmic Spacehead	Mega Drive	Beat the opponent into submission	–
Celebrity (Steve Punt & Hugh Dennis)	Lucky & Wild	Arcade	Complete the level and bust the drug dealer	Lose
Challenge	The Jungle Book	Mega Drive	Collect 4,000 points within 1 minute	Lose
Challenge	Super Pang	SNES	Beat the opponents by popping balloons the longest	–
Celebrity (Sean Maguire)	Striker	SNES	Beat the opponent by scoring the most goals	Win
Challenge	Robocop versus The Terminator	Mega Drive	Complete the level as Robocop within 1 minute	Win
Challenge	Super Mario All Stars	SNES	Beat the opponent by completing the level in the quickest time	–
Celebrity (Monie Love)	Cool Spot	SNES	Beat the opponents with the highest score within 1 minute	Win (Opponent)
Challenge	F1	Mega Drive	Complete the Monte Carlo circuit within 1 minute	Lose
Challenge	Aladdin	SNES	Beat the opponents by collecting the most diamonds within 45 seconds	Win
Celebrity (Nigel Benn & Barry McGuigan)	Sonic Blastman	Arcade	Beat the opponent with the highest combined score	Win (Nigel)
Challenge	Street Fighter II	Mega Drive	Beat the opponents by surviving five single rounds	Win
Challenge	Puggsy	Mega Drive	Beat the opponent in a speed challenge to complete the level	–
Celebrity (Dani Behr)	Monkey Mole Panic	Arcade	Beat the opponent by bashing the most moles	Win (Dani)
Challenge	Batman Returns	Mega CD	Clear two stages and defeat boss	Win
Challenge	Busby in Claws Encounters of the Furred Kind	Mega Drive	Beat the opponent by collecting the most yarn balls within 1 minute	–
Celebrity (Liam Botham)	Graham Gooch World Class Cricket	Amiga	Beat the opponent with the highest combined score	Win (Opponent)
Challenge	Jungle Strike	Mega Drive	Protect the president and reach the White House	Win
Team Championship	Aladdin	Mega Drive	Collect the most apples within 45 seconds	–
Team Championship	Val d'Isère Snowboarding	SNES	Snowboard through the gates in quickest time	–
Celebrity Soccer Championship (Vinnie Jones vs. Les Ferdinand)	Fifa International Soccer	Mega Drive	Beat the opponent by scoring the most goals	–
Team Championship	World Heroes 2	Neo Geo	Beat the opponent in a best-of-three fight	–
Team Championship	Skyblazer	SNES	Collect 50 diamonds in the quickest time	–
Team Championship	Dr. Robotnik's Mean Bean Machine	Mega Drive	Collect as many beans as possible in 45 seconds	–
Celebrity Soccer Championship (Dennis Wise vs. John Barnes)	Fifa International Soccer	Mega Drive	Beat the opponent by scoring the most goals	–
Team Championship	Teenage Mutant Ninja Turtles: Tournament Fighters	SNES	Beat the opponent in a best-of-three fight	–
Team Championship	Street Fighter II: Championship Edition	Mega Drive	Beat the opponent in round-robin tournament	–
Team Championship	Magic Boy	SNES	Bag the most animals in 45 seconds	–
Celebrity Soccer Championship (Vinnie Jones vs. John Barnes)	Fifa International Soccer	Mega Drive	Beat the opponent by scoring the most goals	Win (Vinnie)
Team Championship	Davis Cup World Tour	Mega Drive	Score as many points as possible within ten balls	–
Panto Team Championship	Adventures of Yogi Bear	SNES	Collect as many clocks as possible within 45 seconds	–
Panto Team Championship	Alfred Chicken	SNES	Collect as many diamonds as possible within 45 seconds	–
Celebrity (Frank Bruno)	Greatest Heavyweights	Mega Drive	Beat the opponent into knockout	Win (Opponent)
Panto Team Championship	Holiday Lemmings	Amiga	Beat the opponent to save the highest percentage of Lemmings	Win
Team Championship	Super Star Wars: The Empire Strikes Back	SNES	Collect as many points as possible within 45 seconds	–
Team Championship	Dragon's Revenge	Mega Drive	Render the tree boss armless in the quickest time possible	–
Celebrity (Games Mistress)	Lethal Enforcers	Mega Drive	Collect as many points as possible	Win (Opponent)

APPENDIX/CHALLENGES

EVENT	GAME	FORMAT	CHALLENGE	JOYSTICK
Team Championship	Elfmania	Amiga	Beat the opponent in a best-of-three fight	–
Team Championship	Top Gear 2	SNES	Complete the lap of Australian circuit in the quickest time	–
Team Championship	Tinhead	Mega Drive	Score the highest number of points within 45 seconds	–
Celebrity (Simone Robertson)	Plok	SNES	Beat the opponent by completing the level in the quickest time	Win (Opponent)
Team Championship	3 Count Bout	Neo Geo	Beat the opponent into submission	–
Team Championship	Samurai Shodown	Neo Geo	Beat the opponents in a round-robin tournament	–
Team Championship	Pop'n TwinBee: Rainbow Bell Adventures	SNES	Collect as many coins as possible within 45 seconds	–
Team Championship	Mortal Kombat	Mega Drive	Beat the opponent in a single-round fight	–
Celebrity (Kriss Akabusi)	James Pond 3	Mega Drive	Beat the opponent by completing the level in the quickest time	Win (Kriss)
Team Championship	NBA Jam	SNES	Beat the opponent by scoring the most goals	–
Team Championship	Eternal Champions	Mega Drive	Beat the opponents in a round-robin tournament	–
Team Championship	Bubba 'N' Stix	Mega Drive	Collect as many points as possible within 45 seconds	–
Celebrity (Andrew Paul vs. Lisa Geoghan)	Terminator 2	SNES	Score as many points as possible within 45 seconds	Win (Andrew)
Team Championship	Super Goal 2	SNES	Beat the opponent by scoring the most goals	–
Team Championship	Adventures of Yogi Bear	SNES	Collect as many clocks as possible within 45 seconds	–
Team Championship	Lotus Turbo Challenge 2	Mega Drive	Drive the furthest distance within 45 seconds	–
Celebrity (Ronnie O'Sullivan)	Side Pocket	SNES	Beat the opponent with highest combined score	Win (Opponent)
Team Championship	Jammit	Mega Drive	Beat the opponents as the first to score five baskets	–
Team Championship	Skitcin	Mega Drive	Beat the opponent with the highest ranking position in the race within 45 seconds	–
Team Championship	Jim Power	SNES	Collect as many points as possible within 45 seconds	–
Celebrity (Macho Man Randy Savage)	WWF Rage in the Cage	Sega CD	Beat the opponent into submission	Win (Opponent)
Team Championship	Legends of the Ring	SNES	Beat the opponent into knockout	–
Team Championship Semi-Final #1	Starwing	SNES	Score as many points as possible within 45 seconds	–
Team Championship Semi-Final #1	Sonic the Hedgehog	Mega Drive	Complete the level in the fastest possible time	–
Team Championship Semi-Final #1	World Heroes 2	Neo Geo	Beat the opponent in a single-round fight	–
Celebrity (2 Unlimited)	Fatal Fury 2	Neo Geo	Beat the opponent in a best-of-three fight	Win (Ray)
Team Championship Semi-Final #1	Mario Kart	SNES	Beat the opponent in a race to the finish line	–
Team Championship Semi-Final #2	Mortal Kombat	Mega Drive	Beat the opponent in a round-robin tournament	–
Team Championship Semi-Final #2	Super Mario All Stars	SNES	Complete the level as quickly as possible	–
Celebrity (Crash Dummies)	The Incredible Crash Dummies	Mega Drive	Beat the opponent by completing the level in the quickest time	Win (Spin)
Team Championship Semi-Final #2	Striker	SNES	Beat the opponent by scoring the most goals	–
Team Championship Semi-Final #3	Aladdin	Mega Drive	Collect as many apples as possible within 45 seconds	–
Team Championship Semi-Final #3	Pilotwings	SNES	Steer the parachutist to score the highest points	–
Celebrity (Bad Boys Inc.)	Star Wars: Rebel Assault	PC	Survive the longest duration in the X-Wing	Win (Tony)
Team Championship Semi-Final #3	Street Fighter II Turbo: Hyper Fighting	SNES	Beat the opponent in a best-of-three fight	–
Team Championship Final	Cybermorph	Atari Jaguar	Collect 18 pods within 45 seconds	–
Team Championship Final	Rise of the Robots	PC	Beat the opponent in a round-robin tournament	–

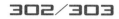

	EVENT	GAME	FORMAT	CHALLENGE	JOYSTICK
	Team Championship Final	Sonic CD	Sega CD	Complete the level in the fastest possible time	–
	Team Championship Final	Street Fighter II Turbo: Hyper Fighting	SNES	Beat the opponent in a best-of-three fight	–
	Team Championship Final	Striker	SNES	Beat the opponent by scoring the most goals	Win
	Challenge	Mortal Kombat II	SNES	Beat Baraka in a best-of-three fight	Lose
	Celebrity (Frank Skinner)	Super Sidekicks 2	Neo Geo	Beat the opponent by scoring the most goals	Win (Opponent)
	Challenge	Earthworm Jim	Mega Drive	Collect the most neutron capsules within 1 minute	Win
	Challenge	Road Rash	3DO	Complete the race in first place	Win
	Celebrity (Bruce Roberts vs. Dan Falzon vs. Sarah Vandenbergh)	Dragon	SNES	Beat the opponents to be the last player standing	Win (Bruce)
	Challenge	Primal Rage	Arcade	Beat the opponent in a best-of-three fight	Win
	Challenge	Novastorm	3DO	Score as many points as possible within 1 minute	Win
	Celebrity (Jimmy White)	Jimmy White's 'Whirlwind' Snooker	Mega Drive	Clear the snooker table before the computer opponent	Win
	Challenge	Top Hunter: Roddy & Cathy	Neo Geo	Score as many points as possible within 1 minute	Win
	Challenge	Sonic 3	Mega Drive	Beat the opponent by completing the level as quickly as possible	Win
	Celebrity (PJ & Duncan)	Street Racer	SNES	Complete the race in first place	Lose
	Challenge	Sonic & Knuckles	Mega Drive	Beat the opponent by collecting the most rings within 45 seconds	Win
	Challenge	Echo the Dolphin 2	Mega Drive	Beat the opponents by completing the level as quickly as possible	Win
	Celebrity Football Tournament (Andrew Cole vs. Kasey Keller)	FIFA Soccer 95	Mega Drive	Beat the opponent by scoring the most goals	Win (Kasey)
	Challenge	Way of the Warrior	3DO	Beat the opponent in a best-of-three fight	Win
	Challenge	Donkey Kong	NES	Beat the opponent by completing the level in the quickest time	Win
	Celebrity Football Tournament (Andy Townsend vs. Vinnie Jones)	FIFA Soccer 95	Mega Drive	Beat the opponent by scoring the most goals	Win (Andy)
	Challenge	Donkey Kong Country	SNES	Beat the opponent by completing the level in the quickest time	Win
	Challenge	The Lion King	Mega Drive	Beat the opponent by completing the level in the quickest time	Win
	Celebrity Football Tournament (Kasey Keller vs. Andy Townsend)	FIFA Soccer 95	Mega Drive	Beat the opponent by scoring the most goals	Win (Andy)
	Challenge	Power Drive	SNES	Perform five precision manoeuvres within 1 minute	Lose
	Celebrity (Ian Kelsey vs. Camilla Power)	Clayfighter 2	SNES	Beat the opponent in a best-of-three fight	Win (Ian)
	Challenge	Super Star Wars: Return of the Jedi	SNES	Beat the opponents by collecting the most points within 45 seconds	Win
	Celebrity (Rupert Moon vs. Dewi Morris)	Rugby World Cup 1995	Mega Drive	Beat the opponent by scoring the most goals	Win (Rupert)
	Challenge	The King of Fighters '94	Neo Geo	Beat the opponent in a best-of-three fight	Win
	Challenge	Mickey Mania	Mega Drive	Collect as many points as possible within 1 minute	Win
	Celebrity (Let Loose)	Vid Grid	PC	Unscramble two music videos within 2 minutes	Lose
	Challenge	Creature Shock	PC	Defeat two monsters before running out of health	Win
	Challenge	PGA Tour Golf III	Mega Drive	Complete the course within 2 minutes	Lose
	Celebrity (C.J. Lewis)	Chaos Control	CDi	Beat the opponent by scoring the most points	Win (C.J. Lewis)
	Challenge	Boogerman: A Pick and Flick Adventure	Mega Drive	Beat the opponent by scoring the most points within 45 seconds	Win
	Challenge	Super Bomberman 2	SNES	Beat the opponents to be the last player standing	Win
	Celebrity (Marcus Alexander Bagwell vs. Del Wilkes)	Fatal Fury Special	SNES	Beat the opponent in a best-of-three fight	Win (Marcus)
	Challenge	Twisted	3DO	Beat the opponents, completing tasks in the quickest time	Win

APPENDIX/CHALLENGES

	EVENT	GAME	FORMAT	CHALLENGE	JOYSTICK
SERIES FOUR	Celebrity (David Coulthard)	Super Karts	PC	Complete the race in first place	Lose
	Christmas Beach Special (John Major vs. Kylie Minogue)	Windjammers	Neo Geo	Beat the opponent by scoring the most points	Win (Kylie)
	Christmas Beach Special (Fake That)	Smash Tennis	SNES	Beat the opponents, best of three games	Win (Jason & Mark)
	Christmas Beach Special (Michael Jackson vs. Macaulay Culkin)	Buggy Ball	Arcade	Beat the opponent by scoring the most points	Abandoned
	Challenge	The Smurfs	SNES	Beat the opponent by completing the level in the quickest time	Win
	Celebrity (Roger Black vs. Du'aine Ladejo)	Numan Athletics	Arcade	Beat the opponent in best of three rounds	Win (Du'aine)
	Challenge	Whizz	Mega Drive	Complete the level within 2 minutes	Win
	Celebrity (Prince Naseem)	Super Punch-Out!!	SNES	Beat the computer opponent to knockout	Win
	Challenge	Darkstalkers: The Night Warriors	Arcade	Beat the opponent in a best-of-three fight	Win
	Celebrity (Natalie Imbruglia)	Kid Klown in Crazy Chase	SNES	Collect as many coins as possible within 1 minute	Win (Opponent)
	Gore Special	Kasumi Ninja	Atari Jaguar	Beat the opponent in a best-of-three fight	Win
	Gore Special	Alien vs. Predator	Atari Jaguar	Score as many points as possible within 1 minute	Abandoned
	Gore Special	Doom II: Hell on Earth	PC	Kill 25 monsters within 2 minutes	Win
SERIES FIVE	Celebrity (The Shamen)	Wipeout	PlayStation	Beat the opponent in race to first place	Win (Mr C)
	Baby Rom	Baby Rom	PC	Collect three clapping babies	Lose
	Cracking Blokes	Tekken 2	Arcade	Beat the opponents with the three best special moves	Win
	Celebrity (Jadene Doran)	Alpine Racer	Arcade	Complete the race before the clock runs out	Win
	Schwiiing (Stephen Hendry)	Smart Golf	Arcade	Par two holes	Win (Opponent)
	Challenge	Mortal Kombat 3	PlayStation	Beat the computer opponent in a best-of-three fight	Win
	Rozzer Rumble	Virtua Cop	Arcade	Complete the game and achieve a perfect score	Win
	Celebrity (Donna Air vs. Vicky Taylor)	King of Fighters '95	Neo Geo	Beat the opponent in a best-of-three fight	Win (Donna)
	Challenge	Destruction Derby	PlayStation	Beat the opponent by lasting the longest without car damage	Win
	Mr & Mrs (Stuart Wade & Tonicha Jeronimo)	Cupid Bug	Arcade Saturn	Correctly guess partner's multiple-choice answers Collect 14 blue crystals while blindfolded	Win Win
	King Combo	Killer Instinct	Arcade	Pull off a combo with the highest number of moves	Win
	Celebrity Football Tournament (Dean Holdsworth vs. David Kerslake)	Winning Eleven	PlayStation	Beat the opponent by scoring the most goals	Win (Dean)
	Three's a Crowd	Puzzle Bobble	Neo Geo	Destroy bubbles across three simultaneous screens	Lose
	Celebrity Football Tournament (Phil Babb vs. Graeme Le Saux)	Winning Eleven	PlayStation	Beat the opponent by scoring the most goals	Win (Phil)
	The Executioner	Mortal Kombat 3 Primal Rage Killer Instinct	SNES 3DO SNES	Complete three death moves from three separate games	Win
	Celebrity Football Tournament (Dean Holdsworth vs. Phil Babb)	Virtua Striker	Arcade	Beat the opponent by scoring the most goals	Win (Dean)
	Is the Net Full of Cak?	The internet	World Wide Web	Find five things of interest on the internet	Win
	Celebrity (Johnny Herbert vs. Mark Blundell)	Sega Rally	Arcade	Beat the opponent in a race to first place	Win (Johnny)
	Gladiators – Hard? Don't Make Me Laugh! (Cobra & Panther)	Victory Boxing WWF WrestleMania: The Arcade Game	Saturn PlayStation	Beat the opponent with most points or knockout Beat the opponent to submission	Win (Opponent)
	Get That Celebrity On the Phone Now! (Ronnie O'Sullivan)	Virtual Pool	PC	Beat the opponent to sink the nine ball	Win
	Oi! Bloke In Suit – Fancy a Fight?	Doom	PC	Beat the opponents in a deathmatch	Win
	Celebrity (E.Y.C.)	Super Bomberman 3	SNES	Beat the opponents to be the last player standing	Win (David)

EVENT	GAME	FORMAT	CHALLENGE	JOYSTICK
Virtually Perfect	Virtua Fighter 2	Saturn	Beat the opponents by defeating the most computer opponents	Win
Celebrity (Whigfield)	Super Mario World 2: Yoshi's Island	SNES	Collect 32 coins from two levels within 2 minutes	Win
PC Impossible (Dean Gaffney vs. Patsy Palmer)	Testing intellect and problem-solving abilities	PC	Set up a new PC and install a game	Lose
Challenge	Duke Nukem 3D	PC	Beat the opponents to blow up a canister in the fastest time	Win
Blokes with Bikes (Mr Motivator)	Virtual Reality Exercise Bike Cyber Cycles	PC Arcade	Beat the opponent with the fastest speed time	Win (Opponent)
Blokes on Film (Stewart Lee vs. Richard Herring)	Director's Lab	PC	Beat the opponent with the best movie masterpiece	Win (Richard)
Challenge	Total NBA '96	PlayStation	Beat the opponent by scoring the most goals	Win
Blokes Who Sweat Rock 'N' Roll (Janick Gers)	Quest for Fame	PC	Inspire six audience members to dance by the end of the song	Win
Challenge	Rave Racer	Arcade	Beat the opponent to win first place	Win
Challenge	Mario 64	N64	Complete the final level within 2 minutes Defeat Bowser within 1 minute	Win
Celebrity (Sam Fox)	Aqua Jet	Arcade	Complete the race before the clock runs out	Win
King of Combos '96	Killer Instinct Gold	N64	Compete against each other to pull off the biggest combo	Win
Celebrity (Danny John-Jules)	Wipeout 2097	PlayStation	Complete the race in first place	Lose
We're Athletic, We Like Lycra (John Regis vs. Tony Jarrett)	Athlete Kings	Saturn	Compete in the 100m/Compete in the long jump Compete in the 110m hurdles/Compete in the javelin	Win (John)
I Have Violence, I Am Happy	Quake	PC	Complete the custom-built GamesMaster level	Win
Celebrity (Paul Leyshon)	Die Hard With a Vengeance	PlayStation	Defuse four bombs	Win
You Only Live Twice	Virtua Cop 2	Arcade	Complete two Virtua Cop 2 machines simultaneously	Lose
Celebrity (Uri Geller)	Mind Drive	PC	Use will power alone to steer the skier through 15 gates	Win
Shoot Down the Shops and Get Us a Paper	Gunblade	Arcade	Complete the game within one credit	Lose
Celebrity Football Tournament (Richard Rufus vs. Michael Duberry)	Sega Worldwide Soccer 97	Saturn	Beat the opponent by scoring the most goals	Win (Richard)
The Boss	Star Gladiators NiGHTS Resident Evil		Beat the Bilstein boss/Beat the Puffy boss Beat the spider boss	Win
Celebrity Football Tournament (Chris Armstrong vs. Rik Henderson)	Sega Worldwide Soccer 97	Saturn	Beat the opponent by scoring the most goals	Win (Chris)
Four Ninja Kids	Virtua Fighter Kids	Saturn	Beat the opponents in a round-robin tournament	Win
Celebrity Football Tournament (Richard Rufus vs. Chris Armstrong)	Sega Worldwide Soccer 97	Saturn	Beat the opponent by scoring the most goals	Win (Richard)
Christmas Quiz	Mario 64	N64	Achieve the best time on the ice slide	Win
Platform Queen	Donkey Kong Country 3: Dixie Kong's Double Spider Crash Bandicoot	SNES PlayStation PlayStation	Collect 30 bananas/Collect 30 DNA triangles Collect 20 apples	Lose
Celebrity (Zoe Ball)	Manx TT Superbike	Arcade	Complete the race in fifth position or above	Lose
Short Sharp Shock	Street Fighter Alpha 2	PlayStation	Beat the opponents in the fastest round to beat Ken	Win
Celebrity (Deepak Verma)	Destruction Derby 2	PlayStation	Survive for 2 minutes in a destruction derby	Win
Tiny Car Kid	Ridge Racer	Arcade	Complete the race within the top three positions	Win
Celebrity (Bear Van Beers)	Sonic 3D	Sega Mega Drive	Rescue five flickies and guide them to safety in 2 minutes	Lose
Tetsujin	Virtua Fighter 2	Arcade	Beat 90 out of 100 opponents	Win
Celebrity (Tracy Shaw)	Alpine Surfer	Arcade	Get to the bottom of the mountain before the time runs out	Win
Til Death Do Us Part	Die Hard	Arcade	Work as a duo to complete all 20 levels within two lives	Win

APPENDIX/CHALLENGES

EVENT	GAME	FORMAT	CHALLENGE	JOYSTICK
Celebrity (Adam Hollioake vs. Phil Tufnell)	Home Run Derby VR	Arcade	Beat the opponent with the highest combined score	Win (Adam)
Some Brothers Do 'Ave 'Em	Sonic Championship	Saturn	Beat the opponents in a best-of-five-round fight	Win
Celebrity (Paul McKenna)	Blast Corps	N64	Protect the nuclear weapon being transported to safety	Lose
Hot 4-way Action	Super EF 2000	PC	Beat three opponents in air combat	Win
Celebrity (The Brotherhood)	Wave Race 64	N64	Beat the opponent with the highest score over two rounds	Win (Shylock)
Things With Wings	Pilotwings	N64	Navigate the gyrocopter through 10 rings/Score a 25-point bullseye on the cannonball level Shoot down 10 balloons	Win
Celebrity (Gene)	Sega Touring Car Championship	Arcade	Beat the opponent in a speed race	Win
Triple XXX Action	Time Crisis	Arcade	Beat the opponent in a speed challenge	Win
Celebrity (Michael Fish)	Prop Cycle	Arcade	Amass 2,000 points before the clock runs out	Lose
The Two Big Tombs of Lara Croft	Tomb Raider II	PC	Beat the opponent in a race to complete the level	Win
Celebrity (Jo Guest)	Rampage World Tour	PlayStation	Earn 10,000 points within 1 minute 30 seconds	Win
Oi Bloke! Fiddle Around With My Character	Mortal Kombat 4	Arcade	Beat the opponents by discovering the highest number of special moves	Win
Celebrity (Kaleef)	PaRappa the Rapper	PlayStation	Finish the rap with a good rating	Win
Three Big Men Get Hard	GoldenEye 007	N64	Rescue two hostages from a hijacked frigate/Race through the city streets in a stolen tank/Stop the train, rescue the hostage and exit the level	Win Win Lose
Celebrity (Ryan Rhodes vs. Khalid Shafiq)	Street Fighter EX Plus a	PlayStation	Beat the opponent in a best-of-three fight	Win (Ryan)
Oi Bloke! Get Off My Halfpipe	Top Skater	Arcade	Beat the opponents with the most trick points within 1 minute	Win
Celebrity (Sol Campbell vs. Christian Dailly)	Sega Worldwide Soccer 98	Saturn	Beat the opponent by scoring the most goals	Win (Christian)
If You Think This Is Hard Just Wait 'Til You Hit Puberty	Crash Bandicoot 2: Cortex Strikes Back	PlayStation	Evade polar bears and complete level riding a baby polar bear	Win Win
Celebrity (Emma Harrison)	Rapid River	Arcade	Win the race before the time runs out	Win
Buff My Helmet For Extra Speed	Motocross Go!	Arcade	Beat the opponent in a race to complete the level	Win
Celebrity (All Saints)	Poy Poy	PlayStation	Beat the opponents to be the last player standing	Win (Nicole)
I'll Move That Gear Stick Manually, If You Don't Mind	Gran Turismo	PlayStation	Beat the opponents by recording the fastest lap	Win
Celebrity (Sarah Vandenbergh vs. Carryl Varley)	Armadillo Racing	Arcade	Beat the opponents in a race to complete the level	Win (Sarah)
Oi, Raptor - Bring Back My Leg	The Lost World: Jurassic Park	Arace	Compete as a team to complete game on a single credit	Win
Celebrity (Catalina Guirado)	Rosco McQueen: Firefighter Extreme	PlayStation	Clear three levels within 2 minutes 30 seconds	Win
Oi, Bloke From Another Country, Are You Starting?	Tekken 3	Arcade	Beat the opponents in a world tournament	Win (Japan)
Celebrity (Emma Noble vs. Debbie Flett)	Final Furlong	Arcade	Beat the opponent in a race to first place	Win (Debbie)

%	GAME	FORMAT	SERIES		%	GAME	FORMAT	SERIES
97%	Sensible Soccer	Amiga	2		90%	Alone in the Dark 2	PC	3
97%	Tekken	PlayStation	5		90%	Sonic 3	Mega Drive	3
96%	Virtua Fighter	Saturn	4		90%	Virtua Racing Deluxe	Sega 32x	4
96%	Killer Instinct	SNES	5		90%	Donkey Kong Country	SNES	4
96%	Hexen	PC	5		90%	Magic Carpet	PC	4
95%	John Madden Football '92	Mega Drive	1		90%	Super Street Fighter II Turbo	3DO	4
95%	FIFA International Soccer	Mega Drive	3		90%	Uni Racers	SNES	4
95%	Smash Tennis	SNES	4		90%	Mortal Kombat III	PlayStation	5
95%	Star Wars: Dark Forces	PC	4		90%	Victory Boxing	Saturn	5
95%	Sega Rally Championship	Saturn	5		90%	Time Crisis	Arcade	5
95%	Virtua Cop	Saturn	5		90%	Worms	Saturn	5
95%	Virtua Fighter II	Saturn	5		90%	Krazy Ivan	PlayStation	5
95%	Donkey Kong Country 2: Diddy's Kong Quest	SNES	5		90%	Turok: Dinosaur Hunter	N64	6
94%	Populous 2: Trials of the Olympian Gods	Amiga	1		90%	Final Fantasy VII	PlayStation	7
					90%	Nightmare Creatures	PlayStation	7
94%	Monkey Island 2: LeChuck's Revenge	PC	1		89%	Formula I Grand Prix	Amiga	1
					89%	Bart Simpson's Escape from Camp Deadly	Game Boy	1
94%	Sim City	SNES	2		89%	Leisure Suit Larry 5: Passionate Patti Does a Little Undercover Work	PC	1
94%	Flashback	Amiga	2					
94%	Comanche: Maximum Overkill	PC	2					
94%	Starfox	SNES	2		89%	Dynamite Headdy	Sega Mega Drive	4
94%	Earthworm Jim	SNES	4					
94%	Wipeout	PlayStation	5		89%	Screamer	PC	5
94%	Super Mario World 2: Yoshi's Island	SNES	5		89%	Viewpoint	PlayStation	5
					89%	X-Men: Children of the Atom	Saturn	5
94%	Earthworm Jim 2	Mega Drive	5		89%	Killer Instinct Gold	N64	6
93%	Indiana Jones and the Fate of Atlantis	PC	1		89%	Shadow Master	PlayStation	7
					88%	Doom II: Hell on Earth	PC	4
93%	Goal Storm	PlayStation	5		88%	Cannon Fodder	Mega Drive	4
93%	Actua Soccer	PC	5		88%	Battle Arena Toshinden	PlayStation	5
93%	Rayman	Saturn	5		88%	The Dig	PC	5
93%	Yoshi's Story	N64	7		88%	Fighting Vipers	Saturn	6
92%	Street Fighter II: Champion Edition	Mega Drive	3		88%	Soul Edge	PlayStation	6
					88%	Screamer Rally	PC	7
92%	Dune II	Mega Drive	3		88%	Crash Bandicoot 2: Cortex Strikes Back	PlayStation	7
92%	Sensible Soccer	Mega Drive	3					
92%	NBA Jam	Mega Drive	3		87%	The Terminator	Mega Drive	1
92%	Micro Machines 2: Turbo Tournament	Mega Drive	4		87%	Krusty's Super Fun House	Mega Drive	2
92%	WWF WrestleMania: The Arcade Game	PlayStation	5		87%	The New Zealand Story	Master System	2
					87%	Legends of Valour	PC	2
92%	Time Gate	PC	5		87%	The Legacy: Realms of Terror	PC	2
91%	Speedball 2: Brutal Deluxe	Master System	2		87%	John Madden Football '93	Mega Drive	2
91%	Tornado	PC	2		87%	Super Swiv	SNES	2
91%	Air Warrior	PC	2		87%	Harrier Jump Jet	PC	2
91%	Sid Meier's Pirates	NES	2		87%	Frontier: Elite II	PC	2
91%	Cyberspace	PC	2		87%	Super Star Wars	SNES	2
91%	Mega Bomberman	Mega Drive	4		87%	Axelay	SNES	2
91%	Street Racer	SNES	4		87%	Front Page Football	PC	2
91%	Sensible World of Soccer	Amiga	4		87%	Dropzone	NES	2
90%	First Samurai	Amiga	1		87%	Mega-Lo Mania	Mega Drive	2
90%	Zombies Ate My Neighbors	SNES	3		87%	Micro Machines	Mega Drive	2
90%	Gunstar Heroes	Mega Drive	3		87%	The Lion King	SNES	4
90%	Cannon Fodder	Amiga	3		87%	Panzer Dragoon Saga	Saturn	7
90%	ToeJam & Earl in Panic on Funkotron	Mega Drive	3					

%	GAME	FORMAT	
86%	Street Fighter II Turbo: Hyper Fighter	SNES	3
86%	Rock 'N' Roll Racing	SNES	3
86%	Lamborghini American Challenge	Game Boy	3
86%	Flashback	SNES	3
86%	RoboCop Versus The Terminator	Mega Drive	3
86%	Young Merlin	SNES	3
86%	Aero the Acrobat	SNES	3
86%	The Lawnmower Man	SNES	3
86%	Soccer Kid	SNES	3
86%	FIFA 96	PC	5
86%	Tintin in Tibet	SNES	5
86%	FIFA 97	PlayStation	6
86%	NBA Jam Extreme	PlayStation	6
85%	Speedball 2: Brutal Deluxe	Mega Drive	1
85%	Sonic Triple Trouble	Game Gear	4
85%	Zeewolf	Amiga	4
85%	Star Wars Deluxe	Sega 32x	4
85%	Ridge Racer Revolution	PlayStation	5
85%	Wave Race 64	N64	6
85%	Soviet Strike	PlayStation	6
85%	Tomb Raider	PlayStation	6
85%	Star Gladiator	PlayStation	6
85%	Virtua Cop 2	Saturn	6
85%	Phantasmagoria 2: A Puzzle of Flesh	PC	6
85%	Destruction Derby II	PlayStation	6
85%	Star Wars: Dark Forces	PlayStation	6
85%	Diddy Kong Racing	N64	7
85%	Postal	PC	7
84%	Darklands	PC	2
84%	KGB	PC	2
84%	World Class Leaderboard	Mega Drive	2
84%	Ragnarok	PC	2
84%	Super Off Road	Game Gear	2
84%	Jeep Jamboree	Game Boy	2
84%	Eye of the Storm	PC	2
84%	Gods	SNES	2
84%	Populous II	Mega Drive	2
84%	FIFA International Soccer	3DO	4
84%	Virtua Fighter Remix	Saturn	5
84%	Jet Rider	PlayStation	6
84%	Bloody Roar	PlayStation	7
83%	Alien vs. Predator	Atari Jaguar	4
83%	Indiana Jones' Greatest Adventures	SNES	4
83%	Virtual On: Cyber Troopers	Saturn	6
83%	Amok	Saturn	6
83%	SkyNET	PC	6
82%	Vectorman	Mega Drive	5
82%	Cool Borders	PlayStation	6
81%	Mortal Kombat	SNES	3
81%	Thunderhawk	Mega CD	3
81%	Pac-Attack	SNES	3

%	GAME	FORMAT	SERIES
81%	Jurassic Park	SNES	3
81%	Top Gear 2	SNES	3
81%	Cybermorph	Atari Jaguar	3
81%	Eternal Champions	Mega Drive	3
81%	The Legend of the Mystical Ninja	SNES	3
81%	Empire Soccer	SNES	3
81%	Twisted	3DO	4
81%	Pitfall: The Mayan Adventure	SNES	4
81%	Zero the Kamikaze Squirrel	SNES	4
81%	Hi-Octane	Saturn	5
81%	Victory Boxing '97	PlayStation	6
80%	The Immortal	NES	1
80%	Birds of Prey	Amiga	1
80%	Knights of the Sky	Amiga	1
80%	Teenage Mutant Ninja Turtles: Turtles in Time	SNES	2
80%	Scrabble	PC	2
80%	Prince of Persia	Master System	2
80%	David Crane's Amazing Tennis	SNES	2
80%	Universal Soldier	Game Boy	2
80%	Star Wars	Game Boy	2
80%	Probotector II: Return of the Evil Forces	NES	2
80%	Jimmy Connors Pro Tennis Tour	SNES	2
80%	The Lost Vikings	SNES	2
80%	Eliminator Boat Duel	NES	2
80%	Ballz	Mega Drive	4
80%	Inferno	PC	4
80%	Animaniacs	SNES	4
80%	Bloodshot	Mega Drive	4
80%	Road Rash 3	Mega Drive	4
80%	Destruction Derby	PlayStation	5
80%	Golden Axe: The Duel	Saturn	5
80%	Pilotwings 64	N64	6
80%	Williams Arcade's Greatest Hits	SNES	6
80%	Mario Kart 64	N64	6
79%	Samurai Shodown	SNES	4
79%	Warhawk	PlayStation	5
79%	Riot	PlayStation	6
78%	Sonic CD	Mega CD	3
78%	Out to Lunch	SNES	3
78%	Aladdin	SNES	3
78%	Legends of the Ring	SNES	3
78%	F1 Pole Position	SNES	3
78%	Virtua Soccer	SNES	3
78%	Choplifter 3	SNES	3
78%	True Lies	SNES	4
78%	Street Racer	Saturn	6
78%	Tobal No. 1	PlayStation	6
77%	Soleil	Mega Drive	4
76%	Hook	SNES	2
76%	Another World	SNES	2
76%	Utopia	SNES	2

%	GAME	FORMAT	
76%	Sonic Blastman	SNES	2
76%	Power Serve 3D Tennis	PlayStation	5
75%	Haunting	Mega Drive	3
75%	Fantastic Dizzy	Mega Drive	3
75%	Mystic Quest	SNES	3
75%	Skyblazer	SNES	3
75%	Teenage Mutant Ninja Turtles: Tournament Fighters	Mega Drive	3
75%	Tiny Toon Adventures: ACME All-Stars	Mega Drive	4
75%	Lethal Enforcers II: Gun Fighters	Mega Drive	4
75%	Trash It	PlayStation	6
74%	Wolverine: Adamantium Rage	SNES	4
73%	James Bond 007: The Duel	Mega Drive	2
73%	Doctor Who	Amiga	2
73%	Best of the Best	SNES	2
73%	Ristar	Mega Drive	4
72%	F-22 Interceptor	Mega Drive	1
72%	Way of the Warrior	3DO	4
72%	Biker Mice from Mars	SNES	4
72%	Criticom	PlayStation	5
72%	Contra	PlayStation	6
70%	Double Dragon 2	Game Boy	1
70%	ToeJam & Earl	Mega Drive	1
70%	Alien Breed	Amiga	1
70%	Space Ace	SNES	3
70%	Spider-Man and the X-Men in Arcade's Revenge	Mega Drive	3
70%	Ghoul Patrol	SNES	4
70%	Bubsy II	SNES	4
70%	World Series Baseball	Saturn	5
70%	Pandamonium	PlayStation	6
69%	NBA All-Star Challenge	Game Boy	1
69%	Plok	SNES	3
69%	World Soccer	SNES	3
69%	Alien Odyssey	PC	5
69%	D	Saturn	5
69%	Twisted Metal Tour	PlayStation	6
68%	Lotus Turbo Challenge 2	Amiga	1
68%	Trivial Pursuit	CDTV	2
68%	Indiana Jones & The Last Crusade	Mega Drive	2
68%	Xenon II	Game Boy	2
68%	Dungeon Master	SNES	2
67%	F-117 (Night Storm)	Mega Drive	3
66%	After Burner	Sega 32x	4
66%	Cosmic Carnage	Sega 32x	4
66%	Assault Riggs	PlayStation	5
65%	Top Banana	Amiga	1
65%	Heroes of the Lance	Master System	1
65%	Fighting Masters	Mega Drive	2
65%	Joe & Mac: Caveman Ninja	Game Boy	2
65%	Shaq Fu	Mega Drive	4

%	GAME	FORMAT	SERIES
65%	Bomberman 64	N64	7
63%	The Addams Family	NES	1
63%	The Fidgetts	Game Boy	3
63%	Lethal Enforcers	Mega CD	3
62%	King's Quest 5: Absence Makes the Heart Go Yonder	Amiga	1
61%	The Dual: Test Drive II	SNES	2
61%	RoboCop 3	SNES	2
61%	Final Fantasy II	SNES	2
60%	Graham Gooch World Class Cricket	Amiga	1
60%	Deluxe Strip Poker 2	Amiga	1
60%	Michael Jordan: Chaos in the Windy City	SNES	4
60%	Newman/Haas Indycar featuring Nigel Mansell	SNES	4
60%	Lone Soldier	PlayStation	5
59%	Pit-Fighter	Amiga	1
59%	Shadow of the Beast	Mega Drive	1
59%	Wing Commander 2: Vengeance of the Kilrathi	PC	1
58%	Dennis the Menace	SNES	3
58%	Total Carnage	Game Boy	3
58%	Hyperdunk	Mega Drive	3
58%	NBA Showdown	Mega Drive	3
57%	Dragon's Lair	SNES	2
57%	Splatterhouse 2	Mega Drive	2
57%	Steel Talons	Mega Drive	2
57%	WarpSpeed	SNES	2
57%	Muhammad Ali Heavyweight Boxing	Mega Drive	2
57%	Track 'N' Field	Game Boy	2
57%	Hebereke's Popoitto	Saturn	5
57%	Automobili Lamborghini	N64	7
55%	Melt	PC	6
54%	George Foreman's KO Boxing	NES	2
54%	Dirty Racing	Game Boy	2
52%	Outrun Europa	Master System	1
51%	Barbie	Game Boy	2
51%	The Blues Brothers	SNES	2
51%	Cluedo	CDi	4
51%	Endorfun	PC	5
51%	Eve	PC	6
50%	The Net	Movie	5
46%	Troddlers	Amiga	2
46%	Drakkhen	SNES	2
46%	Dirty Larry	Lynx	2
43%	Captain America	SNES	3
41%	Geisha	Amiga	1
37%	Goal	Game Boy	3
33%	Mighty Morphin Power Rangers	Mega Drive	4
32%	Street Gangs	NES	2
32%	Paperboy 2	Mega Drive	2
28%	Garfield Labyrinth	Game Boy	3

70%

60%

50%

40%

CONSOLETATION ZONE

Ian Bennyworth. GamesMaster, I'm currently playing *GoldenEye 64*, I'm stuck on the dam level, and I can't seem to find the key to open the gate. Can you help?

Dominik Diamond. Glad to, young Bennyworth. There is no key. I'm not trying to be Zen Buddhist, far from it. You have to shoot the padlock off using manual targeting, not auto. Which is a rule to live by.

Dan Tootill. I briefly appeared on a certain hit TV show in my early teens, thinking it might elevate me from unpopular nerd to local celebrity. This backfired spectacularly because I looked ridiculous in front of around six million viewers. I was never the most confident of people and still struggle with poor self-image 30 years later. Any advice you could give me would be appreciated.

D.D. Au contraire, Dan, with your reviews on *GamesMaster* series two you became part of the greatest TV show of the nineties family. And you were only the second most ridiculous-looking person that series. Did you *see* my red jacket?

Joe Trigg. GamesMaster, in my misspent youth I used to waste the summer hours playing *Sensible Soccer* and *Pro Evo*, but now my girlfriend's younger brother keeps thrashing me at *FIFA* – bar picking a better team than Burton Albion, any advice?

D.D. Psychological warfare can solve many of life's problems. This is one of them. Play a possession game deep in your own half, laughing like a hyena as you do. When you see smoke pouring from his ears, send it long to a ridiculously pacy player to score. Then watch multiple replays until he starts crying. That's what people do to me online anyway, and they all play as Burton Albion. Oh the shame!

Ross Ashley. Hi Dominik, I hope you can help with a puzzle that I've been stuck on since I was 14! In *Little Big Adventure 2*, there is a riddle to solve in order to find Franco's fragment of the key, but I can't figure it out. I know I could look up the answer on the internet, but it doesn't feel like cheating if I ask you.

D.D. This is one of the most irritating riddles in videogame history, Ross. Go to the Bazaar you bought the pickaxe from, face it with your back to the tree, make sure you are in SPORTY mode and walk five to seven paces forward, turn back around and use your pickaxe.

David Binmore. GamesMaster, I heard there was a method of smacking the game cartridge inserted in a powered on Mega Drive that will bring up a debug menu, with which you can gain access to such features as a level select. Is this true? Also do you know if anyone can fix a broken Mega Drive? I really want to see level 2 of *Ecco: Tides of Time*.

D.D. Strange, David. Methods like this, passed on by 'that bloke you met in a train station once late at night' usually work. Try the same thing but this time smack your own head. This will help with your own personal debug from this kind of thing. Broken Mega Drives cannot be fixed any more because it's 2022 and everything is broken everywhere.

Sebastian J. Brook. So, back when I joined the *GamesMaster* club in 1992, I sent in a question in the hope it would be answered. As time went on and as I grew older, it remained unanswered. So that I can finally bring closure to 12-year-old me, here it is again: Dear Games-Master, I've found the first two sets of warp zones in *Super Mario Bros* but cannot find the third. Where is it?

D.D. Defeat one of the Boomerang Brothers in World 2, Sebastian, and he will leave behind a hammer. Use this to destroy a stone in the top right-hand corner of the map and you will find a secret path going to the right. Beat the Fire Bros here to get the whistle. These instructions also work in Swindon.

Glen West. I married an American and I'm very concerned that our little girl won't grow-up to appreciate classic British computer games. How do I correct this? Will she ever master *Elite*?

D.D. As an American this is the least of her problems, Glen, but an Amiga emulator and *Championship Manager 97/98* might help.

Chris Gan. How much wood could a woodchuck chuck if a woodchuck could chuck wood?

D.D. 700 pounds, Chris. Seriously. #science

Lloyd Hiscox. GamesMaster, back in '95 I was a bit tasty on *NBA Jam Tournament Edition* on the Sega Mega Drive. Victories against my brother or mates were always funnier when I had the likes of the Fresh Prince on the court, courtesy of the game's special character cheats. Fast-forward 25 years, and I have a new 'player two' in the form of my son Kian. Which special character would you suggest I use to retain my *NBA Jam* supremacy?

D.D. Nobody likes getting spanked by Hillary Clinton, Mr Hiscox. But be warned, playing your kids is a slippery slope which ends in you smashing joypads when three of them beat you at *Mario Kart*. Apparently. So says ... er ... a friend of mine.

> Milkman Hero. Seemingly everyone is rapidly descending towards a reality where buying new games and leaving them in their wrappers becomes 'the norm'. Would everyone guilty of this be better off spending that money or putting it towards some kind of gaming retirement fund instead?

D.D. I concur, Lord Milkman of the Hero clan. Nothing should be left in its original wrapping unless you have found it in an Egyptian tomb.

> James Chapman. Back in the days of MySpace, you had an excellent page with your band The A.M.s which had such great hits like 'She Likes the Boaby', 'Billy the Dancer' and (if I remember correctly) the Christmas release, 'F*** You'. I'd love to get some inspiration for songwriting. Is there any way I can listen to these songs again?

D.D. You are not alone, James! Many have said our funny little world lit up their own darker one back then, and it moves me greatly. Certainly more than my band moved the charts, although you can still find 'Billy the Dancer' on Apple Music, which is strange and wonderful.

> John Costello. My younger, nineties self is stuck on *Maniac Mansion* for the NES. It was rented from the local videogame club for £5, and I want to get my full money's worth. Do you know how to escape from the dungeon?

D.D. Ah. So few things can be rented for £5 these days, John, unless you frequent really skanky bars. Anyway, make sure you have two characters in the dungeon: one positioned by the door, the other under the left window. Use the WHAT IS command with the latter to locate a loose brick under the window which opens the door, and switch to the other player to run out of it. Later in the game you can obtain a rusty key that solves everything, which once again brings us back to skanky bars.

> Benedict Linley. I am really struggling to complete *Super Mario World* for the SNES. Do you have any tips on completing the game?

D.D. Still? What happened to you Benedict? Did you wander into a dark castle room and prick your finger on a spinning jenny sending you to sleep for 30 years? Do you play wearing mittens? The best advice I can give is to try and keep the little plumber bloke alive, yeah?

> Gareth Gealey. Growing up in the nineties all I ever wanted was a Game Boy, but every Christmas and birthday brought disappointment. Today, as an adult approaching 40, I still bear the mental scars of an unfulfilled youth. How can I get my life back on track?

D.D. Get an expensive therapist and bill your parents, Gareth. That's what my children do.

Tom Dent. Is there anything that can be done about those mother-flipping blue shells in *Mario Kart*?

D.D. This answer is partly gaming and partly a life lesson, Tom. The shell automatically targets whoever is in first place. When you see someone obtain one, slow down until you are in the runner-up position, leaving the shell to hit another player instead. It's the old hare and the tortoise, innit?

Davey Hackett. How can I stop myself reaching for easy excuses every time I lose in an online videogame? Or, am I right that everyone else is just lucky, or has a better connection, and actually I'm great?

D.D. You are right, Davey. You are the best player with the slowest connection on the internet. All the videos on TikTok are saying that. It's all Davey Hackett this, Davey Hackett that. And dancing.

Stuart Mackaness. My partner wants me to find a cooperative videogame we can both enjoy. They say they don't mind what game it is, but nothing I suggest seems to float their boat. Can you help me, GamesMaster?

D.D. Perfect timing, Stuart! I just played through *It Takes Two* with my wife and it is the best coop game ever, albeit with a talking book character that chafes like riding a racing bike. We nearly got divorced on the second last boss though so maybe find a new game or new partner before you reach that part.

Kevin Mackay. What is the best, but not necessarily highest-rated, game you have ever completed? And the one that annoyed you to the point of giving up?

D.D. *Atic Atac* on the ZX Spectrum, because it was the first game I ever completed as a child. *The Outer Worlds* for Xbox One I gave up after my twentieth attempt to defeat the final boss, a fact my children – who all completed the game with ease – mock me with every day, Kevin.

Graham Waters. I've recently become aware of an affliction known as joystick drift. As a keen gamer and a happily married man, should I be worried?

D.D. Ah yes, one of the perils of modern gaming, Graham. The problem arises when the stick sits in an off-centre position for too long. May I suggest sleeping on your back instead?

Lee Abrahams	Paul Barnett	John Boursnell	Catherine Byng	Rees Clissold
Lee Ackerley	Alan Barr	Jon Bowen	Marc Byrne	Jonny Clooney
Fletcher Adamowicz	Alastair Barr	Mark Bowie	Paul Byrne	Pete Closs
Daniel Adams	Wayne Barrett	James Bowman	Rich Byrne	Neil Cobban
Mike Adams	Paul Barrick	Richard Boyd	Scott Byrne-Fraser	Richard Cobbett
Ryan Adams	Graeme Barrie	Stu Boyland	Simon Byron	Andrew Cobley
Terry Adams	Joseph Barron	Dan Boyle	Adam Cadwell	Aaron 'Blowfelt' Cochrane
Adamski	Helen Barry	Gerard Boyle	Anthony Caine	Ian Cockburn
Dennis Agodzo	Kevin Barthaud	Martin Boyle	Martin Caine	Morgan Cockcroft
Ben Ahmady	Edward Barton	James Bracher	Liam Cairney	Gareth Coghlan
Stephanie Ainslie	Neville Bartos	Adam Brackenbury	Michael Culvert	Andrew Coleman
Vic Ainsworth	John Barwood	Gareth Bradley	Liam Cameron	Colin 'Retro-o' Bell
Alistair Aitcheson	Rich Bate	James Bradley	Adam Cammack	Robbie Collin
Adam Aitken	Sel Bates	Tim Bradshaw	Alan Campbell	Pete Collins
Samir Al-Amar	Andrew Baxter	Richard Brady	Andy Campbell	Phil Collins
Christian Albrecht	Daryl Baxter	Alex Brailsford	Duncan Campbell	David Collyer
Daniel Alcorn	Brian Bayes	Toby Braithwaite	Gavin Campbell	Jamie Collyer
Duane Alderton	Richard Baynham	Oliver Branch	Jamie Campbell	Michele Colombo
Phil Alderton	John Beadle	Matt Brandwood	Peter Campbell	Scott Colvey
Andy Aldred	Luke Beaman	Dave Brannan	Richard Campbell	Stuart Combe
Barry Aldridge	Sarah Beamish	Liam Brannan	Scott Cappleman	Commander Jolyon
Gavin Alexander	Daniel Beasley	Mark Brassington	Captain Chaos	Andy Conduit Turner
Hussain Aij	Richard Beckett	Judy Bray	Eamonn Carey	Simon Connell
Craig Allamby	Sid Beckett	Christopher Bree	Sophie Cargill	David Connolly
Darren Allan	Matthew Beckly	James Brennan	Yvonne Cargill	Kye Connolly
Richard Allcock	Alex Beech	Sean Brennan	Leo Carlin	Chris Conroy
Ash Allen	Chris Beeley	Tom Brewer	Bill Carr	Nick Constantinou
Chris Allen	Marcus Beer	James Bridcut	Daniel Carr	Dyl Cook
Dave Allen	Andrew Beggs	Peter Bridger	Martin Carr	Jason Cook
Stuart Allen	Christopher A Bell	Adam Briffett	Ben Carter	Ant Cooke
Steph Allman	Colin Bell	Trevor Briscoe	Matt Carter	Rory Cooke
Mark Allsworth	Mark Bell	Neil Brock	Mark Peter Cartwright	Colin Cooper
James Alston	Robert Bell	Stuart Bromfield	Garry Casey	Damian Cooper
Simon Alty	Ross Bell	Darren Brook	Chris Cassell	Mat Cooper
Ross Anderson	Rikki Belsham	Sebastian J Brook	Andrew Cassells	Paul Cooper
Steven Anderson	Alastair Bennett	Connor Brooke	Ath Cassidy	Steve Cooper
Pete Andrews	Andrew Bennett	Mark Brookes	Christian Cawley	Tom Cooper
ANE/ZWNSBP	Louis Bennett	Richard B Brookes	Marc Chacksfield	Benji Copeman
Andrew Angel	Martin Bennett	Mark Brooks	Avradeep Chakrabarti	Steven Corbin
Steven Angus	Stephen Bennett	Steven Brooks	JV Chamary	Matt Corbishley
Sam Ankers	Ian Benneyworth	Andrew Broome	Peter Chamberlain Cann	Gary Cormack
Tom Anthony	Matthew Bennion	Andy Brown	Barnaby Chambers	Daniel Cornwall
Nicholas Antrobus	Bolin Benny	Andy Brown	Neil Chambers	Marcus Corrieri
Diego Arias	Luke Bensted	David R Brown	Olly Chambers	Jamie Corriveau
Tom Armour	James Bentley	Iain Brown	Mike Channell	Nicholas Cory
Rich Armstrong	Jonathan Bentley	James Brown	Matt Chaplin	Mark Costa
Stuart Armstrong	Benjamin Berry	Jeremy Brown	Chris Chapman	James Costello
David Arnold	Tim Berry	Leighton Brown	James Chapman	John Costello
Gary Arnold	Edward Beswetherick	Mark Brown	Lee AD Chapman	Mark Cotten
Simon Arnold	Greg Beveridge	Richard Brown	William Chapman	William Cottingham
Andrew Arrowsmith	Ian Beveridge	Ryan Brown	Lillian Charles	Graham Coulson
James Ashburn	Jag Bhachu	Spencer Brown	Martin Charles	Tim Coventry-Coyle
Russell Ashby	Adam Bil	Stephen Brown	Stefan Charles	Simon Cowley
Ross Ashley	Martin Binfield	Stephen Brown	Matt Charlesworth	Drew Cox
James Ashton	Moray Binfield	Woz Brown	Paul Charlton	Jeremy Cox
Graham Ashworth	David Binmore	Darren Browne	Luke Charlwood	Martin Cox
James Asker	Chris Birchell	James Browne	James Charnock	Alan Coyle
Nick Askew	Jason Bird	Mathew Browne	Tom Charnock	Paul Craddy
Charles Astwood	David Birkett	Allan Brownie	Was Chaudry	Craig from the 80s
Steven Ather	Steven Birks	Peter Brozyna	Henry Cheese	Tony Crampshee
Jamie Atkinson	Christopher Bishop	Lee Bryan	Riccardo Cherubini	Sarah & Adam Crampton
Michael Atkinson	Philip Bishop	Stan Bryan	Rich Chester	Andy Crane
Neil Atkinson	Scott Bishop	Buckaroo Bonzai	Sam Chester	Mark Cranmer
Daniel Avery	Bitmap Soft	Lee Buckingham	The Chieftain	John Cranston
Chris Aydon	Tony Blackburn	Matt Buckland	Paul Chisholm	Chris Craven
Jason Baigent	David Blair	John Buckley	Colin Chivers	Mark Craven
Alex Bailey	James Blair	Rocco Buffalino	James Chivers	Andrew Crawford
Andy Bailey	Paul Blakeley	Giles Buglass	Lee Chrimes	James A Crewe
Bob Bailey	Neil Blakely	Daniel Bungert	Chris 'GamesYouLoved'	Evan Crichton
David Bailey	Kevin Blakeman	James Burchell	Warren Chrismas	Malcolm Critchell
Jon Bailey	Robin Blamires	Christopher Burgess	Eddie Christie	Blair Crockett
James Bainbridge	Jonathan Blench	Thom Burgess	Andy Chung	David Crookes
Patrick Baird	Stephen Blenkin	Michael Burke	Tom Church	Joel Crookes
Chris Baker	Graham Bliss	Dominic Burnard	Jason Cini	Ben Cross
Colin Baker	Peter Bloomer	Gordon Burnett	Tom Clancy	Rob Crowther
Earl Baker	Danny Blow	Lee Burnett	Brandon Clark	Graham Crump
Stephen Baker	John A Blue	Rob Burnett	Dave Clark	Gary Cullen
James Ballardie	Martin Boddie	Ross Burnett	Kevin Clark	Stuart Cullen
Alfie Bamford	Anthony Boden	Ben Burnham	Paul Clark	Tim Culley
James Bamford	Ken Bodger	William Burns	Richard Clark	Jonny Cumiskey
Andrew Banaszynski	Garry Bodsworth	Girvan Burnside	Matthew James Clarke	Andrew Cummings
David Banton	Alan Boiston	Marc Burrage	Rob Clarke	Laurie Cunningham
David Baptiste	Malcolm Bolton	Tim Burrell-Saward	Thierry Clavel	Peter Curd
Andrew Barker	Peter Borg	Lee Burton	AJ Clay	Dan Curley
Chris Barker	Christopher Borritt	Simon Busby	Jim Clear	Michael Currie
Craig Barker	Simon Borszowski	Christopher Bush	Tom Cleaver	James Cushing
Pete Barker	Ben Borthwick	Steve Bush	Stephen Clegg	DI3TZI3
Stuart Barlow	David Boston	Craig Butcher	Joey Clemens	Christian Dabnor
Rob Barnes	Luke Boulerice	Andy Butterworth	Stu Cleminson	Toby Dale
Chris Barnett	Iain Boulton	Daniel Bygrave	Ed Clews	Gavin Dalton
David Barnett	Oliver Boulton-Lear	Richard Byles	Tom Clint	Neil Danson

Ben Darlow
Ricardo Dartnaill
Mark Daszkiewicz
Perry Davenport
Steven Davidson
Scott Davie
Chris Davies
Jamie Davies
Karl Davies
Kevin Davies
Liam Davies
Rhydian Davies
Richard Davies
Stuart Davies
Ben Davis
Chris Davis
Kevin Davis
Richard Davison
Steven Davison
Brian Dawes
Graham Dawes
Gary Dawson
Justin Day
Keith Day
Alberto De Aveiro
Joseph de Condappa
Tony De Gouveia
Colin Deady
Billy Deakin
Olly Dean
Rob Dean
Dameo Deare
Rob Dearlove
Ceallaigh Dee
Stephen Delaney
Matthew Dempsey
Gordon Dempster
Chris Dennett
Andrew Dennison
Tom Dent
Matthew MF Deputy
Michael Diamond
Robert Dick
Alan Dickson
Bryan 'Brypie' Dickson
Ian Dickson
Diġe
Karl Dillon
Thomas Dillon
Pete Dillon-Trenchard
Declan Dineen
Mike Diver
Christopher Dixon
Paul Dixon
Simon Dixon
Phil JF Dobbing
James Dobrzanski
Tomas Docherty
Ernest Doku
James Donald
Mark Donkey
Donaldson
Andy Donnan
Gerry Donnelly
Kieran Doonan
Matthew Dootson
Adam Doree
Shaun Double
Iain Dougan
Chris Douglas
Jon Douglas
Shem Douglas
Richard Downer
Darren Doyle
Martin Doyle
Phil Doyle
Sedric A Dragon
Ian Dransfield
Matt Driver
Andrew Drummond
Grant Drummond
Matthew J Drury
Phil Drury
Ian Drysdale
Adam Ducker
Selby Duffield
David Duffy
Liam Duffy
Robert Duffy
Alasdair Duncan
Ewan Duncan

Phil Duncan
Stuart K Duncan
Richard Dundas
Sean Dunlop
Alex Dunn
Christian Dunn
Joe Dunn
Jonathan Dunn
Paul Dunn
Abban Dunne
Paddy Dunne
Paul Dunphy
Sam Dymond
Alistair Dyson
Richard Dyson
Charles E
Stefan Eady
Phillip Eccles
Jon Eckersley
Christopher Eden
Alex Edge
Matt Edmonds
Simon Edmundson
Leigh Edwards
Ian Egerton
Sam Egger
Matthew Eilbeck
Stephen Eldridge
Chris Ellingford
John Elliott
Mark Elliott
Christian Ellis
Les Ellis
Mark Ellis
Richard Elsey
Ben Emberley
Corin Ennis
Tom Enright
Jordi Escobar Bonet
Kevin Eva
Benjamin Evans
Chris Evans
David Evans
Doiminic Evans
Gary Evans
Leighton Evans
Neil Evans
Phil Evans
Ian Evenden
Kirk Ewing
Sam Fairley
Stu Fallow
David Farr
Matt Farrell
Danny Faulkner
Mark Fawcett
Duncan Fegredo
Julian Fellows
Joseph Fenech
Graham Fennell
Nick Ferguson
Paul Ferguson
Steven Fergusson
Kevin Ferrie
Ian Ferry
Jonny Ffinch
Fh'yll R'lyeh
Henry Fielder
Pete Fighter II
Michael Filby
Alistair Fildes
Paul Fillery
Alexander Finch
Chris Findlay
Nick Finikin
John Finlay
Thomas Finlay
Andy Finnan
Mark Finney
Will Firmager
Adrian Fisher
Andrew Fisher
Ben Fisher
David Fisher
Mark Fisher
Martin Fisher
Suzanne Fisher
Will Fisher
Stephen Fitch
Casey Fitzgerald
Gregory Fitzgerald

Craig Anthony
Fitzpatrick
Paul Flanagan
Neil Flannery
Sean Flannigan
Tom Flash
Stuart Fleming
Lee Fletcher
Luke Fletcher
Simon Fletcher
David Gilmore Fobrogo
Jonathan Foley
Graeme Foote
Matthew Forbes
Adrian Ford
Keir Ford
Matthew Ford
Tim Ford
Bevan Forrest
Kris Forrest
Chris Forrester
Calum Forsyth
Pete Forsyth
Adam Foster
Alec Foster
Ben Foster
Cliff Foster
Dean Foster
John Foster
Ross Foubister
Joseph Fowler
Chris Fox
Darrel Fox
James Fox
Paul Fox
Nigel France
Wil Francis
Jamie Fraser
Mark Fraser
Stuart Fraser
Dave Frear
Michael Free
Dean Freeman
Ross Freemantle
Simon Freemantle
Jeff Freer
Gareth French
Justin French
Richard Fretwell
Gregor Frew
Cameron Friend
Frantisek Fris
Matt Froggatt
Rob Frood
Will Furdas
Steven G
Papa G'Nelly
Richard Gale
Grahame Gallacher
Ian Gallacher
Chris Gallagher
Chris Gan
Ian Gander
Greg Garbett
Lee Garbutt
Richard Gardiner
Simon Gardner
Stephen Garland
Leigh Garner
Nicholas Garrott
Daniel Gaskin
Steven Gaskin
Frank Gasking
Nick Gatt
David Gaunt
James Gaydon
Gareth Gealy
Vaughan Gerrard
Get Indie Gaming
Andrew Gibbard
Chris Gibbons
Daniel Gibbons
Johnny Gibson
Alan Gibson
Drew Gibson
Kevin Gibson
Mark Gibson
Mike Gibson
Stephen Gibson
Mark Gidley
Simon Gifford

Justin Gilbert
Craig Gilchrist
Warren J Giles
Andrew Gilmour
Kev Gilmour
Stewart Gilray
Ammy 'Midna' Gilroy
Daniel Gintner
Stuart Gipp
Martin Glassborow
Lee Glazebrook
Robin Glennie
James Glover
Jonathan Glover
Russell Glover
Roger Godfrey
Jamie Godsall
Will Goldstone
Danny Golledge
Tim Goodchild
Josh Goolnik
Seth Goolnik
Christian Gorgees
Andrew Gorham
Ben Gorman
Thomas Gorman
Daniel Gosling
Tony Gowland
Denby Grace
James Gradwell
Alan Graham
Ben Graham
Chris Graham
Ian Graham
Ian 'the Fanjo' Graham
Stephen Maurice
Graham
Jesper Granmyr
Andrew Grant
Matthew Grant
Neil Grant
Chris Grapes
Alan Gray
Bruce Gray
David Gray
Mike Gray
Simon Gray
Simon Grayson
Asa Green
Craig Green
Eddie Green
Frankie Green
Mike Green
Harriett Greene
David Greenfield
James E Greenhorn
Paul Andrew Greenop
Maffew Gregg
Simon Gregory
Jacob Gresham-Hill
Brendan Griffin
Mark Griffin
Gareth Griffiths
Ian Griffiths
Steve Griffiths
Dougal Grimes
Keith Grimes
Tim Grindell
Rohan Grove
Gavin Groves
Richard Grubb
Neil Grunshaw
Chris Gudgeon
Mark Guest
Declan Guiney
Christopher Gunn
Sebastian Gurvitsch
Mathew Guy
Rob Gwilliam
Gaz H
Alastair Hackett
Davey Hackett
Tom Hackett
John Haddock
Simon Hadlington
Andy Haigh
Jonathan Haigh
John Hailey
Mark Haines
Vincent Haines
Stephen Hales

Ben Hall
Craig Hall
Les Hall
Phil Hall
Nathan Hallett
Seán Halpin
Michael Halton
Andi Hamilton
Corin Hamilton
David Hamilton
Mark Hamilton
Steven Hamilton
Will 'TwistdRabbit'
Hamilton
Alan Hammond
Mark Hammond
Paul Handley
Séamus Hanly
Iain Hannah
Craig Hannan
Gavin Hansford
Nick Hansford
Christopher Hanson
William Harbison
Martin Harder
Jamie Hardie
Alan Harding
Mark Hardisy
Ben Hardwick
Joe Hardy
James Hare
Bob Harlow
Frances Harputlu
Kevan Harriman
Paul Harrington
Carl Harris
Jamie Harris
Michael Harris
Jonathan Harris-Small
Brendon Harrison
Garrett Harrison
Mark Harrison
Patrick Harrison
Rick Harrison
Chris Hart
Peter Hart
Jim Hartland
Craig Hartley
Tom Hartwell
Hugo Harvey
James Harvey
Joel Harvey
Phillip Harvey
Shaun Harvey
Stephen Harvey
Kenny Haslam
Umair Hassan
Susan Hassle
Peter Hathaway
Gordon Hay
Michael Hay
Nigel Hayes
Pete Haynes
Philip Hayton
Tom Hayward
Richard Hazeldine
Alan Hazlie
Tony Facey Heald
Chris Heath
Mark Heath
Michael Heath
Nick Helweg-Larsen
Andrew Henderson
David Henderson
Grant Henderson
Rik Henderson
Scott Henderson
Stewart Henderson
Ross Hendry
Martin Hennessy
Toby Henry
Iain Hepburn
Adam Hepton
Craig Heritage
Leigh Heseltine
Tony Heugh
Peter Hewitson
Michael Heys
Jamie Heywood
Ben Hieatt-Smith
Sean Higgins

Simon Hildreth
Alastair Hill
Grant Hill
Ian Hill
Julian Hill
Paul Hill
Ross Hill
Sam & LeeAnne Hill
Mark Hillary
Alex Hillel
Andrew Hillel
Steven Hillier
Dan Hills
Joseph Hindhaugh
Chris Hindle
James Hine
Jacob Hinrichsen
HIP P
Colin Hird
Lloyd Hiscox
Scott Hitchcock
Lucien Hoare
Robin Hodges
David Hodgkins
Ben Hodgson
Matthew Hodgson
Paul Hodgson
Mark Hogarth
Jared Holdcroft
Andrew Holder
Bill Holding
David Holdsworth
Gregg Holland
Daniel Hollands
Jody Hollands
Christopher Hollingworth
Alex 'Bonesy' Holmes
Ashley Holmes
Paul Holmes
David Holt
Richard Holt
Tim Holt
Adam Holtby
Adam Holton
Jamie Holyoake
Mark Honeyborne
Matthew Hookey
Andy Hoole
Russ Hope
Alex Hopson
Adam Hopton
Chris Horn
Chris 'CloudLXXXV' Horner
Martin Horton
Andrew Hoskings
Ian Hosler
Laura Hotchkiss
John Houghton
Craig Houston
Luciano Howard
Rhys Howell
Kenny Howie
Ross Howle
Mark Howlett
Philip Hoy
Tim Hugall
Lee Huggett
Nic Hughes
Paul Hughes
Stuart Hughes
Warren Jon Hughes
Dan Humpherson
Adam Humphreys
Adrian Humphris
Dan Hunt
Nicoll Hunt
Adrian Hunter
Steve Hunter
Daniel Huntley
Richard Hunton
Christopher Hutchins
Michael Hutchinson
Colin Hutchison
Grant Hutchison
Hamish Hutchison
Louise Hynd
Stephen Hynds
Zuber Ibrahim
Ike of Spain
Najam Imam

Alastair Ingason
John Ioannou
Luke Ireland
Mark Irwin
Roger Isaac
Dave Isherwood
David Isherwood
Ben Ixer
Scott 'SJI307' J
Pippa Jack
James Jackman
Edward Ashley Jackson
Gareth Jackson
Lee Jackson
Nicholas Jackson
José Jacob
George Jaeger-Wright
Alexis Jago
David James
Ian James
Jonathan James
Mike James
James
Kristian James-Gillum
Alex Jans
Brian Jarvis
Hardip Jasser
Mikey Jay
Adam Jeffcock
Stephen Jeffrey
Tracy Jeffrey
Mike Jelves
Chris Jessee
Damian Johnson
Daniel Johnson
Malcolm Johnson
Neil Johnson
Stephen Johnson
Tom Johnston
Liam Jolly
Gildan Jondal
Alan Jones
Alex Jones
Andrew Jones
Andrew David Jones
Daniel Jones
Darren Jones
Edan Jones
Gaz Jones
Hywel Jones
Jonathan Jones
Nicholas Jones
Nick Jones
Nige Jones
Paul Jones
Peter Jones
Richard Jones
Rob Jones
Neil Jones-Rodway
Alan Jordan
Svend Joscelyne
Marc Jowett
Mark Jowett
Charles Jurd
Simon K
Tasneem Kabir
Caox Kal
Avneet Kandola
Mark Kapelko
Alex Kazam
Thomas Kealy
Alan Kebab
Allan Keddie
Gabriel Keeble-Gagnère
Kieran Keegan
Steve Keen
Kamran Keenan
Lawrence Keenan
Darren Keig
Andrew Keith
Chris Kelly
D Kelly
David Kelly
Doug Kelly
John Kelly
Neon Kelly
Shane Kelly
Stuart Kelly
Thomas Kelly
Al Kennedy
Alister Kennedy

Stu Kennedy
Andrew Kenny
Neil Kenny
Andrew Kenrick
Jonathan Kenworthy
James Kenyon
Tim Kerins
Elliott Kerr
Paul Keward
Simon Roger Key
Steve Key
Graham Kibble-White
Jack Kibble-White
Alexey Kiddo
Elliot Kidner
John Kiely
Sebastian Jon Kiernan
Paul Kilduff-Taylor
Stephen Kilkie
Kimmymari Damacy
Andrew King
Andy King
Hawken King
Matt King
Matthew King
Mike King
Philip King
David Kingsnorth
Ashley Kingston
Dan Kirby
Nick Kirby
Graham Kirk
Billy Kirkwood
Michael Kissane
Peter & Hannah Kissick
Paul Klotschkow
Dan Knight
Leigh Knight
Paul Knights
Daniel Kolodziej
James Kostyszyn
Kris Kowalewski
Stefan Kruger
Richie Kuncyusz
Oleg Kuznetsov
James Ladbrook
Tim Laird
Amar Lal-Sarin
Weng Lam
Dan Lambert
Richie Lambert
Ben Lancaster
Gavin Lane
Patrick Langford
Jason Langridge
Ami Langton
Aaron Larmour
Antony Last
Fletcher Law
Chris Lawlor
Colin Lawlor
Robert Lawlor
David Lawrence
Jim Lawrence
Hugh Lawson
Lee Lawson
Simon Lay
Andrew Layden
Haiminh Le
James Leach
Stuart Leckie
Andrew Lee
Danny Lee
Jamie Lee
Josh Lee
Steve Lee
Xander Lee
Thomas Legg
Joe Legget
Warren Leigh
Rick Lemon
Richard Lenton
Graham Lewis
Joel Gethin Lewis
Matt Lewis
Steven Lewis
Joe Leythorne
Wing See Li
Wing-He Li
Paul Liggett
Andrew Liggins

Benedict Lindley
Andrew Lindsay
Brett Linforth
John Lipari
Neill Liptrott
Blue Littlewood
Anthony Litton
James Lloyd
Keith Lloyd
Matthew Lobb
Frazer Locke
James Lockey
Garry Logue
Ed Lomas
Ewan Lomax
Harry Loney
Ben Long
Wayne Longton-Worley
Chris Lord
Matt Loren
Tim Loton
Neil Lourie
Dean Love
Mark Love-Smith
Danny Loveday
Luis Lozano
Mathew Lucas
Matt Lucas
Benedikt Ludwig
David Lunan
Jamie Lundahl
Nomen Luni
Philip James Lunt
Thomas Lusty
Keith Lutener
David Glenn Lyall
Ben Lynch
Rich Lyons
Michael M
James Macdonald
Scott MacDonald
Jonathan Macey
Alan MacGregor
Stuart Mackaness
Colin MacKenzie
Jonathan Mackenzie
Rob Mackenzie
James Mackie
Alasdair Macmillan
Jamie Madge
MADS 76
Tam Mageean
Paul Magor
Joshua Mahon
Stuart Maine
David Major
Richard Major
AJ Makin
Ian Makowski
Paul Mallett
Ali Maloney
Simon Malpass
Andy Malt
Manic
Ravenel Mansfield
Ross Mansfield
Ian Mardell
Thomas Marinak
Mark 'BetaOne'
Andrew Marney
Edgar Marques
Aiden Marriott
Richard Jon Marsh
Andrew Marshall
Liam Marshall
Stephen Marshall
Christopher John Martin
James Martin
Sam Martin
Steve Martin
Steven Martin
Shaun Marvin
Peter Maskell
Craig Mason
Jon Mason
Kev Mason
Warren Mason
Will Mason
Euan Mathers
Martin Mathers
Ian Matthews

John Matthews
Paul Matthews
Jonny Mattocks
Matthew Maude
Lee Maughan
Giles Maunsell
Chris Mawdsley
Richard Mawle
Jamie Andrew Maxwell
Barry Mayor
Asif Mazumder
Andy McAllister
John McAndrew
Rhys McAteer
Chris McCarthy
Joseph McCarthy
Michael J McCarthy
Paul McCartney
Albert McCausland
Tom McCloy
Si McClure
Kevin McCluskey
Kevin McComiskie
Iain McConchie
Dan 'Dannywhac' McConnell
Luke McCreanor
Kev McCullagh
Andy McDade
Craig McDonald
Nicholas A McDonald
Chris McDonnell
Leigh McDonnell
Roddy McDougall
Bryan McDowall
David McEachan
Neil McFarlane
Stuart McFarlane
Iain McGarry
Ian McGee
Stephen McGibbon
James McGill
Stephen McGill
Stephen McGinty
Joe McGonagle
Mark McGrady
Ryan McGrath
Kristofor Mcgreevy
Ross McGregor
Matt McGrory
Barry McGuigan
Liam McGuigan
Alex McGuinness
Gerry McGuire
Scott McGuire
Wayne Mcguire
Paul McGunnigle
Martin McHugh
Shaun McIlroy
George McInally
Derek McIntosh
Douglas McIntosh
Paul McIntosh
Skye McIntyre
Kevin McKay
Jamie McKeller
Joe McKenna
Scott McKenzie
Darren Mckeown
Andrew McKillen
Mark McKinley
Nathan McKinley
Scott McKinnon
Bruce McLachlan
Rob Mclaine
Fraser, Cameron & Ewan McLaren
Ian Mclaren
Chris McLaughlin
Gareth Mclean
Neil McLean
Peter McLean
Stephen Mcleavey
Steven McLennan
Gavin McMahon
Liam McMahon
John McManus
Andrew McMath
Allan McMillan
Adam McMurchie
Karyn McMurray

James McNab
Dave McNally
Aaron McNamara
Ben McNeill
Iain McNulty
Simon Mealing
Paul Mee
Wyatt Meffert
Niall Meldrum
David Meloy
Steve Merrett
Barry Metcalfe
Tom Methven
Karl Alexander Meyer
Raja Miah
Andrew Middlemas
James Middleton
Chris Miles
John Miles
Milkman Hero
Dave Millar
Adam Miller
Mike Miller
MJ Miller
Terry Miller
Craig Milliken
Thomas J Millington
Graham Mills
Richard Mills
Scott Mills
Simon Mills
Steven Millward
Gav Milne
Will Milner
Bryan Mitchell
David Mitchell
Jeremy Mitchell
Robert Mitchell
Scott Mitchell
Steve Mitchell
David Mitchelson
Andrew Moeren
Steven Mohammed
Kyle Molloy
Paul Monaghan
Stuart Monk
Ian Monkman
James Monkman
Moon Squid
John Mooney
Kevin Mooney
Nick Moor
Evan Moore
Paul Moore
Robin Moore
Warren Moore
James Moorehead
Giles Moorhouse
Paul Moran
Carl Morgan
Craig Morgan
Gareth Morgan
James Morgan
Paul Morgan
Andrew Morley
MaFt Morley
Owen Morley
Ed Morrell
Tim Morrill
James Morris
Stephen Morris
Paul E Morrison
Steven Morrison
Tomas Mosqueira
Andrew Moss
Peter Moss
Richard 'Zelrokyz' Moss
Sam Moss
Tim Moss
Rob Mossop
John Henry Mostyn
Ravi Motha
Rufus & Martha Mowatt
Mr Cheese
Dan Muir
Darren Muir
David Muir
Anthony Muldoon
Ade Mulgrew
Peter Mulholland

Robert Hugh Mullarkey
Andy Mullen
Steve Mumford
Peter Murdie
Andy Murdoch
Niall Murdoch
Ross Murdoch
Peter Murgett
John Murphy
Stephen Murphy
Gregg Gordon Murray
Michael Murray
Kieran Murtha
Xander Myles
Steven Mytum
Matthew Naismith
Danny Nash
Mike Nash
Harrison Nathaniel-Wurie
Chris Neal
Simon Neal
Charlie Needham
Jason Neifeld
Blair Nelson
Jai Nelson
Ambrose Neville
Rich Newbold
Fred Newton
MJ Newton
Steve John Nicholls
Andrew Marc Nicholson
Martyn Nickerson
Andrew Nicklin
Liam D Nicoll
Tom Nicoll
Duncan Nicolson
Iain Nisbet
Andrew Noble
Craig Noble
Kieran Nolan
Stewart Nolan
Zoe Nolan
Rob Norfolk
Jeff Northcott
Nostalgia Chaser
Gareth Noyce
Adie Nunn
Joe Nunn
Steve Nunn
Henry James Nutt
Craig O Connor
Adam O'Brien
Clark O'Brien
Gerard O'Brien
John O'Callaghan
Glen O'Connell
Dan O'Connor
Paul Benedict O'Connor
Stephen O'Donnell
Aaron O'Driscoll
Lee O'Halloran
Simon O'Hanlon
Alan O'Hara
David O'Hara
John O'Leary
Rob O'Mahony
Edward O'Neill
Richard O'Neill
Rorie O'Neill
Tom O'Rourke
Ken O'Toole
Peter Oak
Andrew Oakes
Max Obourne
Andrew Ogier
Gareth Ogilvie
Robin Ogilvie
OJS
Fola Olakunbi
Richard Oldfield
Craig Oldham
Graham Oliver
Craig Oliver-Walsh
Dominic Olszowski
Ryan Omar
Ben Oram
Steven Orr
Tony Orr
Simon Overson
Jonathan Owen

Leonard Owen
Luke Owen
Joe Ozanne
Dan Pacey
Edward Packard
Lewis Packwood
Dean Paddock
James Page
Mark Page
Alexander Palmer
Luke Palmer
Sam Palmer
Tej Pandher
Carl Panter
Zisis Paraskevaidis
Eric Park
Aaron Parker
Adam Parker
Danny Parker
James Parker
Jono Parker
Matthew Parker
Adam Parker-Edmondston
Tom Parker-Shemilt
Stuart Parkins
Craig Parr
Michael Parr
Edd Parris
Brett Parsons
Amar Parvez
Sat Patel
Jill Beattie Paterson
Robbie Paterson
Jason Patrickson
Stuart Patterson
Rich Paxton
Steve Payne
Charlie Pearce
Len Pearce
Mark Pearce
Kris Pearman
Ben Pearson
Matt Pearson
Richard Peck
Fabrizio Pedrazzini
Mick Pell
Rich Pemberton
Stephen Pendleton
Jehane Penfold-Ward
Mawgan Pengelly
Matthew Penney
DJ Isuru Perera
Col Perkins
Justin Perks
Joe Pero
David Perry
Tom Perry
Carl Peters
Chris Peters
Jason Petit
Nick Petrasiti
Barry Petrie
Chris Petticrew
William Pfeiffer
Andy Phillips
Ian Phillips
Peter Philpott
Tony Phipps
Steven Pick
Andrew Pidhajeckyj
Ian Pillay
David Pitcher
Albert Pitter
Si Pittman
Ed Plager
J Playtis
Angelo Pliatsikas
Andy Plucknett
Matthew Pont
Thomas Pook
Colin Poole
Kris Pope
Brad Porter
Niall Porter
Ryan Porter
Antony Potter
Ben Potter
Mark Potter
David Powell

James Powell
Matt Powell
Jean Power
Malcolm Power
Mark Presland
Michael Price
Retro Prime
William Prince
Simon Prior
Les Pritchard
Steve Pritchard
Dean Puckering
Gavin Pugh
Daniel Pullin
Adrian Purser
Ian Quayle
Jonathan Quilter
Alan Quinlen
James Quinn
Sean R
Dave Radband
Graham Raddings
Gareth Radford
Dermot Rafferty
Arman Rahman
Dylan Rajagopal
James Randall
Mark Rawlings
Jake Rawlinson
Adam Ray
Simon L Read
Paul Reaney
Mark Reay
Hammond Reddie
Stuart Reed
Tim & Sara Rees
Dan Reeves
David Regan
Andrew Reid
Malcolm Reid
David Remmington
Olly Rendall
Daniel Renshaw
Dom Reseigh-Lincoln
Kevin Reynolds
Mike Reynolds
Kevin Rhodes
Ben Richards
Jon Richards
Ash Richardson
Mark Richardson
Simon Richardson
Mark Ricketts
Neil Rickus
Alexander Ridler
Malcolm Riedlinger
Adam James Rigby
Daniel Rihoy
Kelvin Riley
Mark Riley
Matt Riley
Alex Rimmer
Derrick Ritchie
Ian Ritchie
Claire Roberts
Danny Roberts
Ed Roberts
Iain Roberts
Lee Roberts
Shaun Lee Roberts
Ste Roberts
Ben Robertson
Doug Robertson
Sam 'UUDDLRLRBAS' Robertson
Andy Robinson
Benjamin Robinson
Gareth Robinson
Matt Robinson
Stu Robinson
Lee Robson
Iain Rockliffe
David Rodden
Derek Roden
James Rodger
Carlos Rodriguez
Milo Rodriguez
Stephen Francis Rooney
Chris Roope
Tom Rosborough

David Rose
Graeme Ross
Richard Ross
Dan Rossati
Meg Rouncefield
Sarah & Mark Rowland
Philip Rowlands
Neil Rowntree
Malachi Royer
Dan Ruck
Colin Rudge
Steve Rudland
Shaun Rudman
Simon Rueben
Twon Ruette
Jacob Rukin
Paul Rush
Leigh Russ
Craig Russell
Danny Russell
Gordon Russell
Kenneth Russell
Ollie Russell
Liam Rutherford
RV DV
Colin Ryan
Daniel Ryan
David Ryan
Nelson Sa
Marc Sach
Shalimar Sahota
Joe Saint
Colin Arthur Sales
Sammy Jankis
David Sanger
David Sarginson
Abhilash Sarhadi
John Saunders
Henry Saunderson
Luke Savage
Chris Sawyer
Daniel Sawyers
Stuart Scaife
David Scarborough
Martin Scent
Dave Schofield
James Schofield
David Schott
Robert Schultz
Liana Scientia
Omid Scobie
Andy Scott
Dan Scott
David John Scott
Jonathan 'Excap' Scott
Simon Scott
Ryan Scoular
Chris Scullion
Miles Seagrove
Adam Sealey
Jason Searle
Michael Seaward
Rob Sedgebeer
James Seldon
Matt Sellors
Mark Selmer
Michael Serieys
Chris Sewell
Paul Seymour
Daniel Seymour-Blackburn
Sunil 'VILLAIN' Sharma
Vikas Sharma
Hannah Sharples
James Shaughnessy
Robert Shaw
Usman Sheikh
Richard Sheller
David Sheppard
Adam Sherring
Peter Sherwood
Peter Shevlin
Rob Shields
Paul Shinn
Kyan Shirazi
Paul Shoebridge
Neil Short
Nick Silversides
Mark Simister
David Simmons

Adam Simpson
Brian Simpson
Harvey Simpson
Graham Sinclair
Simon Sinclair
Amardeep Singh
Jassi 'Singho' Singh
Ben Sironko
Ruban Siva
David Jonathan
    Sivés-Rutherford
Danny Skelton
Marc Skidmore
Matthew Skilton
Gareth Slade
Lee Slade
Robin Sloan
Marc Slorance
Paul Slugocki
Jim Smale
Gordy Small
John Smalley
Ande Smallwood
Alison Smith
Andrew Smith
Andrew John Smith
Ash Smith
Ava Smith
Colin H Smith
Craig Smith
Daniel Smith
Davo Smith
Duncan Smith
Edd Smith
Gordon Smith
Graeme Smith
Iain Smith
James Smith
Justin Smith
Kevin Smith
Marc Smith
Marcus Smith
Mark S Smith
Matt Smith
Matthew Smith
Mike 'PeripheralMike'
    Smith
Peter Smith
Peter 'ZX Renew' Smith
Richard Smith
Rick Smith
Simon Smith
Stephen Smith
Steven Smith
Stewart Smith
Tom Smith
Keith Smyth
Kieran Smyth
Russell Sneezum
Chris Snowden
Socially Distanced Gamer
Jonathan Soden
Audun Sorlie
Darren South
David Southall
Mike Spall
Richard Sparks
Simon Speight
David Jonathan Spence
Antoni Spencer
Chris Spencer
Paul Spencer
Simeon Spencer
Stephen Spencer
Joe Spicer-Fosbrook
Adam Patrick Spring
Springloaded
Ben Squibb
Squiff
Matt Squirrell
Jon Stace
John Stainton
Graham Standing
Daniel Stanford
Jason Stanyer
Stewart Stapleton
Glen Staunton
Jamie Stead
Benedict Steele
Rory Steele
Moshe Steiner

Jim Stephan
Shaun Stephen
Hannah Stephens-Jones
Michael Stephenson
Roberto Stephenson
Scott Stephenson
Shaun Stephenson
Chris Stetz
Joe Stevens
Joe Stevens
Lloyd Stevens
Calum Stevenson
Graeme Stevenson
Stew Sizer
Ian 'Retro-Beats' Stewart
Neil Stewart
Neil 'Wild Snorlax'
    Stewart
Robert Stewart
Simon Stewart
Steve Stiles
Adam Stockton
Damian Stokoe
Clive Stone
Chris Stones
James Stopka
Gavin Storey
Paul Storey
William Stott
Colin Strain
Alistair Strayton
Chris Streatfield
Matthew Stringer
Stephen Strowes
Robert Sturt
Mazen Sukkar
Martin Summerfield
Thomas Summers
Paul Sumner
Misha Sumra
Sean Sunderland
Gordon Sutherland
Jonathan Sutherland
Joseph Sutherland
Richard Sutherland
Aaron Sutton
Adam Sutton
Robert 'Roboyd' Sutton
Carl Swanick
Brian Swann
James Sweatland
Marc Sweeney
Danny Swift
Paul Swift
Adam Tagg
Stuart Tanswell
Tom Tarelli
Ezra Tassone
Colin Tate
Lee Tattam
Adil Tausique
Craig Taylor
Graham Taylor
Mike Taylor
Paul Taylor
Pete Taylor
Peter Taylor
PR Taylor
Robert Taylor
Ross Taylor
Simon Teare
Gideon Tebbutt
Julie Templeton
Lee Tennant
Paul Terry
Chris Tester
Phil Tester
David Tetlow
Chris 'That Retro Video
    Gamer' Thacker
Anthony Thackray
Alastair Thomas
Martyn Thomas
Ben Thompson
Ben Leslie Thompson
Francis Thompson
Ian Thompson
Jonathan Thompson
Michael Thompson
Will Thompson
David Thomson

Douglas 'Wallyman'
    Thomson
James Thomson
JP Thomson
Steve Thone
Keith Thorburn
Tom Thorne
Daniel Thornton
David Tibballs
Arron Timson
Tinnes Tinnes
Barry Tipper
Chris Titchmarsh
David Todd
Iain Todd
Karl Todd
Jack Tomalin
Matthew Tommany
Dafydd Tomos
Nick Tones
Chris Toone
Dan Tootill
Mark Topliss
Mathew Topper
Edward Torkington
Dave Torr
Simon Townsend
Chris Traill
Robert Trainer
Greg Trawinski
Ross Tregoning
Joe Trigg
Michael Trinder
Lynne Triplett
David Trotter
Keith Trotter
Richard Troupe
Jon Truran
Emma Tudor-Pratley
Adam Tuff
Jamie Tunbridge
Ivan Turczak
Andrew Turner
Matt Turner
Richard Turner
Graham Turrall
Jack Tutton
Dan Twining
Paul Tylee
Bill Tyler
Richard Tysoe
Paul Tyson
Nicholas Utting
John van Laer
Karoly Varga
Vitas Varnas
Kevin Vaughan
Kiran Vegad
Rune Vendler
Andrew Verity
Richard Vernon
Ash Versus
Steven Vest
Craig Vickers
Steve Vickers
Peter Vincent
Alex Vissaridis
Dan Voice
Christopher Waddington
Tom Wade
David Wagner
Wagoo Dreamwarper
David Waine
Stephen Wake
Neal Wakenshaw
Chris Walker
Mark Walker
Mick Walker
Peter Walker
Scott Walker
David Wall
Alan Wallace
Dave Wallace
Michael Wallace
Murray Wallace
Andrew Waller
Andy Wallington
William Walllace
Dean Walpole
David Walter
Dom Walter

James Walter
Bruce Walters
John Senua Walton
Nick Walton
William Walton
Shaun Waplington
Daniel Ward
David Simon Ward
Jamie Ward
Max Ward
Rik Ward
Matthew Ware
Dale Warren
Matt Warren
Nathaniel Warren
Phill Warren
Grant Warwick
Graham Waters
David G Watkins
Jack Watkins
Benedict Watson
Christopher Watson
Kay Watson
Marcus Watson
Mark G Watson
Paul Watson
Kevin Watson-Hoy
David Watt
Graham Watts
Iain Weaver
Mark Weaver
Chris Webb
Thomas Webber
Justin Websdale
Mark Webster
Paul Webster
Chris Wedgbrow
Benjamin Weetman
Skyler Weinstein
Simon Welburn
Robert Wells
Sean Welsh
Alan Wen
James Wensley
Marek Werno
Alexis West
Glen West
Neil West
Guy West-McDonald
Marilla Wex
Martin Wharmby
Tim Wheatley
Tom Whiston
Aaron White
Barry White
David White
James White
Jo White
Roland X White
John Whitehouse
Thomas Whitelock
Phillip Whitelow
Alexander Whiteside
Paul Whitingham
Steven Whittle
Mark Whyke
Ben Wicks
Josh Widdicombe
Craig Wighton
Tim Wilcox
Michele Wildey
Dan Wilkin
Dave Wilkinson
David Wilkinson
Joe Wilkinson
Kerry Wilkinson
Scott Willetts
Dan Williams
Darren Williams
David Williams
Ian Williams
Nicholas Williams
Rob Williams
Gemma Williamson
Daniel Willis
Jon Wills
Howard Wilsher
David Wilson
Gavin Wilson
Iain Wilson
Jim Wilson

Lewis Wilson
Nick Wilson
Paul W Wilson
Rob Windmill
John Windress
Kristian Wingfield-
    Bennett
Pete Wisdom
Stuart Withers
Richard Wodehouse
David Wong
Ben Wood
Chris Wood
Dan Wood
James Wood
Jonathan Wood
Marcus Wood
Paul Wood
Robert Wood
Stuart Wood
Will Wood
Rohan Woodcock
Tom Woodhead
Boudicca Woodland
Marc Woodward
Danielle Woodyatt
Adam S Woolford
Michael Woolgar
Jake Worrell
Chris Worthington
John Wotherspoon
Wrexham Gamer
James Wright
Russell Wright
Steven WrightMaster
Rhys Wynne
Kirk Yapp
Glen Yard
Brian Yeo
Gavin Yeo
Andrew Young
Chris Young
Simon Young
Ethan Younger Banks
Tieg Zaharia
Alessandro Zampini
Chris Zerdzinski

318/319

Dominik Diamond would like to thank: Jack Templeton. Not only for coming up with the idea of this book, but for his thoughtful, dogged, insightful editing, where he pushed me to dig deeper and deeper and give an honest account of the show the fans deserved and not just a breezy nobgagfest. It made me a better writer and this a better book. Thanks to publisher Darren Wall for believing in the project and making it such a posh work of art.

Thanks to everyone who contributed their memories of the show, especially Dexter Fletcher, who really didn't have to after all the shit he got, but who is a gentleman, a legend, and as much a part of the *GamesMaster* family as I am.

Thanks to Robbie Williams for the best foreword we could have dreamed of. I wrote a note to his people, never dreaming it would get an answer. A week later I wake up in Calgary to find an email from him in Los Angeles with the whole thing completely written. Superstar. Total superstar.

Thanks to the legends of the gaming industry in the 1990s. You were so generous with me in terms of beer, lunches, launches, dinners and ridiculous nights out in general, especially those who were at Virgin Games, Ocean Software, Interplay, *GamesMaster* magazine and EMAP. They always seemed to be with me at last orders all over the world. Special thanks to Danielle 'Woody' Woodyatt, who was the undisputed Queen of all this, and still is today.

To everyone who backed the project: we couldn't have done it without you. Thanks for remembering the show so fondly. It means the world to me that it meant the world to you.

Jack Templeton would like to thank: Sarah and the boys, Mum, Dad and Anna. The Dickster for your invaluable contribution. Jonny, Kirk and The Games Animal for your kindness, support and humour. Woody and Ami at Outrageous PR, Jane, George, Chris, Simon, Luke and Ash from the excellent Under Consoletation podcast – thank you all. To Kyle for making a childhood dream come true! And to DD, DW and every contributor who allowed this dream's dream of a project to happen. Finally, thank you to the perfectly imperfect nineties and to the television I adored.

Dedicated to the memory of: Julian Wastall, Daemion Barry, Richard Pitt and Sir Patrick Moore. Four glorious members of the *GamesMaster* family who are no longer with us.

Cover illustration: Series Two opening titles (detail)

First published in the UK in 2022 by Read-Only
Memory, an imprint of Thames & Hudson. This edition
published in the United Kingdom in 2022 by Thames
& Hudson Ltd, 181A High Holborn, London WC1V 7QX

GamesMaster: The Oral History © 2022
Thames & Hudson Ltd, London

GamesMaster is the trademark of Future Publishing
Limited. Used under licence. All rights reserved.

Foreword © 2022 Robbie Williams
Text © 2022 Dominik Diamond and Jack Templeton

Designed by Leo Field
Additional design by Bruna Osthoff

Images used with the kind permission of:
The Patrick Moore Estate, Sergio at Learning
on Screen, Dave Perry, Steve Smith at SPS Lighting,
Lindsay Kelso, Steve Carsey, Dan Tootill,
Daniel Pesina, Archer Maclean, Hugh Williams,
Jonny Ffinch, Tanya Kecskes, David Mitchelson,
Peter Sisson and Ben Preece.

British Library Cataloguing-in-Publication Data
A catalogue record for this book is available from
the British Library

ISBN 978-0-500-02591-8

Printed in China by RR Donnelley

Be the first to know about our new releases,
exclusive content and author events by visiting
thamesandhudson.com
thamesandhudsonusa.com
thamesandhudson.com.au